Conversation with the Blues

Conversation with the Blues

Paul Oliver

Illustrated with photographs by the author

CAMBRIDGE
UNIVERSITY PRESS

To the memory of my Parents

PUBLISHED BY THE PRESS SYNDICATE OF THE UNIVERSITY OF CAMBRIDGE
The Pitt Building, Trumpington Street, Cambridge CB2 2RU, United Kingdom

CAMBRIDGE UNIVERSITY PRESS
The Edinburgh Building, Cambridge CB2 2RU, United Kingdom
40 West 20th Street, New York NY 10011–4211, USA
10 Stamford Road, Oakleigh, Melbourne 3166, Australia

Printed in the United Kingdom at the University Press, Cambridge

Design/typography by Emma Smith using QuarkXpress/Adobe Caslon

A catalogue record of this book is available from the British Library

Library of Congress cataloguing in publication data applied for

ISBN 0 521 59181 3 hardback

Blues Standing in My Door
Clarksdale, Mississippi: sharecropper's home

Got up this mornin', got up this mornin', Blues standin' in my door,
Dog-gone you,
Woke up this mornin', Blues standin' in my door,
Says, 'I've come here to stay with you, ain't gonna leave no more.'

I said, 'Blues!' I said, 'Blues, why don't you let me 'lone?'
Oh, Mama,
I said, 'Blues, why don't you let poor me alone?
You been follerin' me ever since the day I were born!'

Mance Lipscomb

Contents

What We Played Is Just All We Know
Butch Cage (fiddle) and Willie Thomas (guitar) playing
on the Old Slaughter Road, Zachary, Louisana

Acknowledgments

The conversations from which this book has been compiled were made on an extensive research tour in the United States from June through September 1960. This trip was made possible with the aid of a Foreign Specialist Grant made under the provisions of the Foreign Specialists Programme of the Bureau of Educational and Cultural Affairs of the United States Department of State. I would like to express my sincere gratitude to Miss Bertha E. Von Allmen, Cultural Affairs Officer at the American Embassy, London, whose interest, efforts and sponsorship initiated the award. My warmest thanks also to Dr Frederick Mangold, Director of the Council on Leaders and Specialists of the American Council on Education, and Mrs Jean T. Davidson, Assistant Programme Specialist in Washington D.C., for their invaluable and continued help and advice throughout my stay.

With very few exceptions the extracts quoted here have been transcribed from field tape-recordings and I am indebted to Anthony Smith, producer, of the British Broadcasting Corporation for affording me the opportunity to use a BBC Midget Tape recorder for this purpose and for subsequently producing the series Conversation with the Blues on the BBC's Third Programme.

Only through the unstinting help of many enthusiasts on both sides of the Atlantic was it possible to make contact with so many blues singers and musicians and I am particularly grateful to Professor Sterling A. Brown and Leon Vogel in Washington; Larry Cohn, Len Kunstadt and Roy Morser in New York; Joe Von Battle in Detroit; Bob Koester and John Steiner in Chicago; Charles O'Brien in St Louis; Dr Harry Oster in Baton Rouge; Herb Friedwald, Dick Allen and Bill Russell in New Orleans and Mack McCormick in Houston for the time and trouble that they took to arrange meetings. I would also like to take this opportunity to thank the very many friends who gave to my wife and myself the benefit of their experience and were so generous to us in their hospitality.

To Chris Strachwitz we are particularly indebted for driving us with unflagging good humour for several thousand miles and for so willingly enabling us to join him on his trip through the South and West. With his recording equipment and skill we were also able to conduct a number of recording sessions with blues singers which might otherwise have proved impossible to effect.

In order that there would be a working capital available for recording sessions with blues artists and to establish connexions with blues specialists in the United States, Robert M. W. Dixon initiated a Blues Research and Recording Project. To him and to the persons who so kindly assisted both in the organization of the project and in the release of the resultant recordings later, my sincere thanks.

Over a long period and with untiring patience and care Mrs Madeleine Cocks processed and printed the photographs and I thank her most warmly for her sensitive and sympathetic work.

I owe a special debt of gratitude to my wife, Valerie, who shared the heat, the humidity and the hazards of the trip as willingly as she shared its pleasures and excitements, and who has always been ready to help with the laborious task of transcribing and checking the contents of nearly a hundred tapes. Finally it is my hope that this compilation will serve in some measure as an expression of my gratitude to the blues singers, musicians and their companions who welcomed us so warmly and who so readily gave of their time to draw upon their experiences in our conversations.

Paul Oliver, 1967

Prologue: Clarksdale, Mississippi

It was a burning July morning and the relentless sun drained the colour from the sidewalk signs, the shop fronts and drawn shades on 4th Street. Inside the Big Six barber shop it was close and the electric fan, the size of a cartwheel, could not dispel the perspiration that glistened on fore-arms and ran down foreheads and chests. Immaculate in putty trousers and tan shirt the barber, Wade Walton, seemed least affected by the oppressive heat. He fingered a slow blues on the guitar for it was Sunday and Clarksdale was quiet.

Two young Blacks entered the barber shop and sat down on the row of metal chairs that lined the side wall. They were evidently tired but unhurried now. It was some time before anyone spoke, and then Wade, who had not met them before, looked up from his instrument and asked, 'Either of you guys play anything?'

'A little guitar . . .' said one, after a pause. He was very dark, good-looking and his hair was cropped but matted. His light clothes were stained with tractor grease and his shoes – sneakers – were slashed to give more freedom to his feet. He reached for the proffered guitar, fingered a run or two and swung into a gentle, rocking blues in an ageless Mississippi tradition. His name, he said, in answer to a question, was Robert Curtis Smith. Right now he had the blues and he was playing the blues. After a while he began to talk about the blues.

'The blues – when you want to sing them, you cain't sing them; and when you don't want to sing them, why, you got to sing them – or hum, or do something. And at the time that you want to sing and you don't feel bad, why you still want to sing . . . and you get to feel that everything goes so wrong that the blues is come in your mind, one thing after another, and you sing songs that – I don't know if they've ever been thought of before – probably have a sound that is real different.'
'Usually it's almost sundown when that thing hits you,' Wade broke in. Curtis agreed.
'Yeah, that's about the time when the blues get kind of heavy.'
'You think about your girl friend . . . .'
'Well, your girl friend, yeah, and then think about the way things is goin', so difficult. I mean, nothin' work right, when you work hard all day, always broke. And when you get off the tractor, nowhere to go, nothin' to do. Just sit up and think, and think about all that has happened how things goin'. That's real difficult. And so, why every time you feel lonely you gets that strange feelin' come up here from nowhere. . . .'
'That's when the blues pops up!'
'That's the blues. And how it goes or where they come from and where they go, I don't know. I haven't been able to explain it yet, but I've felt them a lot.'
'In fact there's a lot of different explanations of the blues. Matter-of-fact it's a feelin' – it's all just come from a feelin' huh?' said Wade, turning to Curtis for confirmation.
'That's all it is, blues. It cain't be, is but a feelin'. Because I have thought I been feelin' good and everythin' worked so backwards, everythin' like down on me: I get a girl friend, somethin' like that, all of them give me a raw deal and I go to lose them tryin' to make them happy and they makin' me unhappy. And it's hard to explain....'
'That's when some people say they gettin' on your teeth. That's real whippin'. The blues is somethin' that is skin deep – is it skin deep or is it somethin' further than that?' Wade asked.
'Well I tell you, the way I feel it's somethin' that is just as deep as it can go. And I think, in fact I know it's from the heart, because if it was skin deep you could forget about it . . . Because the blues hurt you so bad. And you get hot and you find you workin' and ain't makin' nothin'. Half of the time hungry, and when you get the blues on top of that and you get to thinkin' about where can you go, or what can you do for to change. And there is no change. That's when the blues gets you. When there's nothin' else to do but what you doin' . . . and sing the blues:

> I know . . . I know . . . Yes, I know . . .
> I hope one day my luck will change.
>
> I done had to work so hard,
> Nothin' still won't go right,
> I don't have no girl friend,
> The onliest one I had, she lef' me las' night.
>
> That can be bad, and the truth it's sad,
> Oh so sad, when you lose the best girl you ever had . . .'

Big Six Barber Shop Wade Walton outside his shop on 4th Street, Clarksdale, Mississippi

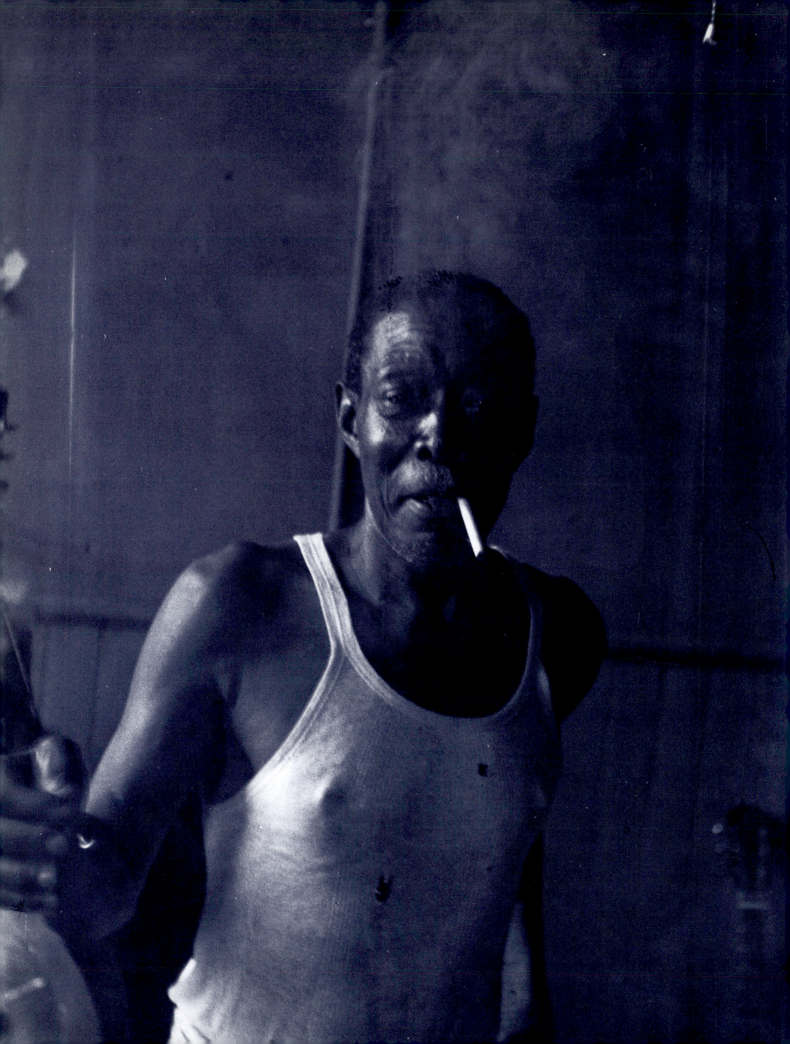

Preface (1996)

That meeting in Clarksdale took place well over thirty-five years ago; an hour or two spent in a Mississippi barber shop which illustrates, as any one of a hundred other encounters might have done, the combination of forward planning and serendipity that led to the conversations from which the extracts in this book have been taken. It was our intention to seek out Wade Walton whose barber shop had reputedly been frequented by Charley Patton; it was pure chance that Robert Curtis Smith should park his tractor, and while he was awaiting his turn for a haircut, should play blues on the guitar that stood in the corner for the pleasure of Wade's clients. Later than night I shared an automobile with Wade as we drove out to a county juke. A literal barrelhouse, the juke joint was a simple, barely furnished, cramped tarpaper and corrugated metal-clad shed where the music came from a jukebox and in the second of two rooms the men played craps. Our presence was welcomed by a few, ignored by others and visibly resented by a couple of young black women, indicative of the tensions and conflicts of emotions that our intervention provoked; Wade was embarrassed by that open hostility. Twenty years later we met once more, as old, if distant, friends, but there was embarrassment again: he had moved his barber shop, lost all his teeth, given up blues and joined the church.

In the intervening years much had happened in the South, in the blues, in American society and in our personal lives. Even by that time many of the singers with whom I had spoken in 1960 had died; today those who are still with us can be counted on the fingers of one hand. In that time-span blues has become a 'world music', sung and played in several languages, avidly followed from Turin to Tokyo, accorded the accolade of being background music to documentaries on poverty (anywhere) and commercials for beer, its predominately white exponents applauded and lauded: Clapton is God. As the background of the blues has indeed become blurred as I anticipated it might, it may be helpful to attempt, briefly, to place these conversations, and the circumstances in which they were recorded, in the contexts of the knowledge of the blues at the time, and of the situation within black society.

As I have explained in the preface to the 1990 edition of *Blues Fell This Morning: Meaning in the Blues*, I had not even visited the United States when I wrote the first edition. Not from a lack of desire to do so, but simply the lack of money to pay for a trip. Its publication prompted Bertha Von Allmen of the American Embassy to draw my attention to the Foreign Specialist grant programme. With a small grant and modest royalties the trip was made possible, though it was not without anxiety that the world that I had described might not be the one which the blues singers had lived in. In fact, the circumstances were often all too painfully accurate. This was in part due to extensive reading, to discussions with Richard Wright and his circle of black expatriates at the Cafe Tournon in Paris, and to my long nights of conversations with the small number of blues singers who had come to London as performers in the previous decade. Then, American musicians were still banned from working in Britain except as variety entertainers. Lonnie Johnson, Josh White, Big Bill Broonzy, Brother John Sellers, Brownie McGhee, Sonny Terry, Jimmy Rushing, Little Brother Montgomery, Muddy Waters and Otis Spann were among them. Though it was rescinded in 1958 the Musicians Union ban against American musicians was still de facto in operation.

Mainly, they performed as 'intermission' artists with Chris Barber's Jazz Band. Blues in the 1950s was still considered as a precursor of jazz, or as a part of it. Though there were 'blues columns' in jazz magazines – like Derrick Stewart-Baxter's in *Jazz Journal*, or my own in *Jazz Monthly*, there was still no blues magazines catering for blues enthusiasts in either the United States or Britain. I wrote occasional articles for the New York *Jazz Review* but in fact, apart from discographical notes, there were few platforms for those who had something to say about blues. Elsewhere, Serge Tonneau had started a small magazine *R & B Panorama* in Belgium and Jacques Demetre wrote a column for the French journal *Jazz Hot*.

Jacques Demetre and discographer Marcel Chauvard had made a 'voyage to the land of the Blues' visiting New York, Detroit and Chicago in 1959. Yannick Bruynogue and Georges Adins from Belgium had also self-financed research trips. To a large extent their intentions were to obtain biographical details of blues singers and to gather discographical data which would fill in some of the numerous gaps in personnel, dates and locations of blues recordings. Researchers in the United States were relatively few. Samuel Charters among American researchers had done extensive field work, gathering material for his book *The Country Blues*, while more localised field recordings had been made by Harry Oster and Mack McCormick in Louisiana and Texas respectively. Alan Lomax had picked up on his work for the Library of Congress and had made return trips to the South in the 1950s to record work songs, folk singers and on occasion, blues singers. Harold Courlander did field work in Alabama recording veteran singers who had been born of slave parents and Frederic Ramsey Jr. had recorded one or two blues singers, though his researches were jazz orientated. My own objectives were different.

In *Blues Fell This Morning* I endeavoured to show that the blues lyrics were directly expressive not only of the singer's thoughts and feelings, but more broadly of the cultural contexts, rural and urban, southern and northern, which blues singers shared with millions of other African Americans. There were many issues that arose from this argument which were unresolved, even if the relation of blues to context that I had described proved to be correct.

Foremost among the questions in my mind concerned the importance of the blues to the singers themselves. It was evident from many blues that the singer speaks as an individual and that the lyrics depict personal involvement. Unlike calypsos, for example, blues rarely comments on contemporary political or historical events except as an aside, with the singer as observer or participant. To what extent the singers drew on personal experience, or poetically projected themselves into the situations and emotions they sang about, remained a major question.

Blues singers that I had already met largely performed semi-professionally in clubs. Even so, most had other occupations – for example, as janitors, like Lonnie Johnson and Big Bill Broonzy. I was anxious to have a clearer idea of how the clubs, juke joints and other social settings like 'frolics' and 'country suppers' related to the blues I had transcribed from records. Were they functionally distinct or were they all expressive of a cultural unity?

It had been my desire to disengage blues from jazz, to release it from its subordinate position to the better-known music which had been enjoying a popularity unprecedented since the 1920s. But I was aware that I may have distorted the picture – I needed to know to what extent blues singers were aware of jazz, and how much jazz musicians acknowledged blues.

It was often asserted (and still is) that 'blues was born in slavery'. Though this seemed to be right I could find no certain evidence that it was so, even if the continuity of church music from spirituals to gospel songs was more apparent. Whether the shadows of slavery and the plantation were still cast over the blues, I realised, would not be easy to investigate. Many historical problems concerning the origins of the blues and the course of its distribution and development challenged me in the 1950s and are still unresolved forty years later. Knowing that Leadbelly had been born in 1889 and Big Bill Broonzy in 1893 I reckoned that there was a good chance that many singers from the earliest years of the blues of which we are aware, might still be around, even perhaps, living in the places of their youth. I had a long-term objective to write a history of blues that would not wholly depend on secondary sources, which meant that singers of all ages should be interviewed, from veterans to my own contemporaries.

In order to understand the blues phenomenon it had been necessary to classify the singers – most frequently by the States from which they came, but also as rural or urban singers. I was never happy with these simple distinctions, but I needed to know to what degree they were valid, and if not, by what means traditions could be distinguished. Among the commonest distinctions was that of the 'classic blues' of the professional women singers of the 1920s, and the 'country blues' of the rural singers of the South. Though the classic blues period had ceased by 1930, at least on record, I was curious to know what became of the women singers, and what other traditions of women's blues existed which had not depended on vaudeville and tent shows. Gospel music was dominated by women singers and it seemed likely that men were more attracted to blues, and women to gospel song. But I was not sure of this, nor certain that the blues was regarded as the 'devil's music', as I had heard said. Whether blues singers considered their way of life as compatible with the church or whether theirs was a deliberate revolt against it, also exercised my interest.

A major problem arose from the very sources from which

Blues Fell This Morning had drawn – 78 r.p.m. blues records. For an enthusiast in Europe who did not live in the United States and in fact, for a middle-class white American too, blues records provided virtually the prime source for the enjoyment of the music and information on its performers and its content. Many singers had interested me greatly as performers and as blues poets – Whistling Alex Moore, Lightnin Hopkins and J. B. Lenoir, who recorded respectively in the 20s, 40s and 50s, among them. It was important to me to try and seek out these singers and many others whose records I had enjoyed and knew by heart.

Whether they were alive, and if so, whether they still lived in their home states or had moved or migrated over the intervening years, was largely unknown to me. Over several years I had collected all the information that I could on recording locations, especially of field units, references on recorded blues to places – the more specific the better – and had questioned each blues artist I had interviewed about the singers they had met on their own travels. All this data I had noted on several hundred file cards which I had also cross-referenced – manually, in those pre-computer days. These were kept in a modified cardboard shoe-box which I carried with me to the States, to refresh my memory everywhere I went. Needless to say, there were neither blues reference works nor comprehensive discographies which I could consult. If finding the singers on whom I had some information might prove difficult, locating those on whom I had none was an unquantifiable problem. Yet I took heart from the fact that field recording units had often worked without previous knowledge of the singers in a region which they visited, as I had previously discussed in an article for *The Jazz Review*, 'Special Agents: how blues got on record'.

Extensive though blues recording had been over some forty years, it seemed unlikely that all blues singers had been recorded. If blues was largely representative of black culture as a whole I reasoned that there should be singers in every black community, recorded or not. I was anxious to meet singers who were unknown to me or the recording studio, but who were significant in their own milieux. I wanted to document their lives and experiences in their own words, and recording on tape was the obvious means. But this raised the question of interview procedure. The advocates of "oral history" had scarcely put

in an appearance then (and have ignored blues and jazz oral histories ever since). There were few guidelines on which I could depend, but a brief course of instruction from the BBC staff who made a heavy ex-army field recorder available to me was a great help. In spite of the many issues which I had identified and to which I hoped I would find some of the answers, I was determined to let the singers give their accounts and make their observations with the minimum of direct questioning. I wanted to keep in the background as much as possible and not to steer the discussions.

It was all too clear that the tasks I had set myself and the objectives I had in planning the trip were far more ambitious than could possibly be accomplished in three months' field work. I was not going to solve the problems of blues history in so short a time. A history is, by definition, diachronic and an historic account must necessitate data collection, much research and processes of reconstruction and interpretation. The opportunity before me was one where I could take a synchronic slice through the blues phenomenon. It might be the last occasion when such a cross-section in time, culture and tradition was possible, I believed. Without doubt, it was imperative to make the trip.

Much was accomplished as I had wished in what proved to be a voyage of personal as well as musical discovery, which has remained with me over three decades as a vivid montage of experiences, sometimes thrilling, sometimes moving, overlaid with planned meetings, chance encounters, much music and many conversations. There were disappointments of course: messages that failed to reach their destinations, musicians who were out of practice, instruments that were in hock, meetings that did not materialise. There were times of anxiety, apprehension, doubts – but not many; most of the time we were sustained by the anticipation of new encounters, new music with each successive day. Some of the experiences and results of research were worked into articles and record sleeve notes. A selection was published in my book *Blues off the Record: Thirty Years of Blues Commentary*. Less evidently, perhaps, a great deal of the information gathered was incorporated into *The Story of the Blues*.

Generally we kept a low profile, especially in the South, though the California Licence plates on Chris Strachwitz's

1953 Plymouth advertised our out-of-state origins. With a naive logic we took rooms in a black motel in Clarksdale, having decided that no Whites would expect to find us there. For it was potentially a dangerous undertaking. In 1960 the Civil Rights movement was gathering momentum. Sit-ins were occurring throughout the South where schools had failed to integrate following the Supreme Court ruling that racial segregation in public schools was unconstitutional. Race riots had occurred in Chattanooga, Tennessee in February 1960 and in Biloxi, Mississippi, in April. The era of lynching had not totally passed – Mark Parker had been lynched by a Mississippi mob the previous year. But the brutal murders and bombing of homes and churches that accompanied the Civil Rights campaign had yet to take place, and the Ku Klux Klan had still to reorganize its forces.

Fortunately, there was a tacit acceptance that record scouts would come by occasionally, looking for talent. Our presence was tolerated. I was well aware of the bald facts of the ghettoising of Blacks in the northern cities and of the injustice of segregation in the South. But still I found it hard to come to terms with the reality of cities that were segmented along colour as well as economic lines, and of southern settlements where 'separate but equal' facilities, from soda fountains to seats in buses were segregated. It continually amazed me, in view of the bitterness of discrimination, that we were treated so generously by the blues singers and their families and that interviewees were so frank in their narratives.

Between the publication of *Blues Fell This Morning* and the proposed date of departure there was little time to prepare. Perhaps it was as well, for if there had been more time, wise counsellors would doubtless have attempted to dissuade me from making the trip, and emphatically, from being accompanied by my wife, Val. But we had shared the years of listening to and transcribing records, the notemaking and research, the house visits of blues singers who came to Britain, and I had no intention of going alone. For several years I had corresponded with collectors on both sides of the Atlantic and the help they gave us was incalculable. I have acknowledged them, inadequately, at the beginning of this book and so I will not repeat my words of gratitude here, except to say that the willingness of Chris Strachwitz for us to join him on the trip that he,

coincidentally, was planning for that period, made all the difference to the prospects of success in our venture. A few speedily exchanged letters, a clutch of transatlantic phone calls, and outline plans were drafted. A two-bunk slot beneath the waterline of the Queen Elizabeth, euphemistically termed a 'Stateroom', was booked – and we were off.

'I'm now engaged in a public demonstration against job discrimination in St Louis, Missouri. There's approximately a dozen people here today trying to let the public know that there exists job discrimination at this particular store and encouraging the prospective patrons not to shop here.'

Neatly-dressed, small and intense, Mrs Marion Oldham spoke into the microphone of the portable BBC tape recorder with the assurance and natural command of language that one so frequently meets when interviewing an American encountered in the street. Now working with an NAACP group she had already spent twelve years as an active demonstrator with the Committee of Racial Equality. Experienced campaigner, she broke off the interview several times to intercept shoppers. Another young woman from the picket joined us.

'Some white person came up and cussed me out just now, and I hadn't made any remarks to him,' she said. 'You have to be careful of the tone of voice you use when you ask them to support your demonstration. You have to ask them the way you usually do.'

Her name was Alice Moore. It was the name of a blues singer once well known in St Louis. Could she be any relation? She was not. Mrs Oldham rose hotly to the suggestion. 'I'm not an avid fan of blues singers or blues. As a Negro, I think that we have been stereotyped – that all Negroes like blues. I think that you might take a look at the noted Negro musicians, and those that have reached fame and popularity are not necessarily blues singers; I think the great majority are not. Radio stations that beam directly to the Negro community in St Louis feel that they have to play blues records all day long, and this isn't so. I think this is a move back as far as the Negro is concerned; among my friends I don't think I know of anyone who is a fan of spirituals or blues.'

Blues is not the music of the black leaders, of the black intelligentsia. The active, militant members of CORE or the NAACP seldom show interest in blues; the music does not feature in the black periodicals except as an occasional success story. Black members of the legal, medical and teaching professions do not consider blues to be their music. It is rare that a blues singer or musician is other than a member of the manual labour groups. A blues pianist who has become an active politician in Harlem, Sam Price, is an exception. He recalled

his youth in the country near Waco, Texas, when he first learned to play the blues: 'The sort of work we did, well, you could pick cotton. We picked the cotton in the fall of the year. You chopped cotton in the spring. The kids would get out of school to chop cotton – early. Then came the summer months and you would go and pick peaches and that sort of thing. And then in the fall you went away to pick cotton. Then you could get a job as a porter, and then you had the middle-class Negroes who were your teachers, and preachers, and a few doctors, and a very few lawyers. And your property owners.'

That was forty-odd years ago and the advances made by the black community have been considerable. But in 1955 the total number of Blacks over fourteen years of age classified as 'professional, technical and kindred workers' was still less than a hundred and eighty thousand. Operatives and kindred workers exceeded a million men and women; the labour force, well over two million more. There is no need to dwell upon the statistics. The unskilled and semi-skilled workers and their wives and families still made up the majority of the black population and it is to them as well as to a great many of their racial group employed in skilled labour that the radio stations beamed their blues and spirituals.

As a folk-song form still, the blues tells much of the society that has produced it, and for good or ill it is an aesthetic expression of that society. Both as music and song, in sounds and words, the blues reveals much of the patterns of behaviour and thought of an underprivileged minority group in a modern state. Records and field studies provide overwhelming testimony to the wide span of the content of the blues and it is valid to make reference to sociological study to determine the relevance of the music. Themes of infidelity and desire in personal relationships have predominated in the blues and can be expected to continue to do so, for these common experiences induce the blues more readily than tenderness or affection which can find more immediate forms of expression. But though such blues may form the major proportion of the total, the blues has had much to say on work and unemployment, on migration and shifting environments, on violence and correction, on sickness and sorrow. If they are sometimes trite because they are commonplace, they are truthful too, just because they are commonplace; often they are

Minor Blues Singer Maxwell Street Jimmy sings and plays guitar while King
David accompanies him on his 'harp' in Maxwell Street, Chicago, Illinois **2**

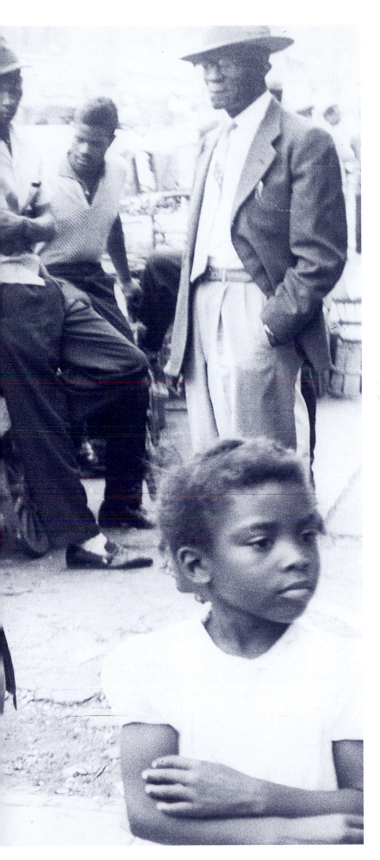

dramatic, frequently poetic and moving, always with the elements of personal experience that are yet shared by a large proportion of the Negro community.

If the blues, like any folk art or indeed almost any art form, is illuminating in terms of a whole group, it is still sung and played by individuals – singers who sing for themselves, who sing for others, who lose the blues through playing the blues, who entertain, who share their music as they share their experience with others whilst singing and playing for dancing or drinking or talking. In the process of examination and recording the history of any large-scale group activity – a school of painting, a battle, a political movement, a religious sect, a folk tradition – or blues itself – the individual tends to become submerged. As the history of the blues is now being belatedly documented in all its styles, its regional characteristics, its themes, its flow and circulation, its creation and development and change must, by the very magnitude of the subject, subordinate the work of countless recorded blues singers, let alone those known by reputation only, to the major patterns and the principal, most influential artists. When the assessment of the major figures is made, the minor blues singer is forgotten.

In total the story of the blues is a story of minor singers rather than major ones, of men with small circles of acquaintances, limited aspirations and humble talents. Present knowledge of the blues is largely conditioned by the records of known blues singers, but the blues man who talks of his home town, of the places that he has worked in and to which he has travelled, brings into the picture the images of men whose reputations were considerable though they stayed within this segregated world of music and, never having the chance or mind to record, are still unknown. Some impression of the migrant blues singers amongst the shifting population of Blacks in the United States may be gained from the reminiscences of some of their number who worked in saw-mills and lumber camps, played in jukes and barrelhouses, sang in labour gangs and hoboed their way from town to town and state to state. Others, who have remained in country communities in semi-isolation from contact with the cities and from the tours of recording executives, tell of the importance of the blues to them today and of the blues singers who hollered in fields and on highways, and who picked out their music in the same clapboard shacks in years past. Certain of these men might well have been influential figures in the blues if means of mass communication had been available to them; others would have remained by any standards truly minor artists, enjoying local reputations, supplying a need, singing and playing for their own satisfaction and the pleasure of their companions. Their esteem for their own music may not have been great but their need to create it is still indicative of the wide significance of the blues in the world of African Americans. To do justice to them and to the blues they deserve attention.

Traditional ballads and songs are recalled in the majority of folk-song forms and are performed by the singers in structures sufficiently intact for their identities to be immediately recognizable or their provenance traceable. Though it is generally implied that the use of traditional verses is evidence of inventive weakness on the part of the blues singer, his borrowing of lines or phrases, even of whole verses, and remodelling them into new blues is part of a creative process which has the elements of traditional folk-song and which is yet more personally expressive. Self-styled songsters find in these remoulded blues the vehicle for individual emotional outlet through performances that are in large part traditional. Such blues take the place of the ballad in Black music today and their aptness, their appropriateness to common experience accounts for their survival. They feature in the work of most blues singers and predominate in that of the minor, less inventive ones. Some blues singers, however, are almost totally original: 'I just sit down, sing and play 'em, unaware to my knowledge or idea or thoughts of 'em until I sit at the keyboard and begin playing and makin' 'em up on the piano,' explained Whistling Alex Moore. A singer like Moore, or Lightnin Hopkins can turn the beam of his own perception on a sudden incident, an immediate phenomenon and highlight it in a spontaneously created blues.

Within the past few years there has been a widespread increase in interest in the blues and an overdue recognition of its musical and poetic merit. Today, 'funk' means blues, 'soul' means blues feeling in the parlance of the modern jazz musician. A music that has become aware of its ultimate sophistication, modern jazz has groped in the earth for its lost roots, and the recent popularity of blues has arisen in part from this.

It has coincided with the eventual realization on the part of the enthusiasts of other forms of American folk music that the blues also merits their consideration. This increase in appreciation of the blues has extended for the first time on any large scale beyond the recording and engagement of blues singers for purely black audiences to their booking for record collector markets and for the concerts of the folk-music coterie. The cultural shock, the impact of modern blues in such settings has often been far from successful.

'They oughta tol' me they didn't want electric guitar. I didn't know they want that ord'nary box, what they call 'coustic guitar. And I only half-done my songs then,' explained Muddy Waters after his performance had shocked a concert-going audience. For the rural Black suddenly transported from the Louisiana back country to the sophisticated, chic bandstand of the Newport Jazz Festival the effect was disturbing.

'What we played is just all we know about them blues. We just learn them people was interested in these things when we went to this Festival. 'Cause you know we thought we weren't doin' nothin' – till the people start to clappin' their hands. You know we felt foolish about things like that,' said Willie Thomas back at his home some time later.

Playing in new circumstances, in a new environment and to white audiences requires an adjustment for the blues singer which some have succeeded in making. Modifying the music, fixing the pattern, establishing routines in performances, giving an emphasis upon the 'act' and the 'performance' changes the nature of the blues and diminishes its traditional function though it may be argued that it creates a new one. Almost inevitably this has carried over to their views on their earlier careers to some degree. The latter-day playing, and one must reluctantly admit, the well-rehearsed pronouncements of the late Huddie Ledbetter and Big Bill Broonzy, were some indication of the process. In the field – whether the field is a Chicago slum or a shack in a watermelon patch – the blues singer is at one with his environment and responds readily to the stimuli of his friends, his immediate surroundings and the associations they induce. It is in the field that his blues are most truly creative so it is here that a conversation with the blues is most rewarding.

'If I knew why I danced, I wouldn't dance,' Pavlova is reported to have said. But about his singing the blues singer has no such sophisticated conceptions even though he may be as puzzled by the closeness of his music to his heart.

'You don't hear blues just for the first time, the blues are just a part of your life. I mean, I can't even remember when I first heard the blues. I can't explain how the blues are – but I do know I like them,' Edith Johnson reflected, when considering the same problem. Even if she is vague about the blues outside the limitations of her immediate experience, the singer is aware of what she means by the blues and why she sings or plays them. There is a similarity of spontaneous observations on the nature of the blues from an unrecorded singer in Detroit with those of an unrecorded singer from Clarksdale, Mississippi, which is in itself testimony to the validity of the idiom and its widespread significance. A more introspective singer is prepared to consider why he gets the blues, what gives him the blues, why the blues as expression takes the form of song or music. He may consider the morality of singing the blues and may hazard a guess at its origins. And he becomes concretely informative when he speaks of his childhood, his upbringing, his hours of work and brief periods of leisure when he began to sing and play. The first experiences of singing, the first experiments at fingering guitar or piano are evidence of the handing on of a tradition and the investing of the traditional form with personal values. The limitations of country entertainment, of social contact and opportunities for recreation define the function of the blues within the community, whilst the tedium of work, the days of poverty, the nights of simple pleasure and the moments of dramatic incident are recalled with nostalgia, anger, amusement, regret and in the recall illumine the meaning of the blues for the individual.

Understandably, some blues singers have more to say about their lives and work than have others. 'I'll tell you, I'll tell you the truth about that,' Willie Thomas would declare before releasing a torrent of words with the dynamic emphasis of a preacher with a liking for the blues. Said Blind Arvella Gray who had packed in his life more bitterness, incident and suffering than most men could endure, 'In short, I just is proud of my life, 'cause I come through with my skin on, an' if I had it to live over, I'd live it all over again.' His graphic, alarming narrative which was made the more stark by his calm and unsensational account contrasted with the laconic words of Robert Lockwood, an amiable but taciturn man: 'What is there to say? – I just make tunes, that's all.' J. B. Lenoir's warm Mississippi accents and easy delivery were notably different from his high, somewhat taut singing voice whilst Henry Brown's guttural syllables seemed to be forced through a constricted throat. John Lee Hooker had much to say but was hindered by a nervous speech impediment which only disappeared when he began to sing. But the majority of blues singers talk easily, naturally and always with an innate dignity. Theirs is an oral tradition, one in which their principal means of communication is vocal, and whilst Lil Son Jackson or Henry Townsend might speak of 'telling it in a song' they are nonetheless articulate and expressive conversationalists.

That the blues singer is more than usually expressive and meaningful in his spoken observations is no source of surprise. The jazz musician is articulate through the medium of his instrument, be it trumpet, clarinet, trombone or flute. But the blues singer communicates in vocal terms. In the simplest forms of blues and hollers the transition from speech to 'moan' or primitive song is a natural and customary one, whilst in the more defined blues the interpolation of spoken phrases between or within verses and the use of longer, spoken passages as a part of the creation of the song is familiar. The blues is of course, only one of several vocal forms in black culture apart from the specific songs of spiritual, gospel and ballad. The narrative and folk tales, the telling of 'lies' or competitive 'tall tales', the heartily obscene 'putting in the dozens', the long and witty 'toasts' and the epigrammatic rhyming couplets which enliven the conversation of folk Black and Harlem hipster alike, have their reflections in the blues. They are evident in the earthy vulgarity, the unexpected and paradoxical images, the appeal of unlikely metaphors, the endless story that makes all blues one, the personification of blues and the lines of rhyming iambic pentameters. The folk Black with time to talk will savour a story and repeat it until he has wrung its humour dry; even the linear repetitions of the blues have some affinity with this age-old habit. Such vocal forms persist in the couplets of Jasper Love, the bawdy repertoire of Edwin Pickens or the tall tales of Wade Walton.

There has been insufficient attention given in the past to the talking and narrative forms of blues – not the humorous couplets and quatrains of the white 'talking blues' which had their exponents in singers from Chris Bouchillon to Woody Guthrie, but the skeletal, bared-down blues spoken to rhythms and patterns that are related to blues verse structure. The extracts, quoted here from the conversation of Robert Curtis Smith or J. B. Lenoir, Edwin Pickens or Little Brother Montgomery who talked whilst they fingered guitar strings or meditatively explored the piano keys, fell naturally into such blues patterns, giving a beauty of form to their utterances that defies any kind of transcription. Song, speech and music are frequently one in the blues. For the blues musician his instrument is a part of his means of expression and for the majority, if not for all blues instrumentalists the piano, guitar, even harmonica is a complement to the voice. Though he may play instrumental solos, the most characteristic blues artist sings through both voice and instrument. For every non-vocal blues instrumentalist there is a non-playing blues singer to speak for him. Whilst the instrumental blues traditions have drawn from other sources – the rhythms and whistles of trains for example which themselves have human attributes – the voice has played a large part in shaping the sounds of the blues. Hollering the blues, screaming the blues, crying the blues, shouting the blues, moaning the blues – these are customary extensions of both singing and playing the blues. The singer's injunctions of 'speak to me, guitar', 'tell 'em, ivories' and similar modes of address to his instrument are evidence of the conception of the strings as an eloquent second voice.

On the technical side of the blues however, the instrumentalist has little to say. 'I just fix on an idea that come to me. And a lot of times I can be sittin' down and different ideas come to me, and I get on up there and I try it out on the box. And if I like it, I never will forget it, but if I don't like it, I just brush it out of the way,' said J. B. Lenoir explaining how he develops a tune. Most blues singers acknowledge their inability to read music and remain totally unconcerned, for their music satisfies them in the form in which they create it. A rudimentary knowledge of musical terms can have some unexpected results. 'Ask anybody around, they say ole Alex Moore plays in more keys than anybody around,' the pianist said proudly.

'I play in A, B, C, D, G, H, I, K, . . . right on up'. Mance Lipscomb, a talented guitarist, declared himself to be 'just an open player, by myself. Play by ear – just ear music', and the few chords for which he had names did not correspond with customary terminology. Talking of pianists of his acquaintance, Little Brother Montgomery recalled Gus Pevsner, adding apologetically, 'Only he was a musicianer like . . . you know, musical. Played by notes and things.'

In the words of Shaky Jake the difficulties of explaining how to play blues on the harmonica became apparent. 'I blow harmonica,' he said, 'but I don't try to blow like nobody but myself, you know. I mean, a lot of guys "cross" it. You can play it straight; you can "cross" it three times; you can "cross" it four times.' Pressed further, he explained, 'You know, you take ten keys and make forty out of them, take ten keys and make thirty, take ten and make twenty – and you can play the ten keys. You cross it with your mouth, with your tongue. I can't show you just how to cross it 'cause I got it in my mouth. Nobody can teach you *how* to blow you just have to pick up on it. You cain't be taught. One thing about it though, I think everybody should have their own style. You know what I mean – be themself.'

Subjecting blues performances to musical analysis is less than satisfactory. On such aspects of the blues the recording remains as the only means for common reference, for the subtleties of timing in voice and instrument, of touch and 'feel', of the peculiar beauty of crushed notes or slid and twisted guitar strings, of the whine of the bottleneck on an unconventionally tuned instrument, can only be appreciated in direct performance or on record. Perfection of tone, purity of voice, accuracy of pitch are not the principal objectives in the singing of blues. Though variations might be indicated by symbols, by graphs and by phonophotography, the subtle qualities of inflection, timbre, throat-humming, gutturals and nasal enunciations, which characterize certain regional and personal styles of blues singing, remain elusive when any attempt at new or conventional notation is attempted. Nor can terminology help, for black singers seldom identify the 'curls', 'bends', 'turns' which the musicologist notes in the blues and field hollers in these words. Sam Price recalled when Mayo Williams introduced him to 'Peetie Wheatstraw, the Devil's Son-in-Law, the High

Sheriff of Hell! He said he would like for Peetie to "bend" his voice. He said that he could "whoop" – I think that's how he described it. " Whooper" he said – whatever that was. I don't know.'

Accepting these limitations, general musical notation is omitted and the recordings made at the time of these interviews and subsequently issued together with others of relevance are included in the Notes on the Recordings and Notes on the Speakers. If blues musicians explain their music best in the performance, their recollections do much to add to our knowledge of the blues. The reminiscences of the individual and his relationship to his community are still the raw material of social research and remain so when this embraces folk-music, explaining the importance of the music in that society, its function, its raison d'être.

'Country blues' and 'city blues' are terms that have relatively little meaning in the blues today for the distinctions have been blurred by the influences of mass media. It is likely however, that undue emphasis has been placed upon them even when reference is made to earlier periods in the history of the blues: some of the best examples of 'country blues' have been recorded by city-dwellers in, for example, Memphis, Birmingham and Atlanta. With the fixed associations of such terms – ones unused by Blacks – are the beliefs that such lateral divisions may also be made by instrumentation. Thus the guitar is 'country', the piano 'city'. That no such simple distinction exists is clearly evident from the testimony of blues singers from rural areas. The guitar was portable and gave freedom to the singer to play where he liked, but the piano was ubiquitous, to be found in every tiny hamlet. The technical skill which many pianists displayed in comparison with their guitar-playing companions may well have arisen from the competitiveness forced on them by the fixed locations of their chosen instrument. Moreover, as Lightnin Hopkins shows, the guitarist was even at a disadvantage in circulating over long distances. Pianos, guitars, harmonicas, fiddles have been the basic instruments of the blues in both country and town it seems.

' They say that blues originated in New Orleans but St Louis had some of the best blues singers that ever there was in the history of blues,' said James Stump Johnson, staking the claim for St Louis. At one time the phrase of George Lee's –

'Beale Street, where the blues began' – had popular currency. Though its reputation is not unassailable, Mississippi has had the most advocates as the source of the blues. Undoubtedly the origins of the blues are far more complex but the 'Mississippi Blues' remains axiomatic as the essence of blues feeling. Whole traditions have sprung up in Texas, in Georgia, in the Carolinas and Tennessee, and Mississippi may owe much to some or all of them. Yet the life-blood of the blues seems to follow the Mississippi River, feeding and nourishing the blues of Louisiana and Mississippi, parts of Arkansas, Tennessee, Missouri and Illinois. The ebb and flow of the blues seems to have run in the hour-glass shape made by Texas, Louisiana and the Gulf Coast, through the narrower waist of the lands bordering on the River, spreading to St Louis, Chicago and Detroit. During the 1950s the exodus of Blacks from the South had been unprecedented in its extent. Mississippi lost more Blacks than any other state as some 323,000 Blacks migrants left in the ten years from 1950 to 1960 and the number was almost as great as the total of immigrants in Illinois and Michigan – which include Chicago and Detroit – during the same period of time. The influx brought blues singers too, and there would be reason enough in an argument that the place to study Mississippi blues was Chicago; for this vast migration is the peak of a continually climbing graph of black movement from Mississippi and elsewhere in the South which has risen steadily over half a century.

Apart from the circulation of migratory Blacks the spread of blues has been assisted by the movement of professional singers. Professional that is, in that they earned their living by singing and playing, but still essentially folk-musicians. At the lower level of entertainment these included the saw-mill and levee camp pianists, the wandering juke and country supper guitarists, the entertainers on doctor shows, minstrel shows and excursion trips alike. The transition from casual to 'professional' playing of this category was a slow one and in very many instances never attained or intended, although the singer supplemented his wage packet by playing.

'I have worked in Houston some, brickyard, lumberyard . . . farmed mostly all my life,' said Mance Lipscomb. 'I've done lots of different kinds of work but I never worked so hard as I did on the farm. Never did work in the musician department,

Farmed Mostly All My Life
Mance Lipscomb sings in his
two-room cabin while his
grandchildren listen

just only in the open air. I played lots of towns but I never did
have any records made, nothing like that.' A Texas sharecropper until a few years before, he worked on the State Highways.

Henry Townsend, who first recorded in the 'twenties and
who maintained a reputation in St Louis ever since, might well
have claimed professional status, but as he explained, 'I have
never depended on the life of a blues singer as for support. I
have always felt that I should do something else and I've always
found other work to do. Well, I drove a taxi for about twelve
years which is very educational for anybody – I mean, dealing

with the public you know.' Some singers have been forced into blues singing as a means of a living, particularly those congenitally blind or blinded by accident, whilst others have found themselves sufficiently in demand playing at jukes and barrelhouses to forsake field labour for work which nonetheless, meant long hours and low pay.

Professional blues singing in these forms hardly compares with the work of the professional jazz musician in New Orleans, St Louis or Memphis when both were working in the same neighbourhoods. To what extent the blues had a formative influence on jazz remains a matter of conjecture. In the absence of any contemporary accounts we are dependent on the reports of surviving musicians who witnessed the music in its early days. That these can be conflicting the sample interviews included here indicate and the time is long overdue for a close examination of this basic assumption. It is salutary to note the paucity of interviews and reported conversations with jazz musicians dating from even the late Chicago period; hardly necessary to add that in this respect blues have been greatly neglected. Even as well-known a blues singer as Bessie Smith is remembered by a hundred songs but only a handful of sentences.

Blues as represented by the truly professional singer such as Bessie Smith probably afforded the closest links with jazz, the musicians meeting the singers in tent shows, circuses, theatre circuits and cabarets. These were the so-called 'classic blues' singers – again a term unfamiliar to those who sing the blues – whose work was linked with and frequently overlapped that of the vaudeville singer and entertainer. Best known to the jazz enthusiast, Bessie Smith had a punching delivery and a timing sense that was close to jazz and left its mark on many musicians. The tragedy of her life had an epic quality and her artistry a magnificence that has assured her place in jazz history. Amongst blues singers she is less frequently recalled than her contemporaries who were nearer the folk idiom, of whom Gertrude Ma Rainey and Ida Cox in earlier years are preeminent. These singers worked in the tent shows and minstrel shows, often employed rural blues singers in their companies and had contact with the 'roughnecks' who sang primitive blues as they raised the tents.

For women, the casual life of the wandering blues singer was generally less practicable; but in the towns, singers like Mary Johnson and Alice Moore could work with semi-professional blues instrumentalists and with their counterparts on the tent shows surviving the bleak years in the entertainment industry after the collapse of vaudeville and the effects of the Depression. Their reputations had been reinforced, sometimes even made, by recording and subsequently the male singers too, depended on recording to shape their careers. In recent years the women singers have devoted their energies to the Church where some of the finest are now to be heard, but, as many blues singers are ready to point out, the association between church songs and blues has often been closer than exterior evidence has suggested.

Recording for commercial firms has provided an effective means of common ground for evaluation of the blues, but as an indication of history it can be an erratic gauge. Depending very much on the initiative of the singers and the energies of the talent scouts, the recording companies introduced 'field ' work comparatively late and then installed themselves in Southern cities two and three hundred miles apart for a few days at a time. The reluctance of some singers to record and the overt enthusiasm of others, the perspicacity of the seekers in the field, the limited circulation of the recording units – these and many other factors conditioned the quantity, quality and nature of the material recorded. They remain so today, and the memories of these who 'got up talent' and the observations of those who still do are instructive. The names of blues singers and musicians, unrecorded but long remembered with admiration and respect by blues artists who are themselves of no mean stature, are mute indication of the vast spread of a tradition of which we can only know a sample. Recording has built reputations with justice in some cases, with rather less merit in others; has brought recognition to some blues singers and passed others by; has given some brief moments of glory; has meant but a few passing and unimportant minutes to still others who have valued more the change in their pockets.

As the blues has brought change for some singers it has also seen change in styles. Here and there in semi-isolation older styles of the blues survive, but mass media have had their effect upon the blues. Widely popular in Chicago the walking bass figures, the amplified guitars, the electric harmonicas and Fender basses have been imitated in even the remoter country districts within the past decade. Day-long sessions of blues and gospel music were beamed from the networks of black radio stations bringing the music of Muddy Waters and Howling Wolf, Little Walter and John Lee Hooker to every home, to be accepted or rejected but always available to be heard and copied. Relying on disc-jockeys with slick names like Houston's Daddy Deep Throat, Vicksburg's Jet Pilot of Jive, Forth Worth's Doctor Jazzbo or Chicago's Big Bill Hill, the stations issued unending blues on record, interspersed only with hip talk and swift, knowing, in-group Negro jive patter salesmanship. Memphis's 50,000 watt WDIA claimed a 'Golden Market' of a potential one and a quarter million black audience; WOKJ in Jackson, Mississippi, claimed the nation's highest audience rated black group – 'the only way to the 107,000 Negroes of the Jackson Metropolitan area'; in Meridian, Mississippi, WQIC beamed to a black audience of 35,000 – car radios, country drive-ins, cafes, jukes and barber shops alike are alive to similar music whilst the mechanical jukeboxes that made 78s obsolete when they switched to 45 rpm rocked a thousand joints interminably to canned blues.

For the folk collector the changes in the nature of the blues, the increasing use of amplification and stereotypes of sound mark the deterioration of the music whilst the lessening of social themes to the common denominator of sexual prowess and unrequited love mark a diminution of the blues as a vehicle of social comment. Live blues flourished however; the young singers and musicians who had been encouraged and stimulated by the blues that they heard. Many younger singers had recently appeared whose popularity threatened the positions held by the famous and older blues men. Some veteran singers and blues musicians retired, others changed their styles to accord with new trends. Some held on, supported by the older black public, others lost their audiences to find new jobs, forget the blues, or go back South. As they returned and retired, aspiring young blues singers inclined to the rock 'n roll, rhythm 'n blues idioms of the day left their homes in Mississippi and Memphis. Native to the Northern cities to which their migrating parents brought them after the First World War, they tested their abilities in the clubs and dives that were always opening, flourishing, closing, reopening and sought a chance to get on record for the brief span of life that

modern media allowed recorded blues. This is how the 1960s blues was in the big cities. Detroit's Hastings Street may have been cleared for an expressway but 12th Street rocked to the blues in its stead; State Street, Chicago, had been laid flat but West Roosevelt, West Lake and 47th Street were packed with teeming bars which pulsed to powerhouse blues, shoulder to shoulder with the store-front churches.

Blues with a church inflexion, gospel songs with a blues beat – to the listener the edges are sometimes blurred – perhaps they always have been. In some churches the preachers militated against the blues and the world it represents; some gospel singers were blues singers too. An uneasy relationship existed between the major thriving forms of music in black society. We talked to Hillary Blunt in his tiny, two-roomed shack in Scotlandville, Louisiana, with its exterior walls lined with tar-paper 'brick veneer' and its interior walls lined with neatly pasted newspapers. He was dust-coated after a long overnight drive in his truck from a Saturday night session deep in the Louisiana country. On the porch sat his wife, resplendent in spotless blue satin dress, red shoes, pink hat, awaiting the arrival of her friends to take her to church. Hillary Blunt nodded in her direction. 'She's mad at me 'cause I'm talkin' to you and singin' the blues and it's Sunday and she's goin' to church,' he explained, wryly commencing to sing *I'm a Thousand Miles from Nowhere*. For many blues singers the conflict of religion and the blues is a matter of real concern; especially for such a singer as Lil Son Jackson who had led the heavily demanding life of a 'professional' blues singer. 'I didn't have time to think about my life,' he said. 'It was every night I had to go and during the day I was resting and sleeping and when I would wake up it was time to go to work again. I mean it was one night after another and one day after another and I never realized – I never had time to think that some day I am going to leave the world, until I had this car wreck and that slowed me down. We was on our way from where we had played in Oklahoma and had the wreck and after that I kind of veered away from music because that was the cause of it. I just told the fellers, " Well, I'm through", and I begin to think of my life.' Convinced that the broken collar-bone and broken jaw-bone that he had suffered were Divine retribution for the life he had led, he was drawn from the blues to the Church.

A mile or two from Hillary Blunt lived Willie Thomas, a preacher who sang the blues. To him the problems confronting black people were of a different order. 'In this latter day here, with all this education, in this space-age, when everybody's lookin' up, the average Negro, the younger Negro is tryin' to imprerate the white man, for he get his things, he try to act like him, talk like him, try to use things like him. But it's nach'al that he can't do it. Like me and Butch Cage here. It's a matter of equalizin' himself, to show the white man he don't have nothin' that he can't do. But nach'lly it's not so,' he declared, accepting up to a point that would be inadmissible to such a leader as Aaron Henry, the drug store proprietor general of the Mississippi Battlefront of the NAACP in Clarksdale, the inequalities that a segregationalist society had imposed.

Such contradictions and differences of opinion are symptomatic of the dilemma in which Blacks found themselves, blues singers no less than their companions. In the widely differing cultural, social and inter-racial climates in which black groups are to be found many shades of opinion exist and these are reflected in the comments of the blues singers which sometimes disagree. In a few months of continual research and concentrated recording it proved possible to gather a vast quantity of material which, whilst confirming some known data on aspects of the blues and substantiating others which had been assumed, also threw new light on many ill-defined areas and added much undocumented material. The continuous conversation with the blues was allowed to take its own course in order to minimize the dangers of interviews steered along predetermined lines. The result was not a series of autobiographies therefore: Henry Townsend displayed a serious concern with the meaning and mobility of the blues, Little Brother Montgomery was unconcerned with the philosophy of the music but could recall with pristine clarity a legion of virtually unknown blues pianists. Whilst a Buster Pickens could evoke the world of freight car and barrelhouse in which he had spent a lifetime, a Blind Brewer displayed an interest in his guitars that reached obsession. Whilst Will Shade recalled the experiences of more than half a century before, Sil Johnson projected the confidence of a youthful blues singer who was making his impression on an excited public. Knowledge of their recordings of twenty-five years before changed Whistling Alex

Moore from a truculent hotel porter to a warm and ebullient personality, and induced Black Ace to laugh over days long past and to pick up the steel guitar and bottleneck which had lain idle for years. Persistent searching led us to them; chance led us to encounter Blind Gray on a street corner and Bo Carter in an unfurnished slum. Different circumstances, different surroundings, different temperaments, different age groups revealed in turn different facets of the blues.

Far from inhibiting the speakers the BBC field recorder excited genuine interest as a piece of equipment and encouraged many a blues singer to summon his memories and address his observations with clarity and confidence. 'I must tell the truth about that, because I'm recordin',' said Mary Johnson half to herself as she began to talk. Frankness was met with honesty: 'You ask me about it, so I'm tellin' you,' said Will Shade when speaking of Beale Street in its lustier and more violent days. 'I can't see you, but I'll tell you about myself because I can tell you're on the level,' said Blind Gray as he commenced his grim narrative. The blues remained the common ground – at the most extreme in the instance of Jewel Long who lived in the tough, unlovely, racially tense little community of Sealy, Texas. 'What kind of language do they speak in your country? How d'ya learn to speak our language so good?' he asked curiously, having never heard of England and not relating 'English' with a nation. But there were other, opposite and even less predictable effects. A European origin was a help rather than a handicap for to most Blacks this implied a liberal approach to the ever-present problems of race and colour. The experiences of quite a few blues singers who had served in European theatres of war and had been stationed at some time in England proved to be an unexpected bond. Above all, the presence of my wife despite the repeated warnings we had received from sources official and unofficial, white and black alike, gave to those we met an immeasurable degree of assurance of our genuine purpose. Coolly and earnestly, with conviction or with passion according to their dispositions, the singers told their stories and expressed their opinions. They were stories that were not without contradictions, not perhaps without errors of fact. The limited horizons of many of the singers produced their own perspective distortions. Time and pride may cause them to embroider some narratives,

We Were With The Red Rose Minstrels
Pianist Speckled Red was a veteran of
the medicine shows

and leave others as sketches. Blues is a folk-music – a music of the people, and much of its history is folk-lore, the mixture of truth and belief which must pass for history in an oral, unlettered tradition.

Change comes slowly to the rural South and the gradual absorption of city idioms is still a slow process in blues evolution. In Chicago, Detroit or Houston, the natural surroundings of the modern living music, the fiercer forms of rhythm and blues continue to maintain their hold over the young African American gatherings. Since these recordings were made, however, certain of the singers represented have reached their peak or passed it, have retired, have been forgotten, have died. Others have achieved a wider fame, moving from the blues environment to that of the college and folk-song club, coming to Europe, touring with package shows. Many have made records with young white accompanists, had been subjected to interviews, and appeared on television. This wider attention was not enjoyed by all their fellows, some of whom, wittingly or unwittingly, having moved into the darker recesses of the blues background. But the more fortunate – materially speaking, at least – witnessed, participated in, and were sometimes adversely affected by the boom in blues popularity. Such changing fortunes seem to be the inevitable lot of the blues singer: as some disappeared others were rediscovered. A happier aspect of the later trend had been the finding of a number of ageing singers who had been brought from relative obscurity to enjoy a brief, belated triumph of recognition in the existing, though alien, environment of the concert platform and the campus. Their stories brought further enrichment of personal detail to the picture of the blues.

It is nevertheless a picture that has been impaired by the extensive imitation and dilution of the blues idioms that the nineteen-sixties brought. Worldwide recognition of the blues has also meant widespread copying of the music and student groups in Liverpool or London played 'rhythm and blues' in R & B clubs whilst their counterparts in the United States, the student 'white blues singers' were acclaimed in the city 'folk-song' clubs. Well intentioned though their efforts, well played and sung though their performances were, theirs was essentially a derivative, eclectic music. Its prevalence brought much confusion and led to considerable misunderstanding of the blues and inadvertently sped its death. The future of the blues as a folk form was not assured by this blood transfusion; it is more likely that it will depend on those whom fame had passed, the little-known and sometimes minor figures for whom creating the blues was a necessary expression in their lives and who kept its heart beating with their rhythm and its life-blood flowing with their inventiveness.

At this stage it is vital that we understand what the blues has meant for those who have created it, see and recognize its background before the image is befogged and the outlines blurred. In retrospect the recorded conversations from which the following transcriptions have been made seem to have been registered at a significant point in the history of the blues. A long musical tradition led to the threshold of the 'sixties; the rapid changes brought about by popularization and imitation were still to come. Far from the close-carpeted artistes' rooms backstage at the concert hall, the coffee lounge or the college auditorium the recordings were made in wooden shot-gun shack and brownstone house, Mississippi barber shop and Memphis pool-room, in black juke and 'colored' hotel, on street corners and front porches, in club and bar-room, basement and tenement, record shop and garage from the Great Lakes to the Gulf of Mexico. Barrelhouse pianists and juke-joint guitarists, street singers and travelling show entertainers, jazz musicians and jug-band players, sharecroppers and mill-workers, vagrants and migrants, mechanics and laborers – these were amongst the speakers. Some had secure jobs, some had none; some were on relief and some in retirement; some played for themselves, some played for others, some had once ridden high and others were going down slow, some were famous, some unknown, some were young and others venerable: all had played their part in shaping the pattern of the blues. It was a pattern that emerged slowly, logically, dictating its own order from the many hundreds of thousands of words transcribed from the results of weeks of recording: a pattern that was not the history of the blues in detailed terms of every personality and style and region, but which was, nonetheless, from the lips of those who made it, the story of the blues.

Blues Country: The Central Stream

Railroads serving the area

Atchison, Topeka & Santa	A T & S F
Baltimore & Ohio	B & O
Chicago, Burlington & Quincy	C B & Q
Gulf, Mobile & Ohio	G M & O
Illinois Central	I C
Louisville & Nashville	L & N
Missouri – Pacific	M P
New York, Chicago & St Louis	N Y C & St L
(Nickel Plate)	
St Louis & South Western	S L & S W
Southern	Sou
Texas & Pacific	T & P
Southern Pacific	S P
Wabash	Wab
Yazoo Delta	Y D
Yazoo & Mississippi Valley	Y & M V (Now I C)

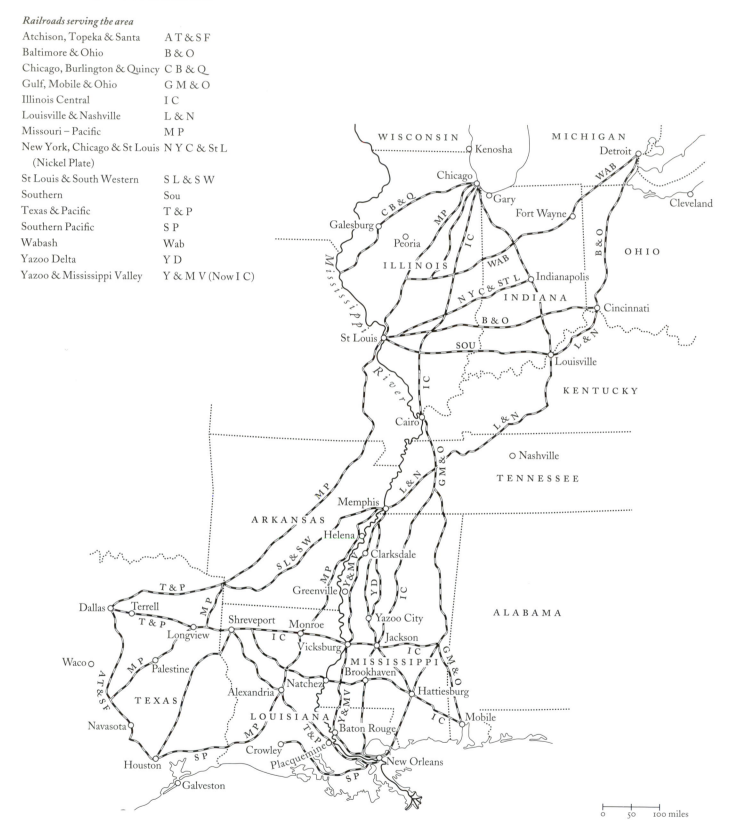

14

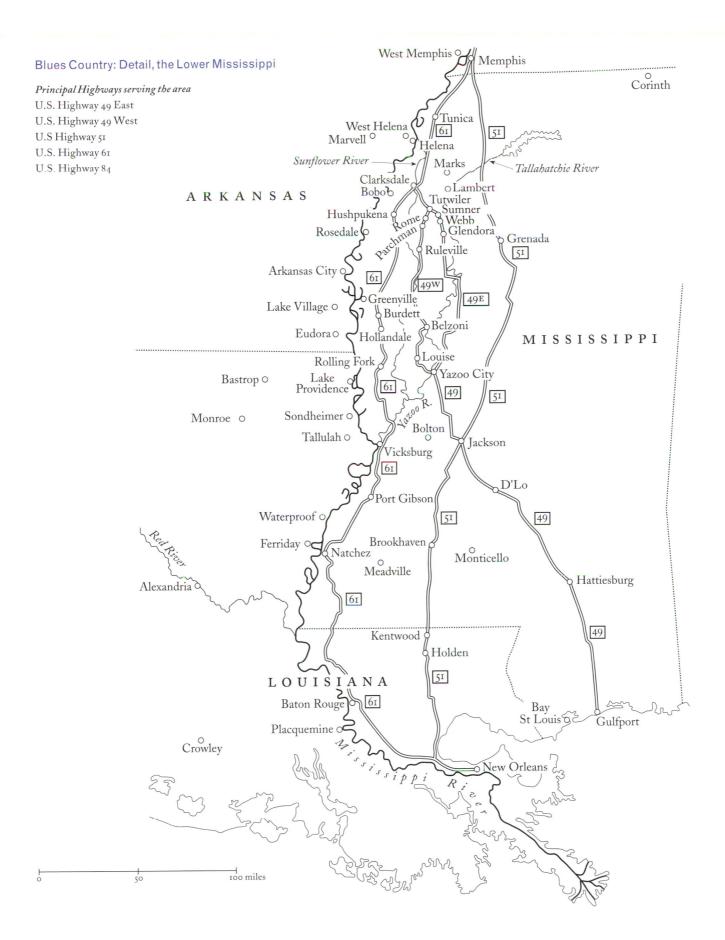

Blues Country: Detail, the Lower Mississippi

Principal Highways serving the area
U.S. Highway 49 East
U.S. Highway 49 West
U.S Highway 51
U.S. Highway 61
U.S. Highway 84

West Memphis
Memphis
Corinth

Tunica
West Helena
Marvell
Helena
Sunflower River
Marks
Tallahatchie River

ARKANSAS
Clarksdale
Bobo
Lambert
Tutwiler
Sumner
Webb
Hushpukena
Rome
Glendora
Grenada
Rosedale
Parchman
Ruleville

Arkansas City
Greenville
Burdett
MISSISSIPPI
Lake Village
Belzoni
Eudora
Hollandale
Louise
Rolling Fork
Yazoo City
Bastrop
Lake Providence
Yazoo R.
Monroe
Sondheimer
Bolton
Tallulah
Jackson
Vicksburg

D'Lo
Port Gibson
Waterproof
Brookhaven
Ferriday
Natchez
Monticello
Meadville
Hattiesburg

Red River
Alexandria

Kentwood

LOUISIANA
Holden
Baton Rouge
Placquemine
Bay St Louis
Gulfport
Crowley
New Orleans
Mississippi River

0   50   100 miles

Conversation with the Blues

It's me as I is
Robert Curtis Smith

Just felt music
Wade Walton

The most reason I sing the blues is because most things in my life and coming up was so difficult, it seemed like I had a harder time than most people. I worked in the fields . . . I lived in Clarksdale, way up to Jackson, working, working, and it mostly keeps me with the blues because everything I go to do it turns out backwards; and the songs that I sing, I sing them from the heart in the way I feel. I hope that the people that do hear me, I hope that they like it because it's me as I is for what I is. I love the blues because the blues is the only thing that gives me relief when I gets to the place where it seems like everything go wrong. So if anybody have the blues like I do – why, I know just how they feel, because it's a feeling that it's hard to do anything about; it's hard to know which way to go, or what to do, the blues . . . I can't explain it: it's a feeling that's deep down inside, it's so deep that I can't possibly get to the bottom of it. The blues is just – the blues, that's all I know.

We play the nach'al blues here in Mississippi, when we say we play the blues here. I haven't had any training for this thing – it's just felt music.

> I have the blues, I have the blues about midnight,
> And I have the blues about the break of day,
> And I have the blues that stay with me all the way.
>
> I have the blues to stay with me all night long,
> And I have the blues with me at my home,
> I have the blues that follow me all along.

I Sing Them from the Heart
Robert Curtis Smith, tractor driver, plays in the Big Six barber shop

You can get to yourself
Little Eddie Kirkland

What gives me the blues? I can say three or four things in life. Unlucky in love for one, and hard to make a success is two; and when a man have a family and it's hard to survive for, and the one thing left to do is to feel sorry for yourself. What's so good about the blues is that when you feel sorry for yourself is that you can get to yourself and sing the blues.

So much good feeling
Boogie Woogie Red

Say for instance you be lonely for your girl friend or your wife, you'd be in a melancholy mood or you'd just want to hear some blues. You'd just go out and relax your nerves; blues is something that relax your nerves. You take a man – he had been prosperous, making lots of money. Ah well, when his money's all gone what else is left but the blues? But there's so much good feeling in the blues, that's the main thing about the blues. And you don't have to have anybody around to have the blues, and you don't have to be around people. You be alone to yourself, time to think about the mistakes you have made in life . . . the money, everything . . . that's what you call the blues.

It kinda helps
Henry Townsend

I feel there's two ways you can go into this: if you have a depressed feeling – that's altogether one thing. Then if you have what you call a happy feeling about a thing, that's altogether another. And they can both give you inspirations to sing, you know what I mean – say if it's joyful you build it one way, but if it's something that kind of puts you 'down in the dumps' as they call it, why you carry it out another way. You express yourself in a different direction. So, of course I can't say that I've found where I'd be feeling down all the time; some of the time there would be joyful things that I would think of. But I tell you, in most cases the way I feel, the song will come to you when you are really depressed you know. I mean, words'll come to you and you feel them and you decide you'll do something about it, so the thing that you do about it is more or less to put it in rhymes and words and make them come out. It gives you relief – it kinda helps somehow. I don't know – it kinda helps.

You have to tell it
Lil Son Jackson

Well I think the blues is more or less a feeling that you get from something that you think is wrong, or something that somebody did wrong to you, or something that somebody did wrong to some of your own people or something like that. That's the way I see the blues. It cause a feeling, more or less a sad feeling about it, and when you have that sort of feeling well, quite naturally you reproduce it. And the onliest way you have to tell it would be through a song, and that would be the blues. That's the way I see it. But the blues is really aimed at an object of some kind or an indirect person. It's not aimed at the whole public; the blues cannot be aimed at the whole public. It's either some person or some object, because you can really aim the blues at an object too you know, like a train or something, or a car for instance. That's right.

Somewhere down the line

John Lee Hooker

There's a lot of things that give you the blues, that give me the blues, that give any man the blues: it's somewhere down the line that you have been hurt some place. I mean it's no certain type of hurtin' but you have been hurt some place and you get to playin' the blues that reaches. And so that's why when I sing the blues I sing it with the big feelin'. I really means it. It's not the manner that I had the hardships that a lot of people had throughout the South and other cities throughout the country, but I do know what they went through. My mother, my daddy and my stepfather, they told me these things and I know that they must have went through those things themselves. And so when you gets the feelin' it's not only what happened to you – it's what happened to your fore-parents and other people. And that's what makes the blues.

Major Blues Singer
John Lee Hooker who
migrated from Mississippi
to Detroit, sings with 'the
big feelin'

A little different
Willie Thomas

It's not very much of song that the Negro got from whites, because Negro people always was a kind of singing group of people through the country. You see, we was kind of a little different; we were kind of a segregated bunch down among the white people. The white man could get education and he could learn to read a note, and the Negro couldn't. All he had to get for his music what God give him in his heart. And that's the only thing he got. And he didn't get that from the white man; God give it to him.

They was always here
Boogie Woogie Red

I'll tell you about the blues – the blues is something that you play when you're in a low mood or something, and the hardships that you have had through life. It's just the mood that you are in. And the average person takes the blues as what you might call a plaything, but the blues is really serious. The blues is something that you have to play coming from your heart. And blues have been goin' on for centuries and centuries, and the blues was written years and centuries ago – they was always here.

On the slavery
James Butch Cage

They comes from back in slavery time. When we was on the slavery – colored time was on the slavery – we was eatin' the bones and the skin and the hog jaws. That's what they eat back there, and the white folks eat all the good meat. They was hard times and they made a song about it. My mama learned it to me; she wasn't a slave but my grandmaw was. She was born the second year of Surrender, my mama was, and they used to sing it:

> Black nigger baby, black feet and shiny eyes,
> Black all over to the bone and india-rubber thighs,
> > Turn that nigger round and knock 'im in the haid,
> > Cause white folks say, 'We're gonna kill that nigger dead.'
> > The white folks eat the hog in the skillet,
> > Niggers was no-good, so very little in it,
> > Old Uncle Dicker-Dagger eat up the grease – say,
> > 'Get up in the mawnin', I'll be free!'
> Black nigger baby gonna take care of myself,
> Always carry a great big razor and a pistol in my vest,
> > Turn that nigger round and knock 'im on the haid,
> > Cause white folks say, 'We're gonna kill that nigger dead.'

Pretty tough on a person
Emma Williams

It's been so long ago, I was quite young then. I don't know how long, many years ago, before nineteen-hundred. I got along pretty well in Mississippi but they didn't pay you nothin' much for your labour and I had to work pretty hard for to live. White folks didn't bother me or nothin' like that; I got on pretty well in that line. But some places in Mississippi you didn't get over three dollars a week; some places you didn't even get that much a week. You know that was pretty tough on a person – living. You didn't pay nothin' much for rent – I had a three-room house, I paid four dollars a month. The rent wasn't high but they just didn't pay you nothin' for your labor. Yazoo City was my main town, Yazoo City. At that time I was livin' in a li'l ole country town 'bout eleven miles from there they call Eden Station. I used to hear 'em playin' on harps, on git-tars and so on like that, some, and whoever was playin' a git-tar or something, they'd sing. But I don't know nothing about them blues much.

He already had five in front
Blind Arvella Gray

I was born in Texas in a little flag-stop town. My people was very poor. When I was born I had sisters and brothers older than I am – and then my mother had triplets and I was one of them. She had a midwife – we didn't have doctors in them days – so when the midwife say to my dad she say, ' Come in an' look an' see the babies.' So my dad come in and he was disgusted 'cause he already had five in front, and when he seen triplets like that he said to my mother, her name was Dora, he said, 'Come and pick out the one you want because I'm gonna drown the other two.' So then I've been swimmin' ever since. That's true. Then as I growed up we was on a plantation and it was pretty rough as far as money was concerned. But we just survived you know. And then after a certain length of time well then, my mother she died in 1918 with twins, you know, childbirth. When she died of childbirth well then my oldest sister taken over and my daddy had deserted us, for no reason at all, just pulled right on out. Then I started at the age of thirteen on my own. So I ran off from my sisters and left them and my brother behind and I went on a plantation called the Dollar Boyd Plantation, that's in the southern part of Texas. And I worked there for a year and he gave me a quarter for my year's work at the end of the season. Now he fed me and he bought me clothes although he didn't buy no shoes. But in the meantime a friend of mine bought me a pair of shoes called Buster Brown shoes – that was the brand name, and they was real shiny. And he told me to put them on and I didn't know what you supposed to do with them because I had never worn no shoes before. And so when I did put them on I stood like half a day before anybody noticed me standin' just in one place and when they told me I was supposed to walk around in them I just didn't understand about walking around in shoes. I was just clumsy when I started walkin' in shoes.

My pa was a fiddler

Mance Lipscomb

An Open Player
Mance Lipscomb
is proud that he has
'got it in the fingers'

I been playin' the git-tar now 'bout forty-nine years, and then I started out by myself, just heard it and learned it. Ear music. And nobody didn't learn me nothin'. Just pick it up myself; I didn't know any notes, just play by ear. And I been playin' 'bout forty-nine years. My pa was a fiddler; he was an old perfessional fiddler. All my people can play some kind of music. Well, my daddy he was a perfessional fiddler and he played way back in olden days. You know, he played at breakdowns, waltzes, shottishes and all like that and music just come from him to me, that's why I learned it from him. Papa were playing for dances out, for white folks and coloured. He played *Missouri Waltz*, *Casey Jones*, just anything you name he played it like I'm playin'. He was just a self player until I was big enough to play behind him, then we two played together. But he played way up from when I was born, and then when I got to size, he took me around to play with him. *Sugar Babe* was the first piece I learned, when I was a li'l boy about thirteen years old. Reason I know this so good, I got a whippin' about it. Come out of the cotton-patch to get some water and I was up at the house playin' the git-tar and my mother come in; whopped me 'cause I didn't come back – I was playin' the git-tar:

> Sugar babe, I'm tired of you,
> Ain't your honey but the way you do,
> Sugar babe . . . it's all over now.
>
> Goin' down town, goin' t'get me a rope,
> Gonna whip my babe till she Buzzard Lope,
> Sugar babe . . . it's all over now.
>
> All I want my babe to do,
> Make five dollars and give me two,
> Sugar babe, oh sugar babe, it's all over now.
>
> Sugar babe I'm tired of you,
> Ain't carin' honey whichaway you do,
> Sugar babe, sugar babe, it's all over now.
>
> Goin' down town, gonna get me a line,
> Whip my babe till she change her mind,
> Sugar babe . . . it's all over town.
>
> Sugar babe, what's the matter with you?
> You don't treat me like you used to do,
> Sugar babe. . . it's all over now.

Yeah, I got a whippin' 'bout *Sugar Babe* – I never will forget that one.

It didn't affect my lungs

J. B. Lenoir

My old man, he was a blues player a long time ago, and I used to sit down and look at him play. And my mother used to say – I must've been 'bout nine months old, when he was playin' the box I would shout in her arms. She just couldn't hold me, I couldn't be still. So when I come to know myself, I was playin' an old number by the name of *Move to Kansas City* then. And the box was bigger than I was, I couldn't sit up, in the chair like this, I had to sit on the flo'. And I was playing' *Move to Kansas City* then. But I was singing all the time. You take my home – my home's in Mississippi – and a lots o' times I used to get out there and whoop and holler just to exercise my lungs, you know? Now you take sometimes I be workin' out there with my daddy on my daddy's peach orchard, or in the yard or in the fields, and I used to holler so loud – just to see how loud I *could* holler. It didn't affect my lungs or nothin' like that. So now it don't never affect it; I can just holler as loud as I *want* to holler sometimes. So I hollered with everything I do. I did just about everything in the work line. I have worked so hard you could hear the water splashin' in my shoe – that's the truth. And I have worked on the railroad . . . in the fields . . . I have run tampers. I have done just about everything a person could name for to make that money for a livin'. So it rocked on, and I used to look at my daddy play, all nights. So my daddy, he got hurt on his job – he was sawing logs – and he made a change. You know how people make a change if they get hurt? And I asked him, 'Well dad, why have you stopped playin' the blues?' He said, 'Well son, I was layin' down and that ole Deevil got at me in my sleep – somethin' with a bukka tail and a shape of a bull but he could talk – and when I spied him I started to run. But the Deevil he said, "You cin run, but you cain't hide"; so that's the reason why I stopped playin' the blues.'

So I guess I took it up from him – playing the blues.

I'd holler too

Muddy Waters

Rolling Fork, Mississippi, was where I was born at. I was the second boy child but my daddy – his name was Ollie Morganfield – went right on makin' children and I had six brothers and five sisters and all but two is livin' yet. My daddy was a farmer; he raised hawgs and chickens. Grew watermelons. We had a li'l – oh, two-room shack and there was a creek – Deer Creek – come right up to the steps at the back porch. I was always playin' in the creek and gettin' dirty and my sisters called me Muddy Waters then. Mama died when I was 'bout three and my grandmammy carr'd me up to Clarksdale and that's where I was raised. I went to school but they didn't give you too much schoolin' because just as soon as you was big enough you get to workin' in the fields. I guess I was a big boy for my age but I was just a boy and they put me to workin' right along side the men. I handled the plough, chopped cotton, did all of them things. Every man would be hollerin' but you don't pay that no mind. Yeah, course I'd holler too. You might call them blues but they was just made-up things. Like a feller be workin' or most likely some gal be workin' near and you want to say somethin' to 'em. So you holler it. Sing it. Or maybe to your mule or something or it's gettin' late and you wanna go home. I can't remember much of what I was singin' now 'ceptin' I do remember I was always singin', 'I cain't be satisfied, I be all troubled in mind.' Seems to me like I was always singin' that, because I was always singin' jest the way I felt, and maybe I didn't exactly *know* it, but I jest didn't like the way things were down there – in Mississippi.

Well ef I feel this mawnin', like I feel today,
I'm gonna pack my suitcase and make my getaway,
 Lord I be troubled, I'm all worried in mind,
  And I never been satisfied, an' I jest can't keep from cryin'.

Yeah, I know my li'l ole babe,
She gonna jump and shout,
That ole train be late babe an' I come walkin' out,
 I'm troubled, I'm all worried in mind,
  And I never be satisfied, I jest can't keep from cryin'.

Yeah I know somebody stop and talk to you
I don't need no tellin' gal, I cin watch the way you do,
 Lord I be's troubled, I be all worried in mind,
  Yeah, I never be satisfied an' I jest can't keep from cryin'.

Start From Monday Plantation field-hands make their way to the cotton-patch

Cotton Field Hollers Workers in the bottomlands near Yazoo City sing 'hollers' and unaccompanied blues. A line of trees marks the Mississippi

Meat and bread
Wade Walton

Ole farm boy livin' out on the plantation, out on a farm. I'm a farm boy and my friends all lived on the farms, and we used to pick cotton . . . . Man! I used to pick two-three hundred pounds a day and then my parents thought that wasn't enough cotton for me to pick. And my boss-man – he didn't think that was enough cotton for me to pick. He used to think I should pick about a bale a day which for this Deltra cotton it doesn't take but twelve hundred pounds to make a bale, see. This Deltra cotton, they call D. P. and L. which means Delta Pine Lands only people call it Damn Poor Livin'. And you put that sack on your back and you pick that cotton and you start from Monday – well some people they start on Sunday and pick all day Sunday and forget about the church – pick them big fleshy bolls and pack it down in our sack; pack it down with our feet and they would pay us fifty cents a hundred for picking. And sometimes we wouldn't get anything; we was sharecroppers on the place – used to have thirty-five or forty acres o' land, depending on the number of dependents that you have in your family, see. And with this cotton, when you get to the plantin' part of it they give you 'furnish' they call it. They give you so much money – two weeks' money and two weeks' grocery. And then you plow this cotton and start choppin' cotton until this cotton matures to bolls, and from that to openin' time. Then they stop furnishin' you see, and you start pickin' cotton and they give you so much for the seed and so much for the lint – which wasn't very much. You had to live very scarcely you know. Just call it meat and bread . . . sounds funny, you might say it's sad but that's what was happenin'. You get a li'l money and by the time you been down town – Clarksdale – and spend it and buy yourself a few clothin' and mama take the rest of it for some of the expenses round home, you have ver' li'l money left for to go to the show. And when settlin' time come, they call 'settle!' When the final settlement come the white man have the pencil behind his ear and he figgered out. And he says, ' I'm gonna check you out. John, you did well, you made a damn good crop. Thirty-five bales, I feel that you did damn good. I'm gonna tell ya now, your furnish' for six or seven weeks run up to such-and-such a thing and I think you did damn good. And a hundred dollars, a hundred and fifty dollars is what I think you cleared and I think you did good, don't you think you did good, John?'

'Yassuh, Ah think Ah did good . . . thas' good money, yassuh.'

'Well how much land do you think you need another year? I think you need more land 'cause thirty-five bales wasn't enough for you and your wife and your five kids. I think you worked hard. The little tiny ones went to school – went to school two months and that was damn good, John, but you need to take on more land. That's what you need to do, John. Now if you take on eight more acres of land and you just clean up that new cut back there I think you'll be doin' all right. And get that all worked up and everything and take about eight or ten more bales, I think that you'll clear fifty more dollars. Don't you think that'll be all right?'

'Yassah . . . Ah think that be all right.'

'I'm gonna give you five more dollars on your issue – and that mean your furnishin' . . . .'

And that kind of thing. Which is quite stupid, I mean if you just look back at it. But those is the kind of things we live by, here.

When Final Settlement Comes
Pause for refreshment at the corrugated iron grocery at Louisa, Mississippi. The mules wait by the cotton gin

I got insulted

Blind Arvella Gray

I got on a farm which was very well known. It was a plantation but they called it Bob Newsome Farm. It's a plantation and there was a few thousand people there. So then I worked there for a year and then a flood came and we had to go to high ground – 1920 I think it was when the flood was in Texas. And then while we was up on the high ground from the plantation another feller – white feller – came along and stole a bunch of us and gave us a line of jive, say, 'We gonna take you out West Texas and you can make some money there and you can be more free and have some money in the bank.' So we went out there, West Texas around Amarillo, sharecroppin'. At the end of the sharecrop we'd made pretty good in them days and I asked the feller, 'Give me seventeen dollars, I want to go see some of my relatives.' And he said, 'No, let your relatives come and see you.' I got insulted about that and I run off from there; got the walkin' blues:

> Said get late of an evenin' feel like blowin' my horn,
> Get late of an evenin' feel like blowin' my horn,
> Say when I woke up this mornin' all I had was gone.
>
> Said don't the moon look pretty when it shinin' through
>   them trees,
> Said the moon look pretty shinin' through them trees,
> Said I can see my baby but she cain't see me.
>
> Now I'm goin' to Heaven, sit down on a stool,
> Said I'm goin' to Heaven, sit down on a stool,
> Said I'm gonna ask poor Moses to play me the walkin' blues.
>
> Now I started to Heaven, Lord but I changed my mind,
> Now I started to Heaven, Lord but I changed my mind,
> Says I'm gonna stay right here where I can have better times.
>
> Now place your deuces, and Lord your fours and fives,
> Said place your deuces, Lord and your fours and fives,
> Say I saw cold water, from the poor boy's eyes.
>
> Now you can always tell when your woman don't want
>   you aroun',
> You can always tell buddy, when your woman don't want
>   you roun',

> She got her head tied up, bed turned upside down – that
>   means get get your hat and go, buddy.
> Said what makes the rooster, crow 'bout dawn a' day,
>
> Say what makes the rooster, crow 'bout dawn a' day,
> Say to let the sweet man know the workin' man's on his way.
>
> Says I'm gonna sing this song pardner, ain't gonna sing
>   much more,
> Says I'll sing this song pardner, ain't gonna sing
>   much more,
> Says I'm gonna pack my suitcase, down the road I'll go.

The onliest way

Lil Son Jackson

We sharecropped out on a farm and more or less that's the onliest way we had of makin' a livin'. I mean my father follered that kind of labor; I mean that's the onliest labor he ever knew. And which and why that was the hard side of life, because in sharecroppin' you work all the year and when the year ends and everything supposed to be divided up, why then you supposed to get half and he's supposed to get the other half. And you don't have but one thing to do and that's go along with him and take whatever the figures showin' whatever you have. You can't argue. You can't prove nothin' so you just go along with him. So you make it out whatever way you can – make it go further.

You know I once was a gambler, boys and I bet my money
   wrong,
You know I once was a gambler and I bet my money wrong,
Ain't got no more money and all I got is, gone.

When I lose that money, sat around with my head hung down,
Lose that money, sat around with my head hung down,
I woke up in the mornin' with my face all full of frowns.

You know I'm through with gamblin', some Jack Stropper
   can have my room
I'm through with gamblin', some Jack Stropper can have
   my room,
Pretty women may kill me but gamblin' will be my doom.

Well I promised my baby that I wouldn't play no more,
I promised my baby that I wouldn't play no more,
Well it seems like gamblin's gonna foller me every place I go.

My father, I think he more or less had a burden of some kind. That was the onliest way he could get relief from it, by singin' them blues. Just like me or anybody. I can get vexed up or somethin' or I have a sad feelin'; seems like to me that if I can sing, I feel better. But my father, he only just played at home and around. More or less at home is all I did know him to play. Now in his comin' up I don't know because that was before my time; I couldn't tell, but after I knew him he just played around at home. They all played music, my father and mother too. And my father was a very good musician especially on the guitar. I never did take music to be a thing that I could make a livin' of; I didn't even think about that because I was a mechanic – mechanic-inclined – I like to work on automobiles. And finally by me playin' behind what I heard my father did and what he showed me and what I picked up I finally begin to like it a bit myself. But I never did take interest enough in it to go to school and try to learn somethin' from the book, I more or less played what I felt.

They burned him

Sam Price

Mechanic-inclined
Lil Son Jackson works at a
salvage and auto-wrecking
yard near Dallas, Texas

When I was a boy I lived in Texas, and it was pretty rugged.
I'll never forget the first song I ever heard to remember. A man
had been lynched near my home in a town called Robinson,
Texas. And at that time we were living in Waco, Texas – my
mother, brother and myself. And they made a parody of this
song and the words were something like this:

> I never have, and I never will
> Pick no more cotton in Robinsonville,
>> Tell me how long will I have to wait,
>> Can I get you now or must I hesitate?

I remember this particular lynching. Now what that meant by
that song was that he would never pick any more cotton in
Robinson – Robinsonville – because a man had been lynched
there. And then shortly after that they lynched a man in
Waco, Texas. I was in the public school you know, as a kid.
And we had to run home and close the door and then they
lynched this man and then they burned him and sewed up his
ashes in a little cloth and sold these ashes to the people. So you
see I'm quite conscious of the – you know – the social pattern
in America. And I'm glad to know that it has gone from all
this horrible record of all the lynching – to last year, I don't
believe there was a Negro lynched in America at all. So the
position must be improving. Well, the sort of work we did . . .
you could pick cotton. We picked cotton in the fall of the year.
You chopped cotton in the spring. The kids would get out of
school to chop cotton – early. Then came the summer months
and you would go and pick peaches and this sort of thing. And
then in the fall you went away to pick cotton. Then you could
get a job as a porter and then you had the middle-class Negroes
who was your teachers, and preachers and a few doctors and a
very few lawyers. And your property owners.

Have to paint my face

Sam Chatman

Say God made us all, he made some at night,
That's why he didn't take time to make us all white,
    I'm bound to change my name, I have to paint my face,
    So I won't be kin to that Ethiopian race.

Say now let me tell you one thing that a Stumptown nigger
    will do,
He'll pull up young cotton and he'll kill baby chickens too.
    I'm bound to change my name, I have to paint my face,
    So I won't be kin to that Ethiopian race.

Say when God made me, the moon was givin' light,
I'm so dog-gone sorry he didn't finish me up white,
    I'm bound to change my name, I have to paint my face,
    So I won't be kin to that Ethiopian race.

Say now when God made people he done pretty well,
But when he made a jet black nigger he made them some hell,
I'm bound to change my name I have to paint my face
So I won't be kin to that Ethiopian race.

We was born on a plantation. It was kinda hard in those days
and it was real hard for colored folks. We was all farmin' crop-
pin' raisin the hawgs and we all just growed up under that.
Come up a bit later I been a yard boy; learned to drive a tractor
did a bit of that. But I can't move away too far now because my
old lady has the paralysis. Can't move you know. So I have to
tend to her. Have to keep the bed by the winder for to ketch
the air because I ain't been able to afford one of them fans.

Kin to the Ethiopian Race
Sam Chatman of Hollandale,
Mississippi, was a member of
the Mississippi Sheiks

Pick up the trash
James Butch Cage

Right now I'm on the whatcha call 'Security' – that's pension money you know. Years back I was sharecroppin' up in Meadville, Mississippi, had to clean up the ground there, put in the seed, chop and do all of that. We were poor folks – yeah, really poor because my mama was a widder-woman 'cause my daddy he died when I was ten year old. So there was thirteen of us chil'ren and my mama raise us all up and I never did have no schoolin' 'cause I was always workin'. Then when the high water come up there in '27 I quit from there an' come to Louisiana and join my brother on his patch. And I did work on the railroad, tampin' the ties and gradin' work, levellin' track and I even pick up the trash for the city – yeah I mean in Baton Rouge, that's right – for to get that money.

> Dried up flour, meat I 'clare it was strong
> That dried up flour and meat I declare it was strong
> People keep your corn-bread; I just can't stick 'roun' long.

> When ya left before day baby, somethin' goin' on wrong,
> When they lef' before day somethin's goin' on wrong,
> But when my right foot itches I mean I just cain't stay
>   here long.

> Tied up my jumper ironed my overhauls
> I tied up my jumper and ironed my overhauls
> My brownie done quit me – God knows, she had it all.

> Well I cannot write baby and I ain't gonna try no more,
> I cannot write baby ain't gonna try no more,
> Blues come to get me – please drive them from my door.

I done everything
Black Ace

Work I done in the past? I done janitor work out on the air base . . . What kinda work I done? Man, I done everything! I picked cotton . . . sure, I went out to try to pick cotton – me *and* my wife. And I think I could pick about three hundred pounds . . . well that kept us eatin'.

> I want you to get up in the mornin' woman, try to find
>   yourself a job,
> I want you to get up in the mornin' woman, find yourself
>   a job,
> And stop sittin' round here tellin' me, baby 'bout the times
>   bein' hard.

> Don't you get no taxi Mama, you must walk over town,
> Don't you get no taxi Mama, you must walk all over town,
> You must find yourself a job woman; babe, before the sun
>   goes down.

> You don't do nothin' but sit on your B.A. and play cards,
> You don't do nothin' but sit on your B.A. and play cards,
> You tell me when I come home, 'Baby the times sure is
>   hard.'

> Now when you get a job Mama, you must work the whole
>   day long,
> When you get a job Mama, you must work the whole day
>   long,
> Now if you don't wanna work woman, you can find you
>   another home.

I picked cotton and then I come out of the cotton-patch and I got a little job janitorin'. And got this job at the air base workin' there five years janitorin'. And got laid off. And went back agin to the cotton-patch, that fall. Well I didn't pick enough cotton to keep my car – you know somep'n: they took my car away from me and I had bought me new set of tyres and they took the car away, tyres and all. I don't know the name of the company that took the car – finance company. I believe they called it Security. Well it must've been *security* – the car was worth $1200!

Half-handers

Mance Lipscomb

Used to work as a sharecropper way back but for fifteen or twenty years I were rentin'. I was a sharecropper before that. On half-handers – that's what we call workin' on halfers – one bale to him and one to me, one load of corn to him and one to me – and that's how we worked about twenty years back. But now if we're workin' on a farm we're workin' rentin' now; 'most everybody's a renter. Most of the time I lost out on my crop when I was sharecroppin' so you owe that. About two, three times I succeeded in a crop – made a profit. Highest money I made was about $700 – then about $150 and $200, somethin' like that – just accordin' to what sort of season you had to farm in. This was in Washington and Brazos Counties – most of my farmin' was there. Well I've done all different kinds of work too. I have worked in Houston some – brick-yard, lumberyard – farmed mostly all my life. I've done lots of different work but I never did as much as I did on the farm. So then I earned me a little bit playin' around different places with my guitar. I never did work in the musicians department, only in the open air. I played in lots o' towns but I never did have any records made, nothin' like that. But I've had lots of experience about bein' round through the country playin' music for different ones – suppers, dances, schools – but I mostly played by myself all the time. Never did have a band. Just an open player by myself. I learned myself to play in different keys. I change my music when I change my songs and you got somethin' new comin' up all the time. I get tired of one key. And I learned some fellers how to play. My sister's boy, I taught him. They all got better voice than me, they all got bet-ter voice because they never had no spell of sickness or any-thing like that. I been near to death with pneumonia. Part of my lungs is gone. My fingers is still 'live. But they ain't got it in the fingers, they got it in the mouth, and they foolin' the people by the way they sing but they don't know the music.

Blues in the bottle, blues in the bottle, stopper's in my hand,
    dog-gone you,
Blues in the bottle, stopper's in my hand,
If you wanta be my woman, gotta come under my
    command.

If you couldn't stand it, you couldn't stand it, you oughta
    stayed at home, dog-gone you
You couldn't stand it, you oughta stayed at home,
To think I killed for you Mama, worked on your daddy's farm.

When I had money, when I had money, my friends all
    ganged around,
When I had money Mama, my friends all ganged around,
Now I'm broke and got no money Mama, friends all turned
    me down.

Then I had my accident – was loadin' timber and the load fell on me and I got hurt. I'm at work now on the highway, State Highway. And I uses three hands – I'm the head of the whole bunch.

Foundation Man
Jewell Long of Sealy,
Texas, does 'just 'bout
any kind of work you
name'

Never had no education

Jewell Long

I've lived all my life in Sealy, Texas. Never had no education and I never been far from Austin County. Well I went up to Dallas a few times and I been to places around in Grimes County and like that. Worked in places, you know where the work took me at. But I ain't never been far from here and I ain't never been out of Texas. Seems I been playin' guitar, little piano most of my life. I come up, under John Thomas, used to play a twelvestring here. And my brother, he was a ragtime player, pianist in these parts. He was a noted musicianer, my brother and I learned a bit of piano from him. I used to play for country suppers in the Brazos Bottoms, play for jukes and like that. *Frankie and Albert*, *Ella Speed* – those old songs, and them old cotton-patch blues. I'm what you call a foundation man; I do just 'bout any kind of work you name. Well, I worked as a mill-hand, in the seedmills here in Austin County. I was a sharecropper years back – been a sharecropper half my life I guess but I can fix automobiles, tractors . . . mechanic work. Worked on the railroad some, been a section hand on the tracks hereabouts. I never played no music for a livin' – you know the peoples round here, they don't want you to advance yourself. You got to know your place, if you get me. So you got to live with 'em you understan', you got to watch yourself.

My baby she went away, my baby she left me a mule to ride,
My baby she went away, she left me nothin' but a mule
    to ride,
Soon as the train pulled off, that ole mule laid down
    and died.
Now baby, I'm goin' away, baby I won't be back until fall,
I'm goin' away, baby I won't be back until fall,
If you don't treat me no better baby, I sure won't be back at all.

Now do it a long time baby, short time sure makes me mad,
Now do it a long time baby, short time makes me mad,
Cause you're the sweetest little baby that your daddy ever had.

Baby, baby do you think that is right?
Baby why don't you tell me? Baby you know that ain't right,
You done left me here waitin' baby and you been drunk
    all night.

Baby why don't you tell me whose muddy shoes is these?
You better hurry up and tell me baby, whose dirty muddy
    shoes is these
Babe, they're here in the corner where your good man's
    ought to be.

I ain't got me, I ain't got me no more baby now,
I ain't got me, I ain't got me no more baby now,
She was a dirty mistreater, didn't mean me no good nohow.

So baby here is your ticket, you understand, your train,
So baby, here is your ticket, you understand, your train.
I'm goin' back to my woman; you better go back to your man.

The way it goes
Robert Curtis Smith

You work from the time right after sun-up until sundown. Other words in choppin' it's three dollars a day, and it's hard to make enough money to practically do anything, because, during the week you got to live and you go to the store and take up a little groceries to carry you that week but when you paid off you owe almost half of that. So there ain't anythin' you can do with the little change you has got, but stay here, because you cain't leave here unless you do leave walkin'. So that's the way it goes. I been makin' crops for 'bout eleven or twelve years straight. I cleared a l'il money two years; for the rest of the time you just work. You get your furnish' and you don't get nothin' else on your crop unless you borrow the money and well it's hard to do that now, and you just workin' and at the end of the year you no doubt come out behind. And if you don't you break even: the whole year's work gone and you ain't got nothin'. And ain't gonna borrow too much because they ain't gonna loan you too much. So it's still hard for you whichever way you go. If you make a lot of cotton why the expenses are goin' to take it up some kind of way. If you don't owe nothin' why the poison, the soda and the fertilizer and whatnot is goin to eat it up still. You don't know what it cost, and if it cost a $1,000 a ton why there's nothin' you can do about it except pay for it because it's put on there and what it costs you never know.

A chance to cut up
Sunnyland Slim

Back in 1924 in Mississippi you know, I was plowin' with the mules. And I was sick of the mules and my stepmother! And I would sit around Clarksdale and Tutwiler and the boys be playin' the blues, and the blues sound so good on Sat'dy nights before day and I always wanted to play. Late around about five o'clock in the mornin' you hear some ole cat lickin' out with the blues:

Lord I got a hard drivin' woman, she drives me all the time,
I got me a hard drivin' woman, Lord she drives me all my days,
And while she gonna drive me I be sinkin' lower an' lower
 in my grave.

She drive me so hard, I'm afraid I lose my mind,
Yes she drive me hard till I'm afraid I'll lose my mind,
Till when the sun starts to sinkin' I start right in to cry.

I wished I could die 'cause my baby treats me like a slave,
Lord I wish I could die, my baby treats me like a slave,
The more she drives me I been sinkin' lower and lower in
 my grave.

Course it was only on Sat'dy nights that you get a chance to cut up all I night and have a little fun like that. See people used to do what Muddy Waters used to do – he used to 'muddy' on Sat'dy and sell fish on Sat'dy nights. And chittlins and hamburgers – sausage sandwiches in them li'l ole honkytonks where you used to have li'l crap games. And that was their day. You know they was happy 'cause they didn't know nothin' else. But you see they would only have one day and that was Sat'dy. On Sunday mornin' and right through to Sunday night everybody have a little silence. 'Bout nine o'clock you get some sleep; everybody had to be kind of a little silent you know – get ready to go catch that mule next mornin'. During the day they be choppin' cotton, plowin', workin.' Some of them work to Sat'dy noon and some of them worked to Sat'dy night.

Sun-up to Sundown
Tar-papered in 'brick veneer', the sharecroppers' homes near Yazoo City are unoccupied during the day

When she come back

Otis Spann

One evenin' my dad said to me, 'You wants to be a blues player?' Because he knew how I bin tryin' to play like Friday Ford. Friday Ford was a great man and a wonderful player, matter-fact I think he was genius. And down to the present time before he died he taught me all I know. I have a real strong feelin' in my heart for him. He was in Belzoni, Mississippi, and he used to take me and put me across his knee and tell me, he says, 'The reason you right here at the piano 'cause I'm tryin' to make you play.' But I couldn't because I was too young and my fingers wasn't develop. After they got develop it were too late because he were dead and gone, but I didn't forget what he taught me . . . I had it in my head. So that's how I picked it up and played it behind him. So my daddy said, 'You want to be a blues player? You want to be a blues singer?' I told him, 'Yes.' He said, 'Well, I buy you a piano.' So he bought me a piano and brought it to the house. It was on a Friday, which my mother didn't know because my mother was a Christian woman, she didn't like blues. That Sat'dy mornin' my mother and daddy went to town from the country and that was the only time they'd go to town. Well I locked the house up – I

wanted no one but myself in the house, and I started to playin' the blues. But my mother forgot her pocket book and she had to come back and get her pocket book before she got to town. And when she come back to the house, well she unlocked the door and I was playin' the blues. She went out and told father, say, 'You know what! You know Otis is playing the blues!' My father say, 'Well that's so, he's playin' the blues, let him play the blues.' And my father kept me up for three nights playin' the blues! And I tell you the type of blues he liked me to play was a real old number:

Out from the Country
At the week-ends country farmers go to town for food, stores and recreation. This farm in Chicot County, Arkansas, is typical

One of these days peoples, and it won't be long,
One of these days peoples, and it won't be long,
You gonna look for me baby, and your daddy be gone.

You know I'm just a poor country boy, right off of Mr
    Rudolph's farm;
You know I'm just a poor country boy, come right off of Mr
    Rudolph's farm,
You know I've never had a chance to get a education, I'm
    only tellin' you where I'm from.

When the moon rise at night, I been layin' down in my bed,
When the moon rise at night I been layin' down, in my bed,
You know I feel I want somebody to come and rub my
    achin' head.

I gets up so early in the mornin' because my boss don't 'low
    me to sleep so late,
I used to rise early in the mornin', my boss don't 'low me to
    sleep so late,
You know that's why I'm from the country and that's why
    I'm goin' back home to stay.

It just kep following me

Blind James Brewer

My home's in Mississippi around Brookhaven, that's a little small flagstop I say; few stores, few people around, mostly come in on a Saturday, don't see them no more till the next Saturday cause they be workin' – that's true. Well, I don't know too much about how I got blind – I was quite small. Fact about it was I never did ask my parents about it because it didn't interest me too much long as I could see some, I was satisfied, and I didn't worry about my affliction. Most of what I was interested in was music. When I was young I started to play one of these git-tars; I started out playin' when I was a kid about twelve, thirteen years old. I paid about three dollars and a half for my first git-tar – looked like the rain done got on it and it was all swolled up and this guy wanted to sell it. The first git-tar I ever owned I didn't know what it was because I was quite a kid. Blind feller come through here with one and my father he bought me one, and I got mad because I couldn't play it like he could, and I just slammed it against a tree and tore it up. Thought no more about it, fact, I didn't care no more about it because I couldn't do no good with it. And he said, 'How you gonna learn, you done tore up your git-tar?' I didn't know that I would have to go *through* something to *learn* something. You don't get nothin' through no flowerbeds of ease; you got to go through something in order to get something, I know that now. But I seen other people since I got up to be about seventeen years old. I begin to go round town and met other fellers that played git-tars. And my father bought me another; and I fooled around with it and traded it for a shot-gun – didn't know what I was doin'. White feller axed me, said, 'Do you want to trade a git-tar for a shot-gun or a suit of clothes?' I say, 'Well, I don't want no clothes, I got plenty of clothes.' I wanted the gun, but what I want with a gun I don't know myself, but I took the gun and he took the git-tar and I took the gun across town and sold it for twelve dollars-and-a-half and went right on back and git me another git-tar. I tried to git away from it but it jest kept follerin' me, and I'm glad it did, and I wouldn't take nothin' for my talent.

Every one of them gave dances

Lightnin Hopkins

I did a little plowin' – not too much; chopped a li'l cotton, pulled a li'l corn. I did a little of it all – picked a li'l cotton. But not too much. Because I jest go from place to place playin' music for them dances. I jest keep on goin' like that, pretty good. I didn't have to do too much cotton pickin'. I be out there most for that Friday night, Saturday night for them dances. They had a farm down there they call Murray Farm one . . . Maples Farm . . . and oh, Brudens Farm – lots of farms. And every one of them farms gave dances. I'd go from farm to farm every Saturday night and every Friday night. They have them dances why, because they be lettin' the boys enjoy theirselves, because they been workin' hard all the week makin' them big crops, and bringin' in them good crops. Yeah, lotta men have their fun down there; that's the way them dances was goin'. No playin' hardly at all durin' the week. They had to rest because they had to work next day. Unnh . . . I'd work too . . . during the week but on that Friday night and Saturday night I'd play. There were singers and players, quite a few, but I couldn't remember their names right now . . . because near about everybody you see around them dances could near about play for them. Be old sets you know, them ole square dances. All you had to do was to rap on your git-tar and they'd pat and holler. Ole sister would shout, 'You swing mine an' I'll swing yours!' and all that. That's the way it was goin' at that time. Well, sometimes they would have the blues played, but they most was really dancin' you see. Have fast songs like *Oh, My Babe, Take Me Back* and

> You swing mine and I'll swing Sue,
> We goin' down to the barbecue . . .

That's jumpin' at that time. Yeah, we had a good time off it, but see, it's all diff'rent now. Everybody wants the blues. They don't want too many boogies . . . they wants you to singin' the blues. More people wants the blues now than they used to be.

Everybody Wants the Blues
Listeners crowd round Lightnin
Hopkins as he plays at the Sputnik
Bar in Houston

We didn't know
Willie Thomas

This is the thing about it: we didn't know nothin' *but* blues. And we – we thought it was common. We had a string band you know, guitars, fiddle, such as that and so lots of times we would go in places where you wouldn't have too much to say about the music, because we don't know nothin' about the blues. We knows nothin' much *about* the blues . . . we called it blues, we called it breakdowns – we called it blues and some people say it's square dances. We didn't know we were playin' square dance music, but that's what we were playin', you know, like *Whoa Mule* and that sort of thing. All those kind of things we just called them blues and some of them breakdowns. We didn't know what it was; the achin'-hearted blues is slow, breakdowns is fast.

A gift that we had
Sam Chatman

We started out from our parents – it's just a gift that we had in the family. Our mother and our father they could both play. And see, he was an old musicianer in slavery time. He played for the white folks in slavery time at square dances and so it was handed down to us. We none of us, well, three or four of us took a few music lessons, but all the rest of us grew with it just by ear. I'm sixty-one years of age. All of us is close to each other in age. All of us was about a year or eleven months apart. And I'm the seventh boy child. My brothers were Lonnie, Edgar, Bo, Willie, Lamar, and me, Sam Chatman, and Laurie, and Harry Chatman, and Charlie Chatman. All of us played together – nine of us. I played bass violin for them, and Lonnie, he played lead violin and Harry he played second violin. And my brother Bo, he played clarinet and my brother Bert played guitar and my brother Larry, he beat the drums. And my brother Harry, he played the piano you see. And my brother Bo he played guitar too and he even used to play tenor banjo. And I played guitar. We just pick up and play any instrument and play one to another. We came from Bolton, Mississippi, we were raised up there; and so, many of us played some numbers and some played others, so we named ourselves the Mississippi Sheiks.

I was a plow hand

Bo Carter

I traveled, I hunt, I farmed. We used to raise cotton, corn, potatoes, stuff like that, before we got to the place where my brothers wouldn't hoe none for me, and that made me quit. I just couldn't hoe that cotton. I could plow it but I couldn't hoe it. I was a plow hand. Well, we called us the Mississippi Sheiks, all of us Chatmans, cause my name's Bo Chatman only they call me Bo Carter. We toured with the band right through the country; through the Delta, through Louisiana down to New Orleans, serenadin':

Baby, if you get married and you marry a real rich man,
Baby if you ever get married and marry a real rich man,
Every day would be Sunday with a piece of money in your
  hand.

But little girl if you ever get married, you marry a farmin' man,
Little girl if you ever get married, and marry a farmin' man,
Every day would be Monday with a plow-handle in yo' hand.

But little girl, if you get married, you marry a workin' man,
Little girl if you get married, an' you marry a farmin' man,
Every Saturday will be pay-day with a few pennies left in
  your han'.

But little girl, if you get married, you marry a jelly-bean man,
Little girl, if you get married, you marry a jelly-bean man,
Every day the women will tell you, you can't have that old
  man.

But little girl if you get married you marry a gamblin' man,
But little girl if you get married you marry a gamblin' man,
Every day will be worry with no money left in your hand.

But little girl if you get married you'll marry a wealthy man,
But baby if you marry it'll be a loafin' man,
Every day will be worry with nothin' t' eat in yo' hand.

All different kinds

Sam Chatman

Then we moved to the Delta and we still had a band. Played for different parties around, so we put out *Corrine Corrine*, *Alberta*, *Stop and Listen*, *I'm the Only Man in Your Town*, *Ants in Your Pants*, *What's the Name of That Thing*. We played all different kinds of music – *Sheiks of Abaree* and *Sittin' on Top of the World* – oh man. We played so many different pieces, I could be here two hours tellin' you about it. We played at Coopers Wells – that's in the hills, and we played at the Whitfield in Jackson. We played at that hotel in Jackson at the Edwards Hotel – if you can call him, we played there. Some were big-big places. Played at some where there was two, three hundred folks there, dancin'. We played for a picnic for Charlie Barrasso. He had a picnic, was down here – three or four thousand dollar picnic they had down here and he had a platform built and they couldn't even hold the people, they was dancin' off the platform. And we played all kinds of music for them. Now when we moved to the Delta in Hollandale here, in '28, we got to playin' up at Leroy Percy Park for the white folks all the week. *Eyes of Blue*, that's what we played for white folks. *Dinah*, that's another for white folks. But we played blues for colored. I just couldn't tell you when I first heard blues, but when I was big enough to hold up a git-tar I went to playin' 'em.

Get away from my winder, knockin' on my door,
Get away from my winder, quit knockin' on my door,
Got a brand new feelin', cain't use you no more.

I be lovin' my sweet mama, like a schoolboy loves his pie,
Don't you heah me pretty mama talkin' to you – like a
  schoolboy loves his pie,
And I love my sweet babe, like to the day I die.

Says my baby's gone, and she won't be back no more,
My baby's gone, and she won't be back no more,
Says now she left me this mawnin', and she caught the B. & O.

There's one thing about my baby that I just cain't under-
  stand myself,
Says there's one thing 'bout my baby, cain't understand myself,
Eeh, that woman I love quit me, but I don't want nobody else.

We played all over
Percy Thomas

Now I want to tell you people, there's something I want you
    to understand,
Want to tell you people, somethin' I want you to understand,
I mean the next woman I love, now, she got to come under
    my command.

Well, we just go from place to place and we commence to
gettin' older and older and we was scatterin' out and commence
to gettin' weaker and weaker until now we cut down to four
brothers. Bo Carter, he went by the name of Carter because he
went to recordin' by himself, so instead of puttin' out Chatman
he put out Carter. Just changed his name as is. Now Walter, he
played with him; he went by Walter Jacobs but he was Walter
Vincent. We was raised together. So now I farmed, I have
night-watched, and fired at a big plant up there in Memphis.
Oh, lots of different kinds of work. I'm a carpenter, I can do
'most any sort of carpenter work you can bring up.

My work is plowin'. Get in my overhauls, go to plowin'. Been
plowin' all my life. I was born in 1896 right here in Clarksdale
and I've lived around here all my life and I'm sixty-four years
old now. We used to to have a li'l band, played all over the
Delta. We named ourselves the Mississippi Corn-Shuckers.
Right behind the Mississippi Sheiks. Mississippi Hot-Footers
– they all the same thing. Well, we called ourselves the
Mississippi Corn-Shuckers. I played the git-tar, and Bill
Johnson here, he played the fiddle. Well he ain't teched no
fiddle for many a year, but he could play it good then. And
there was Sam, he played the harp – sometimes; he's in jail
right now. So we used to play for shuckin'-bees, and when
settlement come. We played at the juke at Rome there down
on the 49 Highway; played at the juke at Louise – all over.
Played for those Sat'dy night fish-fries. We played blues,
breakdowns such as that, and those old tunes like *Comin'*
Round the Mountain Betsy Lee.

We Played for Shuckin'-Bees
Percy Thomas, guitar, and Bill
Johnson, fiddle, had a band called
the Mississippi Corn-Shuckers

They Call Me Banjo Joe
Gus Cannon, ditch-digger,
gum-ball raker, banjo player,
once led his own jug band

Some Banjo
Gus Cannon

I'm goin' round the mountin Charmin' Bessie,
I'm goin' roun' the mountin Cora Lee,
An' if I never, never more see you agin',
Do Lord, remember me.

White girl she wears a thin brown skirt,
Black girl she wears the same,
But that high-brown she don't wear no skirt at all,
But she goin' round the mountin jus' the same.

White girl she wears that sto'-bo'ght scent,
Black girl she's wearin' the same,
That high-brown she don't wear no scent at all
But she smellin' just the same . . .

Well, you goin' round the mountin now boy . . . play it . . .
    little while,

I'm goin' round the mountain Bessie Lee,
If I never no more see you little brownskin,
Brownskin, remember me.

That's the first record I ever made for the Columbia at
Belzoni, Mississippi, puttin' in the wire for the Yeller Dawg
railroad for the first trusses bridge across the Yazoo River.
Now I was playin' some banjo with some kitchen mechanic
down there, for the boys down there then. Up and down the
country with my banjo. I been a ditch digger; I worked for
Pritchett Brothers layin' sewers. I'm a sewer digger – I dug one
the other day for a man they had a contract with. They say I'm
too old to dig no more, but for why, I'm used to doin' it. They
say they won't hire me, but all the fixin's got to be fixed down
here, ole Joe can fix it. My name's Gus Cannon, but they call
me Banjo Joe. Lord have mercy, look what a hole I'm in. But I
still can play some banjo.

Everybody fry up fish
Muddy Waters

All the kids made they own git-tars. Made mine out of a box
and bit of stick for a neck. Couldn't do much with it but you
know, that's how you learn. An' I learn a lot from two other
kids, friends of mine only they were a little older. Sonny
Simms was one and the other was Scott Bowhandle, yeah like
you have a bow and a handle, that was his name. He's livin'
with my aunt in Chicago now but he don't play guitar no
more. But I used to watch them makin' chords and try to copy
them. I made some good at it, but my first real instrument was
the harp. Well I played everywhere I could – any ole place.
Jukes around Clarksdale. Played for those Sat'dy night fish-fries.
I used to sell fish too, then go to playin'. Everybody used to fry
up fish and had one hell of a time. Find me workin' all night',
playin'; workin' till sunrise for fifty cents and a sandwich and
be glad of it, and they really like the low-down blues.

Riverside Roadhouse
Moore's Cafe is a few yards
from the treacherous Yazoo
River. The juke with its open
dance floor is raised on stilts
above flood level

So many bones
Wade Walton

They have lots of fish-fries, 'cause there's lots of fish. Around the Mississippi and usually out on the lakes the type of fish you catch is the white perch, and you catch another fish you call a grinner. He's a very soft fish and the minute you catch him out of the water you ought to eat him 'cause if you don't hurry to get him in a refrigerator system or somethin' in five or six minutes he's spoil. His meat's real soft and he doesn't have too many bones. They have another fish by the name of the shad fish but there's so many bones in him you gotta make a detour, you gotta stop at the red light. I mean you have to have a tooth pick and a pair of tweezers to pull out all his fine bones. It's very good meat. Eating very sweet meat. But you don't enjoy eating very much unless'n you have a lot of time to do it. Take two or three days to eat one shad . . .

A garbage can full
Will Shade

We had plenty of fish-fries, Sat'dy night fish-fries, and I made plenty then. Did pretty good. See at that time you could get fish for a nickel; get a nickel's worth of fish you get a garbage can full. Two pieces of corn bread and all that fish. Used to be a place on Market and Main, you go up there an' buy all that fish for a nickel. Nickel's worth of fish and you get seven or ten pieces of fish. Then you get two piece of corn bread, you could have another piece of fish. In them days you could get anything you want for a nickel. Ain't like it is now, you got to pay a thousand dollars for a piece of fish. Get neckbones at that time for a penny a pound, half a penny a pound. Not like it is now, you got to pay nineteen cents for 'em. So that's why they had plenty of picnics and plenty of fish-fries and we'd go play for 'em.

House parties

Black Ace

In my early days I was raised on a farm. Back where I was born and raised at – it was a li'l ole place called Hughes Springs, Texas, oh, about seven miles this side of Louisiana. I stayed at home with my daddy on the farm down there all my life until I was about thirty years old. That was when I left and started to play the git-tar. I've played on a guitar neck when I was a li'l kid – my brothers had a guitar neck with some wires – strings – on, and I'd make li'l chords on it and I growed up under that. And after I got to be a man, why I bought me an ole git-tar and I learned how to play a piece or two on that – I guess I was around about twenty-two or twenty-three years old. And when I was around about thirty I run up on a feller they call Buddy Woods, but I call him Oscar Woods, and he was playin' git-tar – steel git-tar style but he was playin' with a bottle. And I follered him around, lookin' at how he playin'. I always knowed how to make a few li'l chords on the git-tar but I never seen that kind of way of playin'. He was just messin' aroun' with it and I of course followed him on up and I learned how to play somethin' with that bottle. And he come to playin' this finger playin' up behind me and that's the way it come about. That's the way I started and that was 'long about Depression time. I couldn't get a li'l job nowhere. So I would go aroun' play at house parties with this boy – make a dollar-an'-a-half whilst other folks was gettin' that for one day's work on relief. Dollar-an'-a-half for that one day. I get three or four parties, man – I made a *lot* of money. I was makin' somethin' playin' at li'l ole house parties. Dollar-an'-a-half for fun!

I am the Black Ace
Babe Kyro Turner, the
Black Ace, plays a flat steel
guitar with finger picks
and a small bottle

Now the depression come

Willie Thomas

You see, a woman could get a job at that time, but a man couldn't hardly get it. Want a little money, had to get it from her. That's was in the time of the Depression. And it gave a man the blues: he's been the boss all the time and now the Depression come and she's washin' at the white folk's yard. And she's cookin' there and she can get a little money but she's feedin' him, so he can't cut up too much. So if he wants a little money to go out to gamble, or play the fortune wheel and she won't give him anythin', nachally he says, 'I'm broke, and I ain't got a dime.' And she says, 'Well you ought to have somethin' – I give you two bits last week!' And 'most any man get in hard luck some time.

> Mamma, why do you treat your daddy mean? (three times)
> You the meanes' woman I 'most ever seen.
>
> Well I'm broke and ain't got a dime, (three times)
> Every man get in hard luck some time.
>
> Walkin' down East Cairo Street one day (three times)
> One dime was all I had.
>
> One dime was all I had, (three times)
> For every man get in hard luck some time . . .

And that was Depression time. I remember myself when there was eight of us eatin' out of one pan at the white folk's house. Then the woman had a little money – as much as she had – and the man didn't have nothin'. And she give him two bits to go out on a Saturday night. And he'd try to gamble and try to make a little somethin' and he would lose it and he would come back and ask her for somethin' else. It been hard when a man been boss of his own house and the Depression come and *she* gonna have to be the boss. He had to go to her to get money and she says, 'What do you mean, comin' askin' for money? Didn't I give you two bits las' Saturday night?' He say, 'Yeah, but I lost it.'

'Well you ought to have some kind of money.'

'Well, 'most any man gets in hard luck some time.'

He didn't have any money and his woman wouldn't give him two bits to get in the game, or somethin' – it's pretty hard . . . . He couldn't say too much about it 'cause she paid it. And she eat and had her job at the white folk's house. She bring the pay in there and he's makin' a little dollar-and-a-half a week. She paid everything . . . she didn't have no money, so he had to take it easy, so that's what give him the blues.

Only places they can go
Otis Spann

People Calls Me Lucky
Otis Spann remembers
'barrelhousin'' at his
home town of Belzoni,
Mississippi

When coloured people want to have places to go . . . well, there's places they cain't go. In Belzoni, Mississippi, the only places they could go is to a honkytonk on a week-end. Because that's the only time they have off – at the week-end and so they gits down to the honkytonk and they have a wonderful time amongst theyselves. They have fish-fries and they have gamblin' in the back, and sometimes they be fighting in the back and in the front and so forth. But they be fightin' 'mongst theyselves and don't nothin' ever happen, you understand . . . but what I mean about this is when a musician – they all know one another – they all gets to a place and they sits down to a piano and they starts to barrelhousin'. And what I mean by barrelhousin' – barrelhousin' it mean store-porchin', and storeporchin' it means one man be playin' a piano . . . one be playin' a piano, and when he start to playin' he done either lost all his money at the gamblin' table or he don't have enough money to get in the gamblin' game! And so that's what I mean by barrelhousin'. And so after he lose his money and when nobody won't let him have no more money to gamble with, he sits down at the piano and starts playin':

> Nobody knows, nobody knows people the trouble that
> I've seen,
> Nobody knows people, the trouble that I've seen,
> Now you know I done lost all my money, and my woman
> she treated me so mean.

> So people they call me lucky but to me my luck seems to fail,
> People calls me lucky, but to me my luck begin to fail,
> I been lookin' for that woman, you know, ever since my
> luck been gone.

> I done stopped drinkin' and gamblin' now, and I don't run
> around no more,
> I done stopped drinkin' and gamblin', I don't run aroun' no
> more,
> Yes, you know I'm gonna find my woman, well I don't care
> where she go.

Chock-house days

Whistling Alex Moore

That was what you call chock-house days. You could used to go in them chock-houses and police never used to do anythin' but run in there and raid it, and make them guys break up the chock barrel and throw it away – home brew you know. Like you be in here and there'd be two policemans – one come in the back door and one in the front door. One called Greenlea and the other McLauther, and so they had an automobile with that long board on the side, and so one step on this side and the other guy on the other side, and they so heavy they just beat it to the ground. That runnin' board be on the ground. And when the other feller step in, it straighten up so they both had to step in the same time because man, they weighed somethin' about two hundred a piece or three. Whew! They were the biggest guys . . . and each one of them come runnin' in. I'd be at the piano, 'cause you know you play all night long in those chock-joints, and you hear them people slop and slug and sayin':

'Ooooh, daddy, play it a long time daddy . . . play it . . . .' And the chock be all over the floor and there wouldn't be a good woman in the house! And then finally they come. Police outside the house. They say, 'Who is it?' Man, *they* wouldn't be sayin' nothin'. Man, they so big they just go round there and you hear the front door and the back door crash at the same time, 'cause they time themselves. So they say, 'Who run this joint?' and some time I would just be there a-playin' and everyone be runnin' and some woman be standin' there just *a-howlin'* the blues:

Mmmm, I know my daddy be here, early in the mawnin' . . .
Mmmm, mmm, early in the mawnin . . . .

Then the boys busted in and they shout, 'Hurry on there, 'gainst the wall.' And they bust Joe against the wall. And then you heah me when they throw that pistol on me, 'You get away from me, that stuff ain't none of mine!' 'Cause we have some ole half pint of that corn whisky, White Mule, you know. And they say, 'Who's is this?' Nobody say a word. They say, 'Nobody want this half of whisky?' One of them goes back and into that kitchen and take a hammer and bust that chock right open on the floor. And some of the boys got plenty nerve and they wouldn't care and when the police say, 'Break it!' they grab a glass or somepin' and run forward and get some and go glug-glug . . . . And worst of it was – like me and you be sittin' here, – and if it was a house had some of that home brew, man they'd take it out there and get by one of them brick buildin's and it sound like 'Pow!' Every time they'd hit that barrel see they'd shoot 'Pow! pow! pow!' Glass flyin'. 'Pow! Pow!' And we'd be sittin' there. 'Lawd, listen to that. . . they raidin' somewhere . . . all that good brew you know.' Yeah, they play all night long.

Plenty rugged
Edwin Buster Pickens

Who is the man?
Bo Carter

Barrelhouse is noted from barrel whisky. Back in the late 'twenties, early 'thirties, it would be nothin' strange to see a man have a keg of bootleg whisky. Probably half a barrel of whisky . . . that's why they call it the barrelhouse. You could draw it from the barrel just like you draw keg beer from the keg. They had a chock barrel there – somethin' like beer . . . only two drinks'd knock you out. You had your tin cup – just dip down in the barrel. You just get your chock out – drink it. You won't stand too much of it, but what part you do, it'll move you! Move you around a bit. I don't know what the chock came from; it was made by some of them old bootleggers and they knew what it was all about! We had quite a few tough days, but they weren't imposin' like they are now. People didn't just jump up and do things wrongly just because they *could*. They gambled, they drinked heavily and when there was a fight, there was a good one, but there was a reason for it. They didn't do things just right along so, like some people do nowadays – they jump up and shoot each other down and kill each other just because they can. You were more safer in those days because a man had to have somethin' did to him before he would jump up and do you somethin'. He wouldn't do you somethin' just because he felt he wanted to do it – imposin' on you. But in those days black people got along fine. But it could be rugged when it was; it was plenty rugged – but there was a reason for it.

One time a boy got at me. He run at me with his horse. Then he had his mules set at me and he drove them with his brother one mawnin' right across my cotton-patch, and my lock was taken. My wife and kids was up and I was lyin' in the bed. So I said, ' Gene, why didn't you speak to me, 'stead of come in and gettin' at me this mawnin?'

He said, 'Well I just want to see who is the *man*, this mawnin'. You talk to me like I was a kid, not a man, so I just wanna see who *is* the man.'

Well I did talk big talk 'cause it made me mad, 'cause he run them mules right through my cotton-patch and spoilin' my crop and everythin'. So I say, 'Well heah me mister, you better forgit about it.' Say to my wife, 'Hand me that shot-gun.' He say, 'I wanna see who *is* the *man*!'

Wife handed me that pop-gun and I pointed it out, there to where he was. Wife says, 'He's gone!' I say, 'Who is the man . . . ?' He hollered back, 'You!'

So then me and him made it up and now when I see him he say, 'Who is the best man now, 'cause you can't see, you blind.' But I say, 'No, I can't see no more, but I got my knife in my pocket and I cin reach in my pocket. I got my hand on my knife and I'll open it with my teeth and cut your throat.'

'Would you do that?' I say, 'Sure I'll do it . . .' So me and him we have no more fuss. That's settled. 'Cause I'd do it all right.

Ain't no easy thing
Lightnin Hopkins

I had lots of trouble when I was, you know, young. Kinda
mean. Kinda hard to get along with. Some things – some
places I'd be where we'd have a few fights. One of them cause
me to go to the road . . . ole boys say to the county road –
bridge gang. I worked there for about coupla hundred days.
Working out on the road gang – it ain't no easy thing, I tell ya.
Every evenin' when you come in they would chain you, they'd
lock you with a chain aroun' your leg. And they had a tent
made with a row of bunks on each side. So you had a bunk of
you own and they'd lock you to a post. Lock you up to this
post, next one to that post; all the way down, till they lock all o'
ya up. So therefore you'd be locked that night, and next
mawnin' when you get ready to go out to eatin' breakfast, man
come to unlock you. You go out, eat your breakfast, catch the
mules, hitch the wagon, git right on down to the work. Two
hundred days . . . that was a long time. Had more than that but
I got off befo' . . . . What helped me some while I was there my
wife she come out there and she helped me for a while. She
was cookin' for fifty cents a day. So I was workin' for fifty cents
a day. So you know how much credit I was gettin' for my trouble, for my fine. Got away from there by singin' the blues . . . .
Last one day, the boss man decided – judge at least – he decided
to see I'd get away from there, I could go, and told them to free
me that day, so that's what they did. An' ain't been back ever
since.

Colored Folk's Juke
Across the road from the
juke at Rome, Mississippi,
in Sunflower County, is
the cafe for white patrons

Prisoner song
James Butch Cage

Went to the pen you know, and I was on the penitensha and
I had to serve my time out. Well, some had six months and
some had a solid year, but me and my buddy, we had lifetime
here. That's what it is . . . on the penitensha. That's what they
sing 'cause that's a prisoner song:

> Bring my supper and let me go to bed,
> Fix my supper and let me go to bed,
> Cause I been drinkin' white lightnin' and it's gone to my head.
>
> Some got six months, some got a solid – some got a solid –
> Some got six months, some got a solid year,
> But me and my buddy, we got lifetime here.
>
> Tell me somethin' – tell me how your rollin's done,
> Tell me somethin' – tell me how your rollin's done,
> Because I'm in the jailhouse and I can't have any fun.

Never did like that place

Jasper Love

North of Parchman, that's where I was born, North of Parchman. I always did know what that place was. I was twixt the two camps – down at the State farm at Parchman and up here at Lambertsville. I had a friend up at Lambertsville – 'Camp A' they called it. That was a kind of a rough job at that time – they kinda worked over you and whipped you right where you was if you soever disobeyed or anything, but they cut it down now. It's just like I said, I never did like that place they call Parchman, they treat you kinda bad. Well I have a cousin, I nursed him but he got in a little trouble and he's down there, and I goes down to see him. You turn off at Number One, Highway West I think it is – W for West – and we turn off and they have superintendents and the gunmen and they drive 'em along like that. This boy's down there and he did have real long pretty hair, and when they get him there they shave his hair – other words it's kinda like I imagine you heard what Delilah did to Samson, shaved his head clean as your hand. We had a feller we called Shine, he was down there. He had been a longtime man and they really did work him over you know. They don't only work coloreds though, you know; it's whites and all down there. But of course it's not like it used to been. I remember the time when I was a little boy comin' up they really did treat 'em bad, but now they have a white lady there, superintendent or somethin' like that. They used to be whippin' those boys along the road and she stopped that. In other words if they do enough that they have to be whipped they take them back into the camp and they give them so many licks. But they don't work so hard now as we do in what they call the free world; I passes by there lots of times and they just be workin' ordinary.

Place They Call Parchman
'A Great Institution in a Great State. 22,000 Acres. 17 Units. Mississippi State Penitentiary, Parchman. Fred Jones, Superintendent'

Nowhere to Run to
The station on Parchman Farm is the end of the line for Mississippi's convicted felons

A little scrape
John Henry

Don't quit now!
Whistling Alex Moore

Call me John Henry. It's not my real name but I'm doin' kinda nicely now and I don't want to get in no more trouble. I've done me five years and I've got a twenty year sentence, what they call life. What brought me in here – I was down at the colored folk's juke in Drew you know and we was havin' fun. Music and gamblin' and all such as that and then there got to be a little scrape and this boy got killed. There was some shootin' and they said I done it. Well I dunno, maybe I did. Main thing about it was the Judge sent me down for life here on Parchman Farm and I got about fifteen years to go I guess. Well it ain't too bad but it ain't like being free, what you call liberty. You got to wear these clothes and you cain't do this an' that and they lock you up, nights. No use in runnin' away; ain't nowhere to run to.

I shot at my woman, 'cause I was tired of so much bull corn,
I shot at my woman 'cause I was tired of so much bull corn,
Policeman jumped me, I run like a rabbit from a burnin' barn.

She had red flannel rags, talked about hoodooin' poor me,
She had red flannel rags, talked about hoodooin' poor me,
I believe I'll go to Froggy Bottom so she will let me be.

I don't want no money unless I work for it,
Don't want no money unless I work for it.
Those things you want me to do darlin' – that's why you
   and I quit.

So I'm goin' back home and won't be bothered with you,
Yes, I'm goin' back home and won't be bothered with you,
Because there's someone in Dallas got somethin' else for
   me to do.

Oh, they were tough joints . . . I'd play them all, from North Dallas to the East Side . . . Froggy Bottom . . . Central Tracks . . . Well they had just about everything up and down there from beer joints to saloons. I used to play in some of those places; used to play a lot of social clubs. I wouldn't have learned to play if I hadn't like it and loved it. They used to call out to me, they say, 'You married?' I say, 'Yeah!' They say, 'Who's your wife now?' I say, 'Pianner!' Like me sittin' here now, I sit down and play from seven o' clock to five the next mornin' and never move. Play to seven in the mornin' – be *tryin*! The greatest deal in my life be playin' the piano. They usually say, 'Lord, I sure be glad when he gets off the pianner.' Next place I go they say, 'Lord, I got a headache tonight Alex.' Next place I go they say, 'Alex, we gonna go to bed, come back tomorrow!' And the next place, 'Hmmm – let's go down so-and-so's place so he can't play nothin'!' Then I find one of those places to play and then all you hear is, ' Play it a long time daddy . . . don't quit now . . . don't quit now!' Then after I could play they ask me which one is my piano? And I say, 'The one I'm sittin' at, that's my piano! One I'm sittin' at.' Course, I could play it by then. But you know you couldn't get more than two-and-a-half for playin' all night long in those days, but after you give me a dollar-and-a-half I go right on playin'. You couldn't give me *five* to lose me. Well, those were pretty rough days you know. Plenty of guys want to play; they come up and whisper, 'Give you a dollar right now if you go! Come on Alex, you go now, I give you a couple o' dollars.' But I stay right on there and finish my job. Pay me that some other time, O.K. But I never quit.

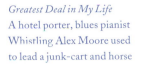

Greatest Deal in My Life
A hotel porter, blues pianist
Whistling Alex Moore used
to lead a junk-cart and horse

They called us Gandy-dancers
Blind Arvella Gray

I got to sellin' moonshine in them days on the side, and gamblin' in my gamblin' joint, and I was a pretty good mixer 'cause I came from the South and I knowed how to say, 'Yes sir' and 'No sir' and git next to my superior which is the white people you know – I just went along with my jive. I knowed how to jive them and they let me get away with a whole lot of stuff that I wouldn't 've if I'd been a little hostile to them. And in the meantime I had whipped my boss on the job which was a white feller. I whopped him a little bit, I was just a guy who liked to fight, oh, just a roughneck all the way round. So then he got to likin' me after then you know, seeing he couldn't push me around like he did the others. So I just had my way, I worked when I got ready, and then I didn't, like that. Well I worked for construction job: I got three dollars and twenty cents a day, of which one dollar, twenty cents went for board and lodging and the other two dollars was clear profit. I did levee camp work; I worked in factories and things and I was a feller never did care for staying on a job, like marrying a job as I would call it in my way. I just jumped from job to job. I did railroad; I was workin' for the B. & O. road out there and that's where I got hurt on the railroad track. One feller got his back broke and several other fellers got their legs broke and things. I just got a little hurt so the B. & O. paid me a few dollars out of that. I was laying track on a extry gang. They called us gandy-dancers on those extry gangs. Now this is a song I used on the railroad when I was laying track, when I was called a gandy-dancer. We used to sing this when we drove steel, and drivin' steel means putting spikes in the rail-road ties to hold the tracks steady, and like that. And we also used to use it when we was linin' up the tracks and we used to have a song like that about linin' up the tracks, we said:

Oh, workin' on the railroad, I'm hammerin' steel,
Hotter the sunshine, Lord the better I feel,
Workin' on the railroad, hammerin' steel,
Hotter the sunshine, Lord the better I feel.

Well I got a letter from Hagerstown,
Saying East St Louis is burnin' down,
Workin' on the railroad, hammerin' steel.
Hotter the sunshine, Lord the better I feel.

But we used to have several songs and one of them was song about, we said,

Well you got your pistol, and I got mine,
Well rap on your cartridge, pardner if you don't mind dyin'.

And the boss would get kinda nervous when we don't have the tracks lined up right for the train, when the fast train come along, and he used to pull out his watch. In them days we had a watch we called a Waterbury, them dollar watches, and we say, we sung a little verse too, we say:

Captain got a Waterbury and it's just like mine,
They both keep runnin', Lord but they won't keep time.

One Shift Goin'...
The saw-mill at Willis,
Texas, In the Piney Woods

They wanted them low

Edwin Buster Pickens

Up and down the Santa Fe tracks in those days was known as the barrelhouse joints. These places was located in the area where the mill was in, and you played all night long in those days. They danced all night long. And the blues was all they wanted; they didn't want anything else. They wanted them low. You didn't have to be fancy at all – you just bear down! Of course they had food in those places, drinks and coffee and so forth, and these men – people that attended them were working at the mill. They worked in shifts: this man's crew is off an' this man's is on; one shift goin' and one barrelhouse. That's what kept it goin'. It would take a couple of rooms, maybe a store. Course they packed 'em in like sardines. People come in and out at all times and of course the piano man, why he'd play a while and rest a while and go back and play again. Sometimes he might have a buddy come along; some of the other piano players – Bo King perhaps – some of these fellers come along, whoever you runs into. If you were tired or got too dizzy to play he might come in and help you out. *The Dirty Dozens* was the openin' number of the house; we opened up with that number. Then we had another number was called *The Ma Grinder*, that was 'first cousin to the Dozens'. Well that number originated right in the barrel-

house. It limited itself to that kind of a life – in other words you couldn't carry it any further. The barrelhouse was as far as you could carry it, because it was a pretty rotten song you know. So it wouldn't fit just anywhere, but it sure worked when it was in the barrelhouse! Mostly though it settled down to the slow, low-down blues and they'd 'slow drag – dance to that you see. Just bear down on the slow blues:

I met Hannah on Colorado Springs,
I met Hannah on Colorado Springs,
Long come her old-time used-to-be, my meat didn't
    mean a thing.

Everyday – we meet on Colorado Springs,
Everyday – we meet on Colorado Springs,
All she want is to hear my music and me to sing.

Colorado Springs – water drinks so good,
Colorado Springs – water drinks so good,
Even over Hannah, I'd be willing to lose my blood.

I'll always sing the Colorado Blues,
Always sing the Colorado Blues,
Even to this day it always be news.

Nothing but pine trees
Speckled Red

They used to have a word they say 'playin' the dozens'. It was talking dirty you know, the boys be together and they'd try and out-talk one and the other till one feller would holler 'you put me in the dozens' because he couldn't think of no more to say. So I made a kind of a song out of the words and I called it *The Dirty Dozens*. But they was real bad words you see; I was playing in one of them turpentine jukes where it didn't matter. Anything I said there was all right in there you see. I had to clean it up for the record but it meaned the same thing but it was a different attitude. Like the *Ma Grinder*, I heard that for years. I don't know where I *first* heard it. In those days and in them places you could say some of them smelly words and don't think nothin' of it, but it's a whole lots different now. So at that time I played in the saw-mill camps and the turpentine, down where there's nothing but pine trees and tap the trees and get the resin and make turpentine out of it. Just like people go out and work every day, they come in at night and they have a good time. And I've worked on levee camps the same way. They've got a big house there where they have some fun when they come in at night. You know they hardly ever go off camp, the camp is so far from town. They come in there until Saturday – Saturday they go to town and all through the week they spend all their money at the camp. There's certain people they have running the house; they go to town and buy all the whisky and all the beer and they run the house and cook, and they have the lunches and everything like that and so they just have that for the people that works on the camp. And you just be there on the camp, you ain't got time, you working there everyday. And everybody comes right there and you play and they dance and sing and have a big time. What I make on the house, that's mine.

The Slow, Low-down Blues
Edwin Buster Pickens was one of
the last of the saw-mill pianists

Juke piano players
Little Brother Montgomery

When I was four or five years old my father bought a pianner. Well I had never seen a pianner before and I tried to play it at the age of five. You know, just simple things on my own. So from then on I tried to create things of my own until I got large enough and was able to hear real people play – such as Son Framion and a guy named Friday Ford. There was another player that was called Papa Lord God and one named Varnado Anderson . . . Leon Bromfield . . . and all those type of players. Well that gave me inspiration of kinda being a piano players like those guys. They were all in Louisiana at this time. This was in Kentwood because my father used to run a barrelhouse juke and the majority of these people used to play for him. It was on a saw-mill firm. You know they had three big sawmills there at that time: Wilkins, Gallaher and Kents. I heard them all on up until I got to be eighteen or twenty years old. They were still there, though I left home when I were eleven years old, first time. Well I worked at jukes; they call 'em jukes, they call 'em barrelhouses, they call 'em honkytonks so that they had three or four names for them. So I worked at Holden, Louisiana, at the juke barrelhouse there for the saw-mill. Saw-mill jobs, logging camps, levee camps – they have places for people to go for – recreation, and at that time they were using piano players only at most of the jukes and barrelhouses so the majority of we blues players were playin' in them. I knew Jelly Roll when I was seven, eight years old. And then I run up against Tommy Jackson – he was Tony Jackson's first cousin, the guy that wrote *Pretty Baby* – he was a great musician. Sudan Washington was a great musician; Cooney Vaughns was one of the best piano players I ever heard and he was from Hattiesburg, Mississippi. They had one called Blind Homer, he was a juke piano player. Blind Jug, he was another. And there was Gus Pevsner, only he was a musicianer like . . . you know, musical, played by notes and things.

A place of business

Edwin Buster Pickens

Turpentine, in the pines . . . you find that around East Texas, but more or less Arkansas. You see, you take Eudora, Arkansas, that's eighteen miles from Bastrop, Louisiana, across the line there. I played up there on the edge of the border of Louisiana and Arkansas: Eudora, Bastrop, Lake Providence and Ferriday which is nine miles from Natchez. Now they used to have roadhouses there and those turpentine camps, they were pretty popular in those days you know. Workers in turpentine they be the same as fellers who work in the saw-mill: they all went along together since that turpentine made from the same stuff anyhow. Turpentine, saw-mills, those were the ones that ruled the barrelhouse. They handled it. Then the oilfields had 'em too. I never did *work* at a mill at all. Garret Stone worked on the saw-mill; Fairbanks, another piano player – *he* did. These men they worked long enough to get in. They had to do something to get in them saw-mills, to play. And after you got in, let the man know you work as well as play the piano – well then you could stay there. I was fortunate enough to know a feller who knew everybody there. He had a place of business at Cowswitch down on the Santa Fe between Navasota and Conroe and he had a big shack there and he sold whisky and food and beer, and he knew the man who owned the saw-mill; fact he worked on the saw-mill himself. So he could bring in anyone to play for him that he wanted. It was all right with the mill owner because he'd say, 'I know him, he's all right.' Mill owner he'd say, 'That's all right, go ahead, just kick 'em on down. You-all just kick 'em on down!' Lots of those fellers though who got established in these places been there a long time and they knew what it's all about; take me along there with them, then if anybody ask any questions they say, 'Robertson brought him in.' They say, 'All right, he can go ahead and play.' They don't want anybody to invade the camp you know.

The blues real down

Little Brother Montgomery

Then so I came up in Arkansas, in Arkansas City and Eudora round up in there. Lake Village – there I run up against a guy they called Burnt Face Jake. His name was Jake Facey but they called him Burnt Face Jake; he was a great piano player, had his own style of playin' but I never got on it. Mostly we kept to our own style of playin'. Blues is a personal feelin' of a person, but I think that the majority of guys that play the blues real *down* have the blues. I don't think a person can play the blues unless'n he *feel* blue. He could play anything but that. So in Lake Village I met Joe Martin, he died one Christmas I think, in 1923 or '22, or something like that. So I run across George Young – Son Young – he got killed at Waterproof, Louisiana. He was a great piano player; Walter Lewis, he was another one. I ran across another guy they called Skinny Head Pete, he was good. And also a boy they called Freddie Coates in Greenville, Mississippi. I thought these guys were great . . . they played terrific to my ideas . . . they played full style, played melody and whatever they played, they played what I thought right, you know.

. . . And One Barrelhouse
Saw-mill workers' homes and
barrelhouse in the logging
'company town' at Willis

Nelsons Street
Daddy Stovepipe

Mississippi Sarah – that was my ole lady, Mississippi Sarah. Name was Sarah Watson; like me, my name's Johnny Watson only they calls me Daddy Stovepipe, and we was livin' down in Greenville there, by the levee. Used to go meet the boats there, me with my box and my harp and my ole lady used to sing to 'em, to the people that come off the boats. An' we used to work in those li'l joints they call jukes on Nelson Street there; plenty of places we would work, and play in the street. There was another lady used to sing – Alice – Alice Pears think her name was and she had a pianner player call him Freddy. They used to be there. Well, I had an ole blues I used to sing:

I woke up this mawnin' Mama, I had the sundown blues,
Woke up this mawnin', I had the sundown blues,
And when my fair brown called me, I refused to go.

I've got nineteen fair browns, but I want one more,
Nineteen fair browns, but I want one more,
Now if you want to see me mama, I'll let the nineteen go.

Then I left Greenville when my ole lady passed. She passed in '37 I think it was. I played aroun' in Mississippi for while . . . then I went down to Old Mexico, played some with them Mexican fellers.

They really started that off

Jasper Love

Like to say – this Willie Love was my first cousin. He died about three years ago. Well he started off with two bands – there was him and this boy James B. Curtis, playin' *Dud Low* – they really started that off. And then this one band was with King Biscuits over in Helena, and this other band was up here in Tunica – Silver King. He was along there with ole Doctor Ross – he played the harp. And I'd make along with him you know, to go to these country balls down here we call them – these clubs, like the Mansatee Club and the Forty-Nine Club down there in Drew. Well then, Willie Love used to play at one time at those joints in Greenville, down there on Nelson Street. Fact of it was he made a blues about that, used to sing somethin' like:

Boys if you ever go to Greenville, please go down on
Nelson Street,
If you ever go to Greenville, please go down on Nelson
Street,
Where you can laugh and have your fun with 'most
everybody you meet.
Now you starts at the top and you walks right down,
Stop at the shoe-shine parlour and get your shoes knocked
down,
Walk right 'cross the street 'cause you still full of vim,
Go to the De Luxe barber shop and get you a fine sharp trim.
Boys if you ever to Greenville, please go down on
Nelson Street,
Where you can laugh and have your fun with every
body you meet.
I walk right 'cross the railroad there, I was a sight to be seen,
I stopped at the Snow White Laundry and got my suit
pressed and cleaned,
Then I went to the Silver Dollar Cafe, that's right on the
corner,
You can stop there boys and have as much fun as you wanna,
Boys if you ever go to Greenville, just go down Nelson
Street,
Cause you can have you fun with just about every
body that you meet.

With My Box and Harp
Daddy Stovepipe – Johnny
Watson – used to play in the
Nelson Street joints

Kind of restless

Muddy Waters

So I'm all dressed up now from my head down to my shoes,
I sit back and relax whilst I play these ole Nelson Street Blues,
So boys if you ever go to Greenville just go down on
Nelson Street,
Where you can laugh and have your fun with 'most
everybody that you meet.

Well that was Willie, my cousin, and then I remember Joe Willie Perkins, now he's a great piano player – they used to call him Pinetop. Then I mind T-Bone Joe Willie Wilson – used to call him T-Bone – he's from back in that time. He's pickin' a great guitar *now*. And of course like in the last past, I remember ole Charlie Patton. He come from down in the Delta – had those ole mules in a team you know. He was always singing an ole blues about, 'What's the matter with that rooster, he won't crow for day'. But there's not too much I can tell you personal about him, but I remember this feller used to play with Charlie Patton – they call him Nate Scott. I used to foller him aroun' a little and he takes up with Charlie Patton. Nate Scott had style a bit like Old Sonny Boy Williams' – had a rack of harps around his belt you know – pick out the one he wanted to play, for the key. He used to come to my daddy's house up at Lambert, Mississippi. You know, daddy give him a dollar and what you call this moonshine. Set down that jug in front of him and he's be playin' all night. Then later on there was this Howlin' Wolf that's makin' all those records now. Well I remember when he used to play out on the streets – he started down here in Ruleville, Mississippi, playin' on the streets and blowin' his harp. So I tried this playin' – tried piano for myself. I went to school a bit, but I didn't get no education – too bad, you know, played hookey and cut out from school. But music, I'm really fond of it, I really do love it. Later on I had a band of my own. We never did cut a record or anything like that . . . piano, harp, horn sometimes, drums . . . we'd cut it up in all sorts of places we'd go . . . Tommy Barnes's place down here on 61 Highway. We use to dig up a lot of trash, you know what I mean? But finally we just got tored up, and I quit it for a while. Went back to hard workin' at the seed-mill.

When I was comin' up, of course I had no ideas as to playin' music for a livin', I just sing the blues 'cause I *had* to – it was just somethin' I had to do. And at that time I used to play harp *and* guitar, either one. Seem like everybody could play some kind of instrument and there were so many fellers playin' in the jukes round Clarksdale I can't remember them all. But the best we had to my ideas was Sonny House. He came from a plantation east of Clarksdale, Marks or Lambert way I think, and I think he's out there yet, farmin'. Well I guess he'd be about in his sixties now. He used to have a neck of a bottle over his finger, little finger, touch the strings with that and make them sing. That's where I got the idea from. You break it off, hold it in a flame until it melts and gets smooth. He made some records you know, Sonny, but to my ideas he never did sound so good on record as he did when you heard him. Then of course there was Robert, Robert Johnson. He used to work the jukes. I don't know what sort of *work* he did. He always had a guitar with him whenever I saw him around. I never did talk to him much. He was the kind of guy you wanted to listen to, get ideas from. Robert was a nice lookin' man. Sort of brownskin, sort of medium height and got good hair. But he didn't seem to stay in any one place too long you know, kind of restless. Think I heard he went to Helena.

Down on Nelson Street
Juke-joints and shoe-shine parlours line Nelson Street, Greenville, for many years a blues centre in Mississippi

Those real stomp-down blues

Roosevelt Sykes

Before I even played around in different joints I learned how to play pianner very nice. I used to work around cafes as a waiter. You know you don't start off as a waiter you start off as a pot washer, and from there to a dish washer and if you doin' a pretty good job they take a chance on you in the dinin'-room. I seemed to do a pretty good job so I become a waiter and that's about all I did until I started to become a music player. This was in Helena, Arkansas, that's my home. And then I started mostly at night spots – most of them were gamblin' houses. They had people runnin' those places and these guys learned that I could play pianner pretty good so they – I was actually too young to go in there, but by me being able to play the pianner – they would let me slip in the joint. So I would go in the joints and listen to those real stomp-down blues-playin' pianists such as one guy named Jesse Bell, in Helena. He never did make a phonograph record but he was one of the outstanding blues players and he made a record playing for himself, just playing around, and I learned how to play just through association with him. So just hearing those fellers and listenin' in to them taught me. They was what you call *real* blues players, always be playin' the blues, and this particular feller, Jesse Bell, he had a blues was somethin' like:

> I got a woman in West Helena, Arkansas,
> Yes, I got a woman, in West Helena, Arkansas,
> She buys me them long-toed shoes, keeps that Brown Mule
>   in my jaw.
>
> She gets beat up on a Saturday, 'long about twelve o'clock,
> She gets beatin' up on a Saturday, 'long about twelve o'clock,
> And from then on, all the joints begin to reel and rock.
>
> She buys peanuts from a blind man, all up and down the line,
> – yes, me and my baby down there –
>
> She buys peanuts from a blind man, all up and down the line.
> She balls Saturday night and Sunday night, Monday
>   mornin' she gets up and rise and shine.
>
> – yeah, she done all the work . . .

This feller Jesse Bell was a notable blues player around Helena. There was another feller around there they called Baby Sneed, he was a pretty good blues player and there was another guy, never made no record at all, Joe Crump. He was a good shoutin' blues singer and player. This town of West Helena was west of the main city, 'bout seven miles away, but nowadays of course it's practically grown together between there. They had a place down there they call Dixie's Drug Store; 'most everybody hung around this corner. I think it was on Walnut and Missouri Streets there. Years back that was a live spot. Most of the people come out of the country from the farms where they raise cotton and corn and hogs mostly. And they all come to town a week-end, like on a Saturday, and they would all meet and after they buy their feed for their stock and get their foods, then they would go for their recreation whilst they were in town. That's the only entertainment they had; these blues players. And they would foller them down, one joint after another. It would be a lot of fun for those country people that only comes in once a week. They come in and they had a good time – something like a Christmas day every six or seven days.

He was a drawing card
Sunnyland Slim

They called it boogie then
Robert Junior Lockwood

I met Robert Johnson in Helena; I met him in *West* Helena and West Memphis and also in Mississippi – all over. There was a lot of guitar players had his style and he was a drawing card for the barrelhouse peoples. He could play those barrelhouse things and he was pretty much movin' all the time. His stepson was famous, Robert Junior Lockwood, and I tell you, he deserve a great deal more credit than he do get. The first real fast blues I ever heard was from Robert Johnson – same thing that Elmore James made famous – *Dust My Broom*, and that was the first thing that had that beat; some kind of a beat you could kinda get around a little fast on – walkin' the basses. Then he used to play a thing with another guy, which was called *Come On and Take a Little Walk with Me* and Robert *Junior*, he put that out. That was somethin' you could get a little faster on too; sort of what you call a fast blues – blues that's got a little motion to it. I don't know just how, but it started people sort of puttin' a little motion of a fast blues – the whole world got in on it. Robert Johnson played guitar but we kinda patterned ourselves on him – played *Dust My Broom* and *Terraplane Blues* – they come out on record too.

He was my stepfather, Robert Johnson, and I learned most of what I knowed behind him. That was at the place I was born at, Marvell, Arkansas, which is about twenty miles out from West Helena. I didn't see too much of him because he wasn't around so much, but I learned quite a bit from watchin' him. So I had a little number then, was *Take a Little Walk with Me*:

> Come on, take a little walk with me,
> Come on babe, take a li'l walk with me
> To same ole place, where we long to be.

> Early one mornin' just about half past three,
> You done somethin's really worrying me,

> Come on, take a little walk with me,
> To the same ole place, where we long to be . . .

Well then in my gettin' around I used to hear that type of music all over the Delta, on through Mississippi, Arkansas, some parts of Missouri, type of tune we used to two-step by back about twenty, thirty years ago. They called it boogie then – right behind *Pinetop's Boogie*. I call it a Mississippi tune 'cause it originated in Mississippi but it's guitar – guitar boogies.

Walking basses
Little Brother Montgomery

On up I learned another blues from a great guy name of Loomis Gibson. We called it the *Loomis Gibson Blues* which is the name of it. When I first tried to play it I was only around the age of nine so I used to only play a walking bass with one finger then, but after I got up around twelve or fourteen I could double up and I could play with all of my hand. Later on, Loomis Gibson passed and I named it the *Crescent City Blues*. We used to call it walkin' basses at the time, but we never called it anything special. I was playin' what you call boogie woogies ever since I was twelve or fourteen years old but then we called it *Dud Low Joe*. I had – see I left home at eleven years old, I was what you call a kid runnin' away – I had played at all sorts of places like I aforesaid. Like I had played at Holden, Louisiana, at the juke barrelhouse, I left there and went to Placquemine. From there I went to Ferriday, Louisiana, and I played there at Henderson's Royal Garden until I were fourteen. I come on up to Tallulah, Louisiana, and then the 1922 high water ran up the side of Louisiana and then I came over – I come over to Vicksburg. That's where I started playing – at 1014 Washington Street for Zack Lewis. That's where I met Ernest Johnson, he was three years older than me and he was playing at Addie's place on Mulberry Street. Well I played there and that's where we originated these numbers like *Vicksburg Blues*, *44 Blues* and things like that – well it's the same thing but I just called it the *Vicksburg Blues*. It's a blues, it's a barrelhouse honkytonk blues. People dance by that, did the shimmy by that. So me and Ernest Johnson and a man they called Friday – well there were three or four of us – Son Crooks (he had a nub hand), Johnny Eager – we all played it. It's a thing we made up; you could keep addin' to it. Ernest Forty-Four, well he and I and Robert Johnson, that was his cousin, we invented the *44 Blues*. His name was Ernest Johnson but we nicknamed him Ernest Forty-Four or we used to call him Forty-Four Kid, and we called him Flunkey too. He always wanted to work on the railroad; fact he did later on up. Dehlco Robert Johnson was his cousin and he played with us and he played the *44 Blues* too. So there was a feller there by the name of Lee Green used to be always hangin' around us tryin' to get in on it. He was pressin' clothes – he was a clothes-presser in Vicksburg. So then I met him again at Sondheimer, Louisiana, and I taught him to play the *44 Blues* then, and later years he taught them to Roosevelt so they beat me to Chicago and put them out. So after they put them out as the *44 Blues* I came up to Chicago and made it the *Vicksburg Blues*. I changed the name because – well, you know they were ours in front.

44 blues
Roosevelt Sykes

That's kinda old
Jasper Love

There was a feller by the name of Lee Green – they called him Pork Chops – and he was the first guy I ever heard play the *44 Blues*. Several people had been playing it all through the country of course – Little Brother Montgomery and several others but nobody had ever recorded it and there was no words to it, no words or lyrics at all. So Lee Green, he took a lot of time out to teach me how to play it, to use my left hand on tenth bass. In music it takes a pretty good stretch to stretch ten keys with your one left hand. But my hands were kind of small. Well I could skip and jump 'em but he showed me how it was done, but of course, he's passed now. But Lee Green was a mighty fine feller, he was a stylist, he had his own style and wrote his own tunes, like he was a great pianist. He had a nickname of Pork Chops and at times when he felt devilish he would always crack jokes. So he'd call the girls over, so she'd come over to see what he want. And he'd have one of the women there and she'd want to know what he wanted and he'd tell her to turn all the way round. And she'd want to know why, and well . . . he'd just do that thing! And the girl turn round and smack his face! And then we used to call him Turpentine Joe because that was one of them bad men. You know we had a picture 'bout him, once upon a time, Turpentine Joe, so we called him that because he didn't mind getting smashed. He was full of devilment you know. He was a nice guy – he taught me, started me on the *44 Blues*. Lee Green he had one about *Train Number 44*. He made several other blues, *Memphis Fives*, *Railroad Blues* – tunes like that. Green taught me how to finger 'em but we still play 'em different. I mean, I put my soul to it which was different from his. But he was the one responsible for *44 Blues* as far as I'm concerned. But I wrote the words.

I was born down there on the Tallahatchie River and I growed up around a little place they call Webb, and Sumner, and when I was goin' on, got to be a man around Clarksdale. But now, when I first heard this Roosevelt Sykes when he was first playin' I was working what you call about fifteen miles south of Helena, between Wabash and Helena I'd say. That was round about '25. I was quite young, mannish, in my prime, you know what I mean? Well I started back about then with the real late Roosevelt Sykes, started back with him with that old *Four O'Clock*. He had three brothers, I can remember Jess and Wyle. I even got the pattern of the way Wyle used to play . . . that's kinda old I guess. That was his key at the time. I used to stand by the piano and watch him . . . he was makin' music for my auntie. That was a long time ago. And so I started out tryin' to do it. I never been taught, I always do all mine by ear you know – sounds I hear and so on. So I tried the kind of type Willie – Wyle used to play, the old *Vicksburg*. Then when he got over in the night he played what you call a *Road Blues*, kinda slow and easy . . . So I kinda take over, had an old blues which I used to play in Drew – made it up:

I said the Smoky Mountains, the Smoky Mountains
  darlin', where I belong to be,
I said the Smoky Mountains, Smoky Mountains darlin'
  where I long to be,
I can't stay here no longer baby, 'cause you know this ain't
  no place for me.

I said out on the desert, out on the desert, you know the
  rain darlin' was fallin' down,
Out on the desert, out on the desert, you know the cold rain
  was fallin' down,
Wasn't nothin' I could do, wasn't nothin' I could do darlin'
  because you know I swear I was Chicago bound.

I hated to go boys, but I had to. I had got busted down in my home town – you know what I mean? Ragged, dirty, broke, didn't have no job – I had to do somethin'. Even walked up to my friend's door, he wouldn't even give me a helpin' hand . . . .

You can't go too far
Robert Curtis Smith

I have moved quite a bit and the polices haven't been at me as far as I knows of. But I have knowed a lots of people in Mississippi who cain't leave. Because if you make a crop and don't clear nothin' and you still wound up owin' on your share-crop and on your furnish' and you try to move, well the police be after you then all right. But if you're clear well mostly, you can't go too far because of the money. If you move, or if you try to move, they know if they like the way you work they make you pay somethin' just for holdin' the house up. If, after you pay that you want to move, well you cain't go too far because you got to pay them. You gonna need money to carry you on to the place where you can get work. And if you cain't get work at one place you go on to the next place, but you cain't go too far, because you ain't got enough in hand *to* go that far.

When I left Mississippi
Walter Davis

When I left Mississippi I was around thirteen years old. My father sent me down to cut some cotton stalks one day. And I got on the stalk cutter and rode the mules down to the back-side of the fence. Then I got off the stalk cutter and got under the fence and tied the mules to the fence and walked about thirty miles and caught a ride on a wagon! Ha! Walked about another twenty miles and I caught holt of a truck goin' uphill and I caught on the back of it. I run off and I don't know what! They didn't see me no more in three years!

I Used to Stand by the Piano
Children listen as Jasper Love plays. The two older girls can both play piano blues

Walk a while, ride a while

Edwin Buster Pickens

You know I heard the Santa Fe blow one mornin' . . . It cried like a child – that engine was shootin' up steam . . . an' I talked with the conductor, the brakesman, in the caboose – and he said, 'Where ya goin' boy?'

   I said, 'I'm goin' to Cowswitch!'

   He said, ' I don't 'llow nobody to ride this train.'

   I said, 'Boss, I'm hungry.'

   'What can you do?'

   I said, ' I can fiddle a li'l bit.'

   He said, 'All right, go on . . . and fiddle . . . How – how
      do you do that?'

   I said, 'I do it on the piano.'

   He said, 'All right – but you ain't got no pi-ano!'

   'That's right – but if I catch the Santa Fe, I'm gonna find one.'

He said, 'I'll let you ride . . .'

All right . . . then she blowed . . .

Number Fourteen-Thirty-Five . . . Mountain Jack. So he let me ride, but it was another stop there, and I quit her. And I met ole Robertson there – he was 'n old-time piano player and the saw-mills had rode him out. He said, 'Son, take my place!'

I said, 'I will.'

He said, 'What'cha come in here on . . . ?'

I said, 'On the Santa Fe . . . ain't but one road . . .'

He said, 'How did you get by the brakesman?'

   'I told him who I was.'

   'Who is you?'

I say, 'Well, I ain't much' – but I try to say what I can do. 'Well, what'cha go tell him? . . . what'cha do when you tell him?' 'Well, I say, Looka here!'

   I says, 'I'm just here tryin' to ketch this train.' He says, 'I don't want you to ride my train!' I says, 'I know it's against the law to do that, but – I – I'm on my way!' He says to me, he says, 'Get on – and ride! Where ya goin?' Cowswitch!'

   That's where they make real saw-lumber. Change shifts, one shift goin' and one barrelhouse . . . in the saw-mill. Brakesman said he wanna barrelhouse too, but he didn't have the time, he was on the train. I says, ' I'm on here too. So, when you get off there, come by and see me sometime!' He says, 'I will. . . .'

I traveled by freight trains. I rode freight trains practically all over the country. I flag rides and so forth. I might go to Tomball an' I might stay there until things dull down. Then I hear of another camp where it's booming. I leave there and probably go to Raccoon Bend – oil-field. Then I leave there and probably go to Longview . . . Kilgore . . . Silsbee . . . Just wherever it was booming. Big boom out there, I'd hear about it. Money in operation there – why, I'd go . . . oh, freight train, truck sometimes, even walk a while, ride a while . . . . These other piano players – Son Becky, Conish Burks, Black Boy Shine, Andy Boy and all these men – they went out different routes – hardly ever paired up. Each lookin' for his own bread.

Ain't But One Road
The Santa Fe tracks, Tyler in East Texas

They Were Small Places
Honkytonks front on the
tracks in the 'wide-open '
town of Richmond, Texas.
Hoboes swing off the freight
cars as the trains pass through

Ain't But One Road
The Santa Fe tracks, Tyler in East Texas

Ride and play
Lightnin Hopkins

Places I was playin' – they were *small* places. Oh, four or five stores and nearly each of them didn't have much more than that. Quite nach'ly I imagine they built up some more, five or six stores larger now, but at that time they was about three or four stores. And they call Buffalo – that sounds a big place: small. Brenham, Texas: small place. Crockett, it was small. But to listen to all them names you'd think they was great big places. They're small. Well, sometimes we jump on top of freight trains, run over there from Buffalo to Palestine. Get off there, play there, ketch the freight back to Buffalo. Sometimes we get on an old T-model truck and go; we'd had several different ways we go. Had friends pick us up from time to time. Had to wait my time to get on those freight trains. I'd always get on whilst it was standin' still; I didn't like takin' off in the air none, I'd wait till it stopped. Other boys, they'd run, swing on them things. I couldn't do that. See I always take my git-tar with me; I'm scared I'm gonna bust it. So when it was standin' still I'd slip in the box car and ride. When it stopped, I'd slip out. When it take off they ketch you so I'd already be on there. They did ketch me one time. They put us off. We had to walk about five miles; real hot that day. Put us off, made us walk. But that was about the only trouble I had with the railroad dicks. Otherwise, I used to ride buses – yeah, free. They'd see me goin' down the street with my git-tar. They'd say 'Hurry on boy! Jump on there! Let's go!' I'd jump up there, ring down on that ole git-tar there, make me a little piece of change between Dowling Street and West Dallas and back. I did that for years. See all the bus drivers on that line they knowed me far as they'd see me. They'd blow or call me, say, 'Git on!' I'd just ride and play . . . lots of fun at that time.

Canned heat
Blind Arvella Gray

This was immediately after the Scottsburg boys way back in 'twenty – I don't know exactly which year it was because I never kep' up with those data. Anyway, it was about eleven o'clock at night. Well real hoboes they have certain ways they do. When they get into a town they don't go roamin' around in the city an' things at night because if some of the people in the city would break in stores or do anything, well, they would take the hobo and he could be sent up for what somebody else do. Get the rap. And so a bunch of us hoboes we just said well we'd stay here and make ourselves a little canned heat and drink here by the railroad. So anyway, we weren't payin' any attention. So two girls, two white girls passed by us and so they immediately called the police. And the police come down there – oh, 'bout a dozen police – and they surrounded us and they say, 'You-all around here been meddlin' girls!' And we say, 'No, there ain't ben no girls been by here.' And they say, 'Well the girls reported that you-all had meddled with them.' And so that's when we had to start talkin' and had to talk fast, and we sweated whilst we was talkin'! So they kept us overnight at the jailhouse and the next mornin' they carried us to the railroad track and they told us to get out of there and get out fast. Which we did. And I never went back there no more. But I hoboed all over the country; catch the freight trains as they slowed down to go into one of those tunnels.

Ride on into town

Speckled Red

I never did flag many rides 'cause I never did like it. But I hoboed on trains – I'd catch a train right now, if I feel like it, go anywhere I want to go. My eyesight ain't too good and I couldn't see it very well but I could see it good enough. I wouldn't wait till it get started too much; catch it before it started off if I could, then I'd hobo my way. Well I got put off so *many* times – run like a rabbit! I've got shot at and everything at night. Run down the hill – down it – you don't know which way you're runnin' – cross the railroad, anything – anywhere to get out of the way. I remember one time I was going down from Memphis Tennessee. Caught a train, caught the Illinois Central going down to Cairo. And I got to Cairo and got out at the junction. The train always stop there, let 'em search the train – seize anybody before they go into town. The brakesman sees a gang of 'bout twelve of us there. They got lights searchlights by the fireman's bell or something. And they shine these lights and caught us and they were shootin' down there. And you could hear them bullets going ping . . . ping . . . ping . . . ping . . . and I just fell down and come over and over and over down hill. The hill was steep – steep like just going down in a gutter. Down, way down there. Well I rolled right down in there – well they can't see you in the weeds and things. So I got away. Wait a good while. Then get out on the road, catch one of them trucks and ride into town. You get into town but maybe you don't get no job. You just go around somewhere where there's joints if you got it good. If they got somebody playin' why you play two or three pieces and maybe somebody else'll pick you up at another place where they ain't doin' so good, see? Then you build the place up. I remember one time I didn't have a job, hoboed into town and there was a secondhand furniture store there had some pianos. I asked the man could I play a piece or two and he said, 'Yeah you go ahead and play – *if* you can play'. So I played a couple of pieces on the pianner that was in the winder. It was on a Saturday afternoon. I played that Saturday afternoon up in the winder and people comin' into town – the store was full of people. Full of people – I mean everybody. And I made about sixty dollars there playin' in the winder. And that night, that evenin' a newspaper man came and asked me did I want to play in a contest. I told him sure, I wanted to do anything. And I had on some old smoky clothes from riding the train. I went and bought me some clothes with some of the money I had from playin' and cleaned up and went over there and played that night. And I won first prize and won $125 – sure did. Of course I wasn't always a hobo on the trains. I played on the train too. See once a year the Illinois Central used to have an excursion, they go down to the Mardi Gras in New Orleans you see. It was just a big train, with big cars. Big train and the cars would be crowded full of people just all over the train – be about sixteen or eighteen car loads of people. And they have a car where you can dance and sing and go on and play. And I was playing with a little three-piece orchestra on the excursion. I played piano all the time. I was in something like a baggage car. Just an open car where they dance and sing. All the way down to New Orleans. Of course I liked it all right because it was mighty noisy and everything. A whole lot of people they have cut-rate fare. You could go right down there, stay overnight and come back next day. Everything was pretty cheap in New Orleans. You could take fifteen cents and you couldn't eat the whole meal – everything was cheap. I played on that excursion train for three years. Then they finally broke it up on account of a boy and a girl got killed on that train and so they don't have that no more.

People throw water

Dédé Pierce

During the Carnival season in New Orleans a lot of these Creole men go round with guitars and if they see somebody they knew and they wanted to talk to them they'd sing Creole songs and Creole blues at them. Most of the time people throw water at them or whatever they had handy. During the Carnival season. But what clothes she wear, what she buy in the street – everything they could think of they sing about. Anyone they didn't like they'd pick up their guitars and serenade them like that – in Creole. They had these blues singers in the streets. I can't remember what they sang – but they did it.

The Railroad Blues A folk artist at the Beale Street Rescue Mission, Memphis, gives expression to a familiar blues theme

They'd be singing

Charles Love

Up town in New Orleans they had a lot of country guitar players used to come to town and sit around and in barber shops you know, and play. But they never did play any real music with the band orchestras. They hear 'em playing and they sit around in the barber shops and if they catch the piece they pick it out on the guitar. You know they pick the guitar like you do a pianner and some of them sounded very nice. They sing blues and such songs and they sing all them songs like they play and sing on the steamboats – them roustabouts – and on the railroads. While they were unloading the cotton they'd be singing and then they were resting they'd be playing them guitars. It was very nice and I used to enjoy that, but I never liked the blues much.

We Run Together Dédé Pierce and his wife Billie Pierce at their home, back of North Galves Street, New Orleans

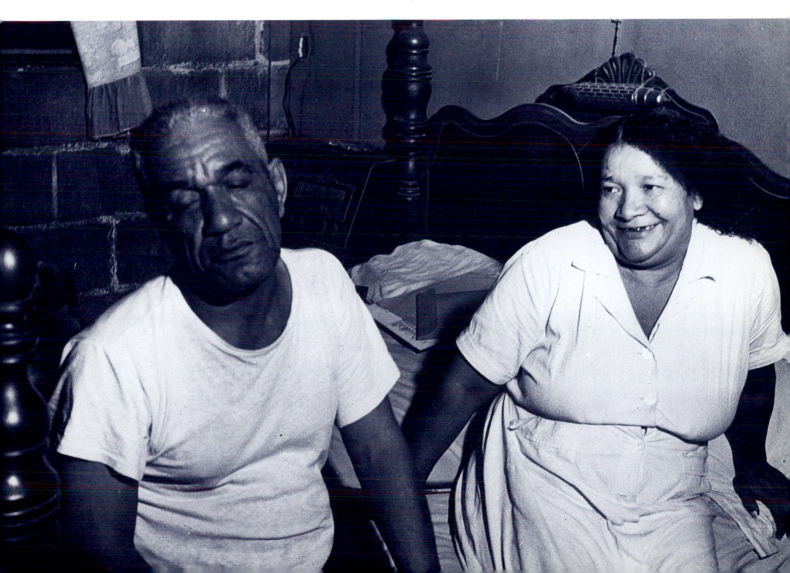

Only thing we cared for
Billie Pierce

I tell you, from my remembrance I was quite a kid, very young, when I first started to play the piano. I just learned my style – just come up with it. My mother, she was a great pianist and songster, my mother. She played a little rags but not too much, mostly played hymns. My father, he too did play hymns most of the time. But when all we seven sisters come along we all was ragtime and blues players – only thing we cared for. Now I have a niece and a nephew and they play the same things, jazz and blues just like I do. And they all sings. We was all the same – we was all jazz piano players: blues, jazz, ragtime, all that. When I wanted to play the piano I was playing a little, but the first thing I learned was the blues; and I started to singing the one words to the blues I knew, and I sung it, I say:

I never loved but one man in my life,
I never loved but one man in my life,
He was a married man an' I stole him from his wife.

That's when I started playing the blues, and I was quite a kid – must have been around seven years old at the time.

Blues was all the go
Lonnie Johnson

Early days of the blues – as far back as I can get is 1914. That's when I was at home in New Orleans and my family was alive then. We all played music – five sisters and six brothers, mother and father. We played for banquets and weddings and things like that all around and then finally I lost most of my entire family in World War I, when I come back from overseas. And so I started out on my own. I had to then, there wasn't anything else to do. So I started playing music for a living. And the blues was all the go then and from then on I loved blues and I just continued to playing them. And finally I got so I could make a living by singing the blues – and I loved them and I still love the blues. I worked all sorts of places – I worked at the Iroquois Theater for a long time and I worked at Frank Pineri's place on Iberville and Burgundy, oh God, I don't know *how* long – 'bout four and a half years or something like that. Strictly blues all the way – on the violin. And I made several numbers on the piano – I used to play piano for a while, but only blues, no popular songs. Then I bought my guitar. I bought it in 1917. It's a beautiful instrument, but oh when you tune it up you got a beautiful instrument. And at night, if you want to get the real effect of it, take a small tub – you know, a small washtub. Fill it up with water, sit down on the steps and set that tub of water down. You set down there and play it and let that sound come through that water and you talkin' about somethin' beautiful. Oh brother. . . I'm not kidding . . . and I'm talkin' about a *feelin'* . . . it sounds sweeter, goes further . . . You know how an instrument sounds on the water? That's what I'm talking about, it's more effective on the water than it is anywhere else.

You Got Little Money
Lonnie Johnson had seen
good times and bad in fifty
years of singing the blues

It wasn't gloomy then

Billie Pierce

Play right on

Dédé Pierce

When I met Dédé he was workin' with my sister on Decatur Street for Charlie Palooka, and I was workin' on Ursulines and Decatur for Vince St Cyr and Milton Shotts, and the name of the place was the Kingfish. Dédé's workin' on the next block for a woman named Corrine. Well Dédé and I runnin' together. Well anyhow, Corrine, she goes to sleep and forget to pay the band off and Dédé got mad one night and he was about to quit. So before he quit I went down to get Dédé and bring him back from Corrine's to the Kingfish because I had no trumpet player – come and work with me. We run together about a week and then we decided to get married. Well, we married, and when I was workin' at the Kingfish and my boss was very glad that day I got married because he figgered by Dédé playin' trumpet and me playin' pianner he's have a band all the time, see. My drummer was McGhee – he's out in California now – well, McGhee was workin' for us. It was just a jitney, so it didn't seem like they want to give me a chance to ketch my breath at all – just music, music, music all the time. So I say I quit. My boss say, 'What you say?' I say, 'I'll tell you, I'm gonna quit', and McGhee says he's gonna quit too. So he says, 'All right', 'cause he figgered Dédé was goin' quit too, but Dédé wouldn't quit; he stayed on there and they bought a pianner player to play in my place with Dédé. This pianner player liked the liquor you know, so Dédé made him so drunk he just couldn't play the pianner, just because I wasn't there to play the pianner with him. So finally they wanted me to come back to work. I tell you, it was a thing on Decatur Street. Right next door, everywhere you go it was bands, bands, bands. Cross the street more bands. You work three or four places on one block at that time – keep runnin'. You go out of one place into the other and you could quit a job and the band go right next door and go to work. I did that plenty of times. I leave one job go next door. Say I'm fired, I quit, I need a job. They let me go to work. I go right back and get me old job back again later on. And around Decatur Street we had all kinds of nationalities. Everybody go round Decatur Street, come to the French market. All roll up – just about everyone: soldiers, sailors, merchant marine – everybody go till the wagon come. But I know one thing, it wasn't gloomy then! I'm tellin' you we had lots of fun down there! Anything would happen on Decatur Street at that time!

Well at that time merchant seamen come in, get in some argument, try to tear up the place but the band continue playin' the blues, don't stop! Mostly the bands did that – if somebody did come in to tear up the place the bands continue playin'. Stop after a while when the law broke it up you know. Tear up tables, glasses, beer bottles – all that went! Feller we called Poppa had a nice spot but somebody started a fight in his place. Then somebody put all the lights out and ran over to our place for pertection. Kingfish was goin' to give him some help you know, put order in his place. So our boss went over there and our band went over and everybody was drinkin' up all the beer whilst they had those fuses burnt out. Until they put order in there those fellers cleaned out everything they had in the place. Everybody took what they wanted. It was raided 'cause of the fight they had. Billie come home with a gallon of wine! Took her a whole gallon of wine and come on away! Joe Gleason too – that was the Cat and the Fiddle. They had two entrances – a front and a back entrance. And the sailors got to fightin' in there and they throwed every table out of the house – throw it on the roadside. So the boss, Joe Gleason, when the sailors want to know who was the boss, Joe says, 'I'm the boss!' So two sailors was fightin' in there picked him up bodily and threw him through a plate-glass door out on the balcony – the boss! Lost his wrist watch and I went out there and pick it up and give it to him. And all the time the band would play right on; and the singers would sing right on. Mostly at that time the bands would consist of clarinet, piano, banjo and drums and they would play a lot of blues. In other words blues is mostly make-up songs. Just make up songs by puttin' anything in you know. They wife done left them and all that . . . just plain blues is all I call it. Put words together, call it some one blues or other but it's all the same blues. And all they call it is blues. Only difference is the instruments and the key of the number they played it in. Makes a difference in the sound. Play it in E♭, play it some in B♭, some blues in C, some blues in D, and that's the way they call'em.

We'd play rags
Sweet Emma Barrett

I started out with Papa Celestin; played piano for him with the Original Tuxedo. We used to play those blues numbers – *St Louis Blues*, *Careless Love* and things like that. And we'd play rags and those old tunes. Well, I'm a jazz player, a rag player. So we'd feature a number of blues and I'd play those, and I had a little blues or two of my own. But I never fooled around with those blues players. *Strictly* blues players; never did have much to do with them at all. I can't tell you nothing about them. I never did pay them no mind. Fact is, I didn't like their blues.

Pete's Blue Heaven
On South Rampart Street,
New Orleans, the juke-box
replaced the blues pianist

Evil-spirited music

Charles Love

I don't like the blues myself, but I've been playin' them all my life. You see blues is the evil of music, evil-spirited music. Why I say that is because wherever the blues is played there's a fight right after. You know the blues apt to get them all bewildered some kind of way, makes 'em wild, they want to fight. They want to dance and fight and everything; I never did like blues but I noticed that. Everywhere we played and started playing the blues the dance would be all right until right up to the time we put the blues on. When you start with the blues it breaks up the dancin' and they stop. We used to play rags like we do now – *Maple Leaf Rag* and all of that. We had an eight-piece band and we'd play some swell rags that wasn't in the books you know. And the fellers all enjoyed it. I remember one time we were playing those rags and then they wanted to hear the blues. I had a little brown derby I used to use on the blues and we started to playin' the blues and everythin' come down, you know. Got way down, and I commenced to fannin' the trumpet with that little brown derby puttin' in all kinds of stuff in there, growlin' and everythin' and I made it as low-down as I could make it you know. And after a while some-body hit the policeman and downstairs, there comes the wagons, about eleven wagons puttin' everybody in jail. That broke the dance up. People was fightin' and usin' razors and everything else. I had to run, get out of there, get under some trees! I say I ain't gonna play the blues no more, but I did. I played 'em, but somethin' happen all the time. Every time I played the blues somethin' happen. That's what I said, that's the evil spirit of music. That's not good music, not to me.

People fall for that

Billie Pierce

Charlie Segar came from my home town in Pensacola, Florida. He was a great piano player, also a nice trumpet player. Well Charlie used to be quite smart on the piano. He learned me to cover the piano with a sheet and learned for me to play on top of the piano with the sheet coverin' it up. And Charlie played nice trumpet hisself. He would play trumpet and piano at once. They would blindfold his eyes and he'd play trumpet with one hand and piano with his other – he had his own band! He was really good too. It was just somethin' to be showin', advertisin' yourself. Lots of people fall for that kind of stuff, you see. Cover the piano altogether and play through the sheet or blindfold yourself like that. That was kind of a novelty and I used to do that behind him. See there was so many good blues pianists and songsters and musicianers that you had to be able to do somethin' special to get yourself noticed. Lots of competition at that time.

King of the blues

Dédé Pierce

I imagine the trumpet players get that feeling of the singers at times from playing with them. They kind of imitate them. I follow the singers as close as possible, myself. Then they'd alternate and put whatever come to their minds during that time you know, the breaks, in between the singing. In the line of blues players as far as I know, Kid Rena played a lot of blues, and this Chris Kelly was called King of the Blues in his time. There was Kid Rena, Kid Shots Madison – Joe Nicholas, he was a blues man too. At times they'd play a second behind the singers; second as *we'd* call it. They played an obligato it's called, fill in behind the singers. In other words they make the music prettier behind the songster, that's the way they played it. Chris Kelly begin to play a blues and he'd take a rubber stopper, a plunger they call it, and work it in and out of the horn till he could almost make it talk. Just like a young baby want to say 'Mama' or talk or so forth, he could use that plunger that way on the trumpet. Sometimes he use a tin can, and the more delapidated the tin can the better it sound. Take that to the bell of his horn and take it away to make different sounds almost like a human voice'd talk or sing the sound. Make it sound like 'Yes' or 'No' and simple words like that he'd make on it too.

Selling his medicine

Charles Love

Of course they had blues singers on those medicine shows. Matter-of fact if you worked on one of those shows you had to be ready to do just about anything yourself in the entertainment line. I got on a medicine show, playing trumpet, and the feller was sellin' medicines you know, and linaments and stuff like that, and every time he make a sale people would start to go, and then the band would start to play to draw more people. And we would play along you know and the cornet player that he had already, he would get up and sing and dance. He had two or three fellers working regular for him and they would put on a little show and by that time he had a big crowd again, and he'd start off selling his medicine. But I didn't like being on that show because it wasn't enough show for me, and I wanted to get away.

Good for a thousand things
Speckled Red

Me and Jim Jackson played on the shows together, all down the Mississippi and through Arkansas, Alabama, all over. We were with the Red Rose Minstrels it was called but it was a medicine show. It was just a show where the man sold all kinds of medicine and soap and stuff. One medicine good for a thousand things – and wasn't good for *nothin'*. A whole lot of pills, everything. He had a big show where there was a whole lot of women and I was playing pianner. Sometimes I was on the stage, trying to dance, and I could talk, crack a whole lot of jokes – me and Jim. And there were lots of girls dancing up there, chorus girls. Aw . . . just something like a vaudeville act, like there used to be years ago. Well Jim Jackson was a great fella, and if it hadn't been for him I never would have made a record. He was a big fat feller, weighed about 235 pounds. Tall, stately feller too, and he danced, sang, played git-tar, crack jokes. I used to go visit his family too, they lived where he was born at, Hernando, Mississippi. That's not so far from Memphis. And he died there. He died back in 1937.

Tight, like that
Bo Carter

I worked on doctor shows, I used to play for doctors one time. I'd say, 'What did the rooster say to the hen?' Ask the doctor that. Then I'd sing a little song:

> Big red rooster said to the little guinea hen,
> 'You ain't laid an egg since God knows when,'

> Little guinea hen said to the rooster,
> Say, 'You don't come aroun' as often as you usta.'

> The great big rat say to the itty bitty mouse,
> 'I don't want you creepin' roun' my house,'

> And the itty bitty mouse tol' that big ole rat,
> 'When I comes aroun', well it's tight like that . . .'

Then I'd fix on one of them gals out in front and I'd sing a little blues:

> She's a little bitty woman, built pretty from the ground,
> She's a little bitty woman, she's pretty from the ground,
> And every time she loves you, she'll turn your damper down.

> I said, ' Good mornin', tell me what be your name?'
> Said, 'Good mornin' little woman, tell me what be your name?
> Before many more questions won't you make a little hole in
>   the world for me?'

> You'se a real pretty woman, lightnin's when you smile,
> You'se a real pretty woman an' it lightnin's when you smile,
> You five foot six inches, just a good lovin' size.

> Every time you walk the streets, yo' hips shakes like a leaf
>   on a tree,
> When you shake your hips they shake just like the leaves on
>   a tree,
> One thing nice about you, all your lovin' belongs to me.

Sell a lots of medicine then . . .

I Used to Play for Doctors
Once a 'medicine show' guitarist,
Bo Carter became sick and blind,
scarcely able to play his old
'National' steel guitar

Say, doc!
Gus Cannon

Way on the medicine shows . . . I can give you a sample of that:

'Yes sir! Here I is . . . way on this medicine show, ole Banjo
Joe. Now folkses, you know one thing? I just cain't see you all
over there! Looks 'bout as if I'm gonna go blind lookin' at
them brownskins! Ha! Yeeesuh!'

' Say, Doc!'

'Yeah?'

'Now listen? Can you tell me how far is up?'

'Up where?'

'Up anywhere . . . anywhere. You know *down* don't you?
How far is up?'

'Oh yeah! I know *all* about bein' *down*. I don't know nothin'
about up!'

'Now I tell you one thing. I'm in the medicine show, but
I tell you one thing. Now looka here, Doc. I'm gonna axe
you somethin'. I'm gonna axe you a question. Are you gonna
answer?'

'Yeah, I'm gonna answer . . . I reckon.'

'Why not Doc? Say now listen.' (I turns around.) 'If I had
four dollars and give you one . . . ' (He say, 'Hmm . . . mmm.')
'How many would that leave me?'

'You say, if you had four dollars and give me one, how many
would that leave you?' (I say, 'Yassuh!') 'That'd leave you three!'

' Uh-oh! Nooo, white folks! If I act the *fool*, and give you
one, I'd *still* have my four!'

I worked with the doctors. I worked for Dr C. Hangerson,
I worked for Dr Stokey right here on South Parkway,
Memphis. I worked with a man out of Louisville. I worked
through Mississippi, I worked through Virginia, I worked
through Alabama, I worked through Mobile, Gulfport, Bay
St Louis – far as I been down, playin' my banjo on them
doctor shows. I'm *old* time. And I worked right back here to
Memphis. I used to play *John Henry, Old John Booker* . . .
I used to play all them things.

When the Boats Come in
The excursion steamer Memphis
Queen docks at the levee where
the *Katy Adams* used to come in

Days of nineteen-hundred

Will Shade

Beale Street, Memphis – there used to be a red light district, so forth like that. Used to be wide open houses in them days. You could used to walk down the street in days of 1900 and like that and you could find a man wit' throat cut from y'ear to ear. Also you could find people lyin' dead wit' not their throat cut, money took and everything in their pockets, took out of their pockets and thrown outside the house. Sometimes you find them with no clothes on and such as that. Sometimes you find them throwed out of winders and so forth, here on Beale Street. Sportin' class o' women runnin' up and down the street all night long . . . git knocked in the head with bricks and hatchets and hammers. Git cut with pocket knives and razors and so forth. Run off to the foot of Beale and some of them run into the River and drown. Roustabouts on the boats would come in at three and four and five in the mornin', when the boats come in. The *Katy Adams*, they used to call that a woman's boat, a woman's boat on the water. All the women would foller that boat . . . jest pay fifty cents for cabin fare and ride that boat from Memphis down to Rosedale and that's the way they made they money – go up and down the River. Which the boat was carryin' Uncle Sam's mail so all them women was pertected . . . They used to come back in – and they used to wear 'Nation' sacks in them days – and they used to wear their money twixt their legs, hung on a sack tied round their waists. Put their money in there – and they didn't tote nothin' but gold dollars in them days – and they had so much money, when they got back to Memphis they be hump-backedted, they couldn't straighten up. That's right, I'm tellin' you the truth. Then when they meet those roustabouts – they'd make a hundred and fifty dollars a trip totin' all that cotton – and then when they come, in the boat would blow and they get up and go out and meet that boat and all they friends. Next mornin' when they wake up they'd have so much money they had more money than the law allowed.

Tickled to death
Sunnyland Slim

Born talented
John Lee Hooker

In 19 and '24 at Lambert, Mississippi, a feller found me by the name of Hot Shots and I was playin' at a juke down there. So he asked me what was I doin' and would I like to play for him. I went down to his place and we went on down to a motion picture show and he had me play the blues and boogie woogie whilst the pictures were showin' – from eight until around eleven-thirty. And then he paid me a few dollars and I was tickled to death. And while I was workin' at that motion picture show a man was standin' there – from a roadhouse out in the country. And he was waitin' on me to finish and then he commenced to talk to me because he liked my playin'. So *he* hired me to play out at his roadhouse for two dollars a time from twelve o'clock until day. And I was tickled to death again. And after that I felt I was gettin' some place. I was doin' little things, blues, like:

Well it's early in the mornin' when the blues really do
    come down,
It's early in the mornin', you know when the blues really
    come down,
Well, if you aren't aroun' darlin' I just don't feel satisfied.

Standin' at four o'clock in the mornin' and my baby she
    ain't returned,
It's four o'clock in the mornin' and my baby she has
    not returned,
I'm kinda worried 'bout that girl and wonder where she
    could be found.

Well, leavin' you baby, you'll have to do the best you can,
Mmmm, leavin' you baby, so you'll have to do the best
    you can,
I'm leavin' you li'l girl, you'd better find you another
    sweet man.

And I did leave. After two or three weeks I got ready to leave Mississippi, got ready to go to Memphis, go up North.

I was livin' in a little town you call Clarksdale, Mississippi, with my dad and mother. That's where I was born, August 1917. Well then I had a stepfather and his name was William Moore and he played guitar and he taught me a little; I took my firs' inspirations from him. I left home in my early days when I was aroun' twelve or thirteen years old; I left when I come to Memphis, Tennessee. Well I got a little job there when I come to the New Daisy picture show just down on Beale Street, and I was workin' there as an usher in the movies, playin' my music as time would omit me to do. And my mother and my dad come and got me from there and brought me back home, so I never did get away from that farmwork too much. But I was born talented I guess, so I messed around with the guitar, and singin' and run away from home again and come up to Memphis again.

New Daisy Picture Show
The Daisy Theater still stands,
but the building on the left is
on the site of Pee Wee's place

A Place Wide Open
The Monarch gambling
house where Benny Frenchy
and Sonny Butts were heard
by Jelly Roll Morton and
W. C. Handy

Boys, get together
Robert Henry

Now I'm speakin' from 335 Beale. I've been on Beale Street for more than forty-seven years. I've seen Beale Street to its peak at three o'clock in the mornin' that you could hardly get through it. I knew when the musicians on Beale Street was only gettin' two dollars and sixty cents for their work. A dime of it was for car fare and the rest for the musicians. W. C. Handy and I was very good friends. We stayed together, run together for years to come. We had a place – they called it Pee Wee's where Handy come from. Pee Wee's place was a great spot for musicians – all the musicians hung out there. And when Handy used to say, 'Boys, get together!' he would put a cap on anybody who was a musician and say he belong to Handy's Band. Now at that particular time we had what you call Midnight Shows: we had one night for White and the others for Colored. We had Charlie Williamson and his band – they called it the Palace Band. Aw, but they were wonderful, and it was a great day when they give that Midnight Show. The white people packed the street and nothin' too much happened, they got along fine, when they come to that Midnight Show. Charlie Williamson he passed, and the Palace is a picture-show place now. The Monarch – the Monarch was a place wide open. This was on 340 Beale and the Monarch was a place where we called it a gamblin' house at that particular time. They played piano there, blues goin' all the time. They searched you just like you would be if you were goin' to jail. It was a great time then, the streets were full of gamblin' houses where they shot craps. You could do nothin' then to control gamblin'. While we mention about gamblin' there – if you got out of order, that's what it was – Bad Sam! Feller there who'd deal with you and everybody called him Bad Sam. We had another crap house, they called it the Panama. A boy named Howard Evans operated it for years. Aw, it was great in those days.

So much excitement
Will Shade

Pee Wee's was the name of a – the name they used to call 'em was joints; some people used to call 'em honkytonks – that's where I learned to play the blues at the honkytonks which was originally called the joints. Some people called them saloons. Pee Wee's was wide open in there in them days, and they had crap games in there and runnin' policy games, bootleg whisky and everything like that. Come on down there used to be a place on Beale Street called the Monarch and that was a crap shootin' joint. There used to be a man there they called him Bad Sam. He got into a shootin' duel there one time. Shot a man who was causin' bit of trouble and the man fell downstairs. But he raised up enough to shoot back at Sam, so both of them fell; one went one way and the other went the other way and both of them died. I dunno, there was so much excitement down there on Beale Street it'd take me a year and a day to tell you about all that excitement. 'Nother place, joint, was called the Red Onion, and another place called the Vintage – used to prize-fight there. Used to knock 'em out of the ring and break their necks. Go up to Jim Canands they used to be a woman there, used to call her Razor-Cuttin' Fanny. Every time you see her if you didn't give her that piece of bread and piece of fish she cut your throat. You go there and ask for bootleg whisky and they don't give you none, you used to high-jack it. Used to take a car and go round to where it was stashed away and take all the whisky they got. You come and try to get your money for the whisky they stole and they knock you out with a bat, or like a pool cue: the butt end of a pool cue would knock your brains out. It wasn't too bad to see somebody's throat cut. That was the main part of it: you see somebody knocked on the haid the ambulance 'd come and take 'em in. They'd all be in line, those ambulances, you wouldn't have to call 'em. They line up because they know what's gonna happen on a Sat'dy night. They all gonna be in line and race at the bodies. If you wasn't dead, well they'd have two drivers in there and one driver take a needle and stick it in you and you'd be dead before you reached the hospital. Oh, they had plenty ways of makin' money round here. I'm just tellin' you – you ask me about it, and I'm just tellin' you, that's true. If you get hurt they get an ambulance – they even had an ambulance at the police station down there. Come feel your pulse and say, 'Aw . . . he's dead; come on' let's take 'im to the

No closin' at that time
Sunnyland Slim

morgue.' That's the last of you. You automatically dead. No use you kill yourself because the ambulance driver done kill you. Aw, we used to have a rough kind of crowd.

Come up to Memphis
Where Highway 51 meets
Beale Street was a goal for
migrants from Mississippi

Beale Street was real tough in them days. There were some real rough joints: one at the Panama, and at the Harlem Night Club – that's at South Memphis at 1128 Florida. And then too the Goshorn Quarters was another we had. Down at 4th and Beale, Pee Wee's had one open. The Hole in the Wall, that was a rough joint. I used to make all them joints and there was no closin' at that time. When I come into Memphis I got into the Hole in the Wall, sat down at the pianner, begin to play. I was sittin' there and a great big woman called Jenny – she had the blues. And that night I started playin' my li'l *Four O'Clock Blues* and started to hollerin' loud. And then there started to be a crowd gatherin' roun' the pianner and I just sit there playin' the blues, and I just sit there and drink that White Mule – moonshine – and I start to cut rough myself.

> Four o'clock in the mornin', the blues come fallin' down,
> Four o'clock in the mornin' and the blues they come fallin' down,
> I was all locked up in jail, and I was prisoner bound.
>
> Baby you will never, never see my smilin' face again,
> You will never baby, see my smilin' face again,
> I always want you to remember that you have been my friend.
>
> Sometimes I wonder Mama, why you don't write to me,
> Sometimes I wonder baby, baby, why don't you write to me,
> Well if I been a bad feller, I did not intend to be.

You could see anybody, anybody you wanted to see at that time on Beale. That's how I run up on Piano Gibson, Loomis Gibson, the most famous piano-player in the world in those days. I tell you, I met Shaky Head Walter there too, the guy who was more or less whipped by Buddy Doyle, the man that made 'Grief'll kill you, get you down to skin and bone' – he was playin' that steel guitar in the streets then; I remember him. Buddy Doyle made some records too. At that time you had to stick your head in a barrel and holler and sing you know, and then you pick your guitar and hope it come out. The voice they get but you had to stick your guitar close to that barrel to be heard. They had sheets hung up there and if I make no mistake it was at that Hotel Joseph. A whole lot of people remembers Room 254–3–1. That was when they were making records of that jug band. They had jug bands they called them, and several of them made records I remember, in Memphis.

They feel too good
Robert Henry

Well one of the jug band players is still livin' right in the rear of my place of business here; that's Son Brimmer. His name's Will Shade but we called him Son Brimmer. It was a joke – one time I had some people out of New York come to listen to the jug men. So they tol' me, the jug band did, 'All right, but all we need now is for us to have a few drinks so we be feelin' good.' So they did and we went along to hear the jug men start makin' records. Well, but the boys were so drunk that they wasn't able to stand. The people out of New York laughed and said, 'Well, they wanted to feel good, but they feel too good. Well we have to leave you; this ain't the people we was lookin' for!' But since then Son Brimmer has made several records of the old timers. So it is not many of them is living yet of the original jug bands. We lost one about two years ago – Willie Batts. He had one of the biggest jug bands – and they usually carry from four to five pieces in the band. Made some records with Jack Kelly once; he was a blues man come up from Mississippi. Willie Batts that was. Most of them uses the can for the bass, there's hardly nothing else left in there for them! Some of them do use a jug. There's not much left of them now, but they was mostly men play for parties, picnics and things; elections, for people won a race, and parties of that kind. People who drink and have a good time – mostly the jug band plays for that, they don't play for dances. So that's why the jug band is made for the people, understand me, to have a good time, people who is havin' parties. At one time Batts' Jug Band used to play for conventions at Peabody Hotel. That's our biggest hotel. So we had a jubilee . . . to entertain the people. Most of the people – it was a hardware convention – was out of the East. So I went downstairs to send the people home in a taxi and when I got back upstairs the jug band had a hat down in the middle of the Peabody Hotel ballroom. But the money was piled in the hat, so I said, 'Well you-all ain't gettin' paid tonight for your act; I'm cuttin' in with you. Because you've got too much money in that hat there. You expect to draw ten dollars for your work!' Aw, it was fun. They played the Peabody for a night or so at a time. I used to book the jug bands on the jobs, but I'd always notify the people who they were workin' for, to be particular about them drinkin' because if they showed they'd got a bottle of whisky they'd have a bunch of drunken people on they hands. Now they like to play but

they sure like to get drunk. So you watch for the jug bands. When they don't get drunk, there's not much pep in them. But they really likes to drink that hooch.

The great big idea
Will Shade

I been practically doing blues singin' and workin' as a talent scout all my life. I started from a kid up, and I got to be of age where I commenced to learn to play music. Learned from different people you know. I first learned from my mother – she learned me how to play *On the Road Again* – 'I'm a nachul born Eastman, on the road 'gain.' Learned me that and I come from that to –

Here we're goin' round and roun'
Me an' my babe is Louisiana boun'.

Learned me how to play that. And after that I got to learn from a feller by the name of Hucklebones; he learned me how to play guitar. And from then on up I heard a great feller by the name Tee Wee Blackman which was the first one gave me the great big idea to play the blues. I got some ideas from him and he showed me how to play. I begin to, you know, pull out for myself, and I rigged me a li'l ole three-piece band, and after riggin' up a three-piece band I met a feller by the name of Lionhouse but his real name was Elijah; old man of about sixty-five so me and him got together. He was playin' a bottle, wasn't playin' no gallon jug; he was playin' an ole whisky bottle you pick up anywhere. So we said, 'Let's get a gallon jug.' So after we got a gallon jug we commenced to play it an' I dubbed: I played harmonica, guitar and also a can. Some people call it a garbage can but I calls it streamline bass. Streamline bass, but some folks say garbage can. I made pretty good at it. Kep' on playin' up and down Beale Street. First blues I learned was

Newport News, Stingy Woman, Son Brimmer's Blues,
Kansas City Blues and all such as that.

I'm goin' to Newport News Mama, catch a battleship
    across that dog-gone sea,
Goin' to Newport News Mama, ketch a battleship across
    that dog-gone sea,
Ah, you know that woman that I'm lovin', 'clare that fool
    don't care for po' me.

She got a man on a man boy, got a kid on a dog-gone kid,
She got a man on a man boy, got a kid on a dog-gone kid,
Kid man done got so buggy, 'clare that fool just could not
    keep it hid.

Now don't you wish your easy-roller, was both li'l and cute
    like mine,
Don't you wish your easy-roller, was both li'l and cute like
    mine,
Lord every time she walks, 'clare she reelin' and she rock behin'.

I'm goin' to Newport News baby, goin' to see Aunt
    Caroline Dye,
Goin' to Newport News baby, goin' to see Aunt Caroline Dye,
You know she's a fortune-tellin' woman, 'clare that fool,
    she never tol' no dog-gone lie.

Oh babe I can sit right here, look on Carlton Avenue,
Babe I can sit right here, look down on Carlton Avenue,
I can see 'most every li'l ole thing 'clare my easy rider do.

I mean your teeth ain't pearl baby, low-down eyes ain't
    navy blue,
Mean your teeth ain't pearl baby, your low-down eyes ain't
    navy blue,
You know you three times seven, 'clare you never know
    which way you wanna do.

Aunt Caroline Dye was a fortune-tellin' woman. See Aunt
Caroline Dye 'she's a fortune-tellin' woman never tol' no lie' –
I made that up my own right, my own song, nobody knowed it
but me. She was a fortune-tellin' woman – two-headed woman.
She call you, she'd fix you so you better come; she didn't have
to come to fetch you. That's the kind of woman she was, had
that much power – 'fore she died. White and Colored would
go to her . . . you sick in bed, she raise the sick. Conjure, hoodoo
that's what some people say, but that's what you call it, conjure.
Yeah, she could make a 'hand' so you could win anybody's
money. Take her 'hand' wit'ya, win everybody's money wit'
that spell. Had that much brains – smart lady. She break up all
kinds of spells you had: she could have you walkin' like a hawg;
any kinda whichaway, she could make you walk on two legs
again. That's the kind of woman she was. Aunt Caroline Dye,
she was the worst woman in the world . . . had that much sense.
Seven Sisters ain't nowhere wit' Aunt Caroline Dye; she was
the onliest one could break the record with the hoodoo.

Salaries was very cheap

Eddie Boyd

Well I started out in Memphis on Beale Street . . . leastways I was playing piano before that in my home town of Clarksdale, Mississippi. There was a barrelhouse joint there on the edge of Clarksdale run by a feller by the name of Hoskin – Hoskin's Juke we used to call it. I got me a job there as pianist, playing the blues, barrelhouse blues. They seemed to like the way I played so I stayed there for about four years, and I guess I was about seventeen years old when I started there. But I was really inspired by Roosevelt Sykes – he was the guy that inspired me to play blues on the piano, only in those days there were so many guys that were playing the blues and I guess I learned from all of them. So I got on to be pretty good I guess and I came up to Memphis, Tennessee on Beale Street. When I first started out I used to work in those honkytonks in Memphis like Pee Wee's and Jodie Farnley's and the Big Four. Those were honkytonks – kind of a low-class place where the people would come every night and where the salaries was very cheap – I used to work for seven dollars a week, seven nights a week. I stayed there about five years, came there in 1936. Well, then I met up with some boys and I was workin' at that time with a feller by the name of Willie Heard. He played drums and we had a feller name of Eddie Childs, played trumpet. So Willie Heard had a band they called the Dixie Rhythm Boys and then later on I took it over. Well I was with them for about four years and then I branched off in 1941 and came on up north.

I was tops

Speckled Red

After I left Memphis I went all over the country. I played any-where I could make a nickel. Wasn't makin' much – I played for fourteen hours for maybe a dollar and a half, two dollars. Boy, if I got five dollars I was tops. I was amazed when I got five dollars. All in them days you played from three o'clock in the evenin' to three o'clock the next mornin' – or three o'clock the next evenin' – you got the same price. You got plenty of whisky and everything. Well, it wasn't whisky – they call it lightnin'. Plenty of lightnin' but you didn't get too much money. Course back in them days you didn't need too much money but you could make enough to get along. So I played around until 1939 when I come to St Louis. Left there, come back to St Louis and I been around there since 1941 about. I started playin' at the Dixie Tavern – different joints, first one thing, then another. Then I quit. Quit for about ten years. Wasn't makin' nothin' so I went to work on Market, St Louis – I got to be a shippin' clerk. So after I got to be a shippin' clerk I didn't play nowhere.

Catch-catch operation
Charles Thompson

Big time sports
James Stump Johnson

In the days that I come up in I was well acquainted with the late Scott Joplin, I knew Tom Turpin, Jelly Roll Morton, James P. Johnson, Ell-Zee Young, Robert Hampton, Speckled Red and any number of blues players. Blues and ragtime music in those days was a sort of catch-catch operation; each player would foller the others to try to see what he'd learned overnight and try to steal it from him, and in that way everybody seemed to get along a little ahead. One was always trying to be ahead of the other. The old Chauffeur's Club on Pine Street and Compton Avenue was a regular hangout for all the musicians in that day. They would all gather in there at night and each one would try to show off before the other ones which one had learned the most during the day. Jelly Roll Morton spent the winter here in St Louis in 1911 before he went to New York and he was a very apt musician, very quick to catch up almost anything. I think that when he went to New York he took all the ragtime players' music that they played along with him to New York. I'm a ragtime pianist although I never took a lesson in my life. In 1916 I played in a piano contest held at the Booker T. Washington Theater in which there were sixty-eight contestants. It was an elimination contest. We played three shows a night, four names were drawn from a hat and the winner was held over to play the following week. It lasted about eight weeks and I finally won it. After that I had to play Tom Turpin who was a close friend of Scott Joplin for the Championship of the State of Missouri, and I beat him in the final contest. I was awarded two hundred and fifty dollars and a beautiful gold medal for that effort and I won that on the *Lily Rag*. That was my big piece but I made *Hop Alley Dream* and *Ragtime Humming Bird* and oh, *Buffet Flat Rag* and others I forget now. I've been a make-up pianist all my life and *Lily Rag* is the only one I had was published. Now I had a piece I called *Deep Lawton* which sort of had a blues sound to it and I have another now which is a blues number and a ragtime number combined which I hope to record. I'd like to say that blues – the blues is very original because there's always some improvisation that can be made in the blues such as fancy runs, different chords that you wouldn't ordinarily make in ragtime music, although ragtime music can be placed and improvised and made in a style of its own. They are both of a different style altogether. And jazz is a combination of both only in slower time – the time is slower, that's the way I find it.

They say that blues originated in New Orleans but St Louis had some of the best blues singers that ever there was in the history of blues. There was Son Long, the man that originated the boogie woogie. He's dead now, and he never had a chance to record but he was the originator of what they call the boogie woogie. And the boy who recorded it – he is dead, Pinetop Smith, he was a friend of mine back in early days but he wasn't the originator. It was a boy by the name of Son Long. He learned to play by ear and he was one of the best pianists around the city of St Louis or anywhere else. He was born around and lived around 15th and Morgan at the time, and I used to hear him there. That was the coloured limelight. That was where all the sporting people congregated – from there back to the Mississippi Levee to a place they called Boots'. The levee at St Louis was known throughout the country as the origination of blues. When I was young I used to play around for the sporting houses and the only thing I would get would be fifty cents and a chance to be there and look at all the big-time sports comin' in and spendin' their money. And at that time there weren't any taverns and very few saloons. They just had what they call the 'good time houses' and that's where you could find anybody in the 'life' in St Louis was at the sportin' houses. I played – I didn't make no livin' out of playin' blues – but I played and I was just quite young and glad to be around the sportin' people. I had learned to play the blues by just hangin' roun' the poolroom where they had an ole piano, just pickin' it up for myself, nobody gave me lessons and to be around the old people I'd have to go in with them, and they'd ask me to play the blues for 'em. And sometimes we'd start around two o'clock in the evenin' and stay there round the clock until two o'clock the next evenin' and wouldn't even come out of the house or stop. So down there on Johnson Street, where *Frankie and Albert* was originated – where they used to be – there used to be a house that I would go to and play the blues as a kid. And just all around St Louis, down to Boots' on the levee I'd be. And Boots' was one of the most popular places in the city of St Louis because all the riverboats would come in there and dock and all the 'ristocratic people would come down there for slummin' and enjoyment. They were very, very tough places though, and they were shootin' dice and drinkin' whisky and enjoyin' themselves and it could get kind o' rough.

Nothing but the blues
Charles Thompson

Some of the early blues pianists that I remember – well there was a feller by the name of Louis Chauvin. He was a ragtime player and he was a blues player too. He played real blues and he also was an ear man. In fact, he could play anything – in any key. He was so good until when the Smarter Set came to St Louis and the show was stricken with ptomaine poisoning, and the pianist for the show was ill too, he went to one dress rehearsal. They hummed the different songs over to him; the orchestra played the overture to him without the piano, and that night he played the show, and played it the whole week they were here. So he could play anything, and he was a good blues man too. But other great blues players here at that time was a youngster by the name of Conroy Casey, and there was Raymond Hine, and Willie Franklin. And they were boys who played nothing but the blues – no songs, no rags – only blues. They played in the buffet flats and at the sporting houses you see, and in those places it was strictly blues all the way. All of those fellers is dead. They all passed and in fact it's very hard to find a blues player or a ragtime player living now who lived in the days of Joplin or Turpin or Louis Chauvin.

I'm still poor
Mary Johnson

My mother's been a widder-woman ever since I was a small kid, about that high I guess. And I wanted to stay around with her and I was the only child my mother had, and she has only one sister so I just stuck aroun' with her and didn't try to go other places. So I was born in Mississippi, aroun' Jackson, Mississippi, in 1900; come to St Louis in 1915. My mother was a widder and of course, when I were nineteen years old I began to workin'. I couldn't work and earn enough money at the factory to support us both, so after I was about twenty – oh, twenty-five or somethin' – well that was when I first started to goin' out entertainin' . . . night clubs and places. I used to go to a place they call Jazzland was owned by Charlie Turpin, that was Tom Turpin's elder brother. Jazzland, it was on 23rd and Market, and I seen the girls singin' and dancin' and entertain-in' so good that I just decided I'd do the same. That's been so long I don't recall who was there, but I did know a girl name of Jessie White, she was a very good blues singer. She sing there extrally once in a while you know, they fix her in as a guest. And later on there was Victoria Spivey. You know her? Well she was singin' and Victoria and I were very good friends. All this singin' make me think of tryin' to make me some money, an' I ain't got nowhere yet! And I'm still poor, and right now I'm goin' from bad to worse I guess. Right now I don't have anythin' now – I did have it, but I spent it; throwed it away fast. I gave some to my mother and for my part I throwed it away. I can't remember all the places I was singin' at: I was appearin' at 17th and Carr, they had a club there and that's where Mister Mayo Williams pick me up. Then I was at the Chauffeurs Club that was out on Lawton and Jefferson Avenue. And I was at 9th and Carr, I was workin' at a night club there, entertainin'. I can't remember all the clubs and these particular places where I worked at in St Louis. I didn't play no instruments at all. Henry Brown was my piano player – I liked his style very well. And Ike Rodgers, and Georgia Tom and Tamp' Red: they all worked with me and I really liked to have them playin' when I was entertainin'.

From Memphis down to Rosedale
The Wolf River at the foot of Beale
where it joins the Mississippi

Stomp 'em down to the bricks

Henry Brown

Deep Morgan, that's where I was raised up at; that was low class. Oh man . . . they call it Delmar Avenue now, try to forget it was Deep Morgan you know. That was all just them low-down sportin' houses and recreation parlours you know, call 'em recreation parlours. Like a barrelhouse joint. I was born in Troy, Tennessee, but I came here when I was twelve years old. Went to the Del-Lin school a little bit. But I wasn't too interested in that education 'cause I wanted to play the blues. There was a man by the name of Blackmouth used to play in places on Morgan and Market, Franklin, places like that. And I used to follow him on *down*, you know, listen to him and try to catch what he was playin'. He was a real old-time blues player and he'd stomp 'em down to the bricks there on Deep Morgan. If he ever had another name I didn't know it; everybody called him Blackmouth and he was some blues player . . . oh, man . . . . Then there was Joe Cross, used to hear ole Joe Cross's blues; he was down there on 23rd and Market Street. Boy, we had some times . . . and this is still ole Henry Brown kickin' 'em on down just a li'l bit. So I come up under these men, tried to play the same way as they did. Listen to them . . . go on down to Jim McMann's down on Market Street there – listen to them blues . . . .

Good whisky's back

Blind James Brewer

I went on down to St Louis, spent four or five years down there, woofin' and beefin' aroun' and blowin' my top as usually. An' I met a feller there down on Market and Main and places in East St Louis, name of Peetie Wheatstraw. And he was a great pianner player and used to sing the blues; they really used to like his way of playin'. I used to run aroun' with him quite a bit. Of course he played pianner and I played git-tar. Well, this piece here reminds me of my old friend, used to play pianner, but I ain't got no pianner and if I had one I doubt if I could play it, and if I played it I wouldn't know what I was playin' – but this piece here is called *I'm So Glad Good Whisky's Back*; *I Don't Have To Drink This Hooch No Mo'*:

> Well, well, I'm so glad good whisky has come to be,
> Well, well, good whisky has come to be,
> Well, well, I'm so glad, ooh, well I don't have to drink this
>   hooch no mo'.

That's what they call moonshine . . .

> Well, well, I tol' my baby, one more ha'f a pint,
> Well, well, I tol' my baby, 'I just want more ha'f a pint',
> Well, give me one mo' ha'f a pint well, well boys an' I'll
>   wreck the j'int.

Put out all the lights an' I'll call the police . . .

> Well I want my woman, I want her right here by my side,

Yes, but she's a long way from here tho' . . .

> Well I want my woman, I want her right here by my side,
> Well, since she ain't here, ooh, well man, I'm dissatisfied.

My improvement come

Henry Townsend

I could play it better if you were here baby . . . .
Put me in mind of when I was in East St Louis down there on
Main and Broadway; I didn't play with but three things when I
was down there – that's women, whisky and slot machines. . . .

Well I love my women, and I want them all to myself,
Ooh, well, and I want them all to myself,
Well I can take care o' them, oh God, man I don't need no help.

Now play it baby . . . yees, I know . . . one more pint and I'll
wreck the j'int . . . .
I'm gonna play this song, an' I believe I'll play no mo'.
I'm gonna play this song, an' I believe I'll play no mo'.
Cause I'm worried blue and disgusted, oh, well an' I don't
care where I go.

I was originally born in Shelby, Mississippi, but I have claimed Cairo, Illinois, for my home because I came there rather young and that's where I had all my schoolin'. And from there my parents came over here to St Louis and well, I been here in St Louis and aroun' ever since. In the beginnin' – I mean of course I was quite young at this time – I guess I must have been just into teenage when I began to listen to a particular musicianer who was Lonnie Johnson, and I liked his method. I used to listen to him in East St Louis and I thought that he was a wonderful guitar player. So he and his brother, we called his brother Steady Roll at that time, well he was what you might call a great guy too, he played wonderful piano – so that kind of inspired me to get over to this instrument and get to work on it. I worked around from place to place until I bought me a cheap guitar, and I used to keep the family awake all night trying to learn and eventually I learned a few chords. And from then on I begin to annoy the public – you know, trying to force something on them, trying to get them to listen. And then, well, later I played for house parties so that's where my improvement come. So from time to time as I got older, why I run into the things that would give me the inspiration so I started to build in from that. You know you have to like a thing to devote heart and soul into it, so well, I like it so that's what I put into it. There has been other musicians of course that I admired and thought they were great people – regardless to what others thought of them. For instance, Cecil Gant, I thought he was a wonderful guy and speakin' of my old partner Roosevelt Sykes, I still think he's one of the ace fellas. And Henry Brown – sometimes he forgets to devote his time to what he's talented to do, but he is a great guy and one time I've known him to be one of the greatest blues pianists in the city of St Louis you know; I mean, the city catered to him as a musicianer in the field. And then there was my old buddy Sylvester Palmer. He was an awful fine fella and I thought he would have been one of the top musicianers if he had still been alive, but unfortunately he died. I don't recall exactly how long, the time that he died, but it's been about eight or ten years longer that he died.

We would switch it round
Lonnie Johnson

I got inspiration
St Louis Jimmy

Jelly Roll Morton, I knew him in St Louis, Missouri. We were playing on the excursion boats out of St Louis. Well I played a couple of times on it but after that I started playin' violin with Charlie Creath's band on the steamer St Paul – he taken it over. I was with Charlie Creath I think it was seven years. I played violin then, but I never went back to violin any more after that. I gave it away. My brother, he played piano, *and* violin, *and* guitar. He was better than me . . . my brother, Steady Roll. De Loise Searcy was my piano player and my brother was playing piano at the time until De Loise was with me. Then De Loise would play the piano and my brother was playing the violin and I was playing guitar. Then my brother would play guitar and I would play violin. We would switch it round that way. Lord sakes, yes, he was better than me. He played violin for Ethyl Waters – he was her first violinist. He's been at one club near St Louis – Newport, Illinois, it's called, where he plays piano, and if I can remember closely, he's been there twenty-nine years. He's still there . . . twenty-nine years. It's called the Waterfront Club. I don't know why it's named that because it's on the Boulevard, but that's what it's called. But it's not near the Mississippi River, so you just figger it out . . . but I guess people drink so much liquor there . . . .

You Have to Like It
Henry Townsend first recorded in 1929 and though he had many jobs, always played the blues

There were just so many good piano players in St Louis in those days. I used to play piano myself a little bit but I never did play piano on record or like that. See there were so many that were really good: Peetie Wheatstraw and Roosevelt, and Steady Roll Johnson and all those guys. But I used to write blues for some of them. Of course all blues singers make up their own blues you know, but I used to give them blues too. Blues – I think it's a soul feeling. It's accordin' to the way you feel, to sing blues. Some people get up and sing and don't have no inspiration behind it. You know blues is somethin' that give a person a – well, if *you* feel it, the public feel it. Or some parts of the public *got* to feel it 'cause someone's in there feeling just about like you do. And my blues came mostly from women, and I've had quite a few to give me lots of trouble, but nevertheless I'd always write from them and that's the reason why I started out to writin' blues. *Goin' Down Slow* started from a girl in St Louis – it wasn't me – I've never been sick a day in my life, but I seen her in the condition she was in – pregnant, trying to lose a kid see. And she looked like she was goin' down, slow. And I made that remark to my sister and it came in my mind and I started to writin' it like that and it was the first number I wrote that made a hit. But I got writin' a little bit more and a little bit better. I got inspiration from writin', and I looked at other people's troubles and I writes from that, and I writes from my own troubles. Not from the other feller much – 'cause I think I've had more than the other feller had. At times anyway. See I was an orphan when I was eleven year old. I was born in Nashville in 1905, 26th June it was, and I came there to St Louis after my parents died in 1914 'cause my sister raised me and my two brothers. But I had it pretty hard then and I started to workin' in a barber shop. That's what give me the idea to singin'. I'd hear those boys singin' whilst they were waitin' to have their hair fixed you know. They had what they called 'barber shop fours', it was quite a thing in those days. And they'd have a guitar layin' around. Play it if you want to. Well then I used to sing at house rent parties with this feller from Mississippi, Big Joe Williams. I started around 1929 doin' that; just singin'. And me and Roosevelt Sykes were doing that. He told me that I had a voice for singin' and I just started out practising with him and writin' – I never sung no one's number but my own and I been writin' songs for the last thirty years. So me and Roosevelt started out in 'thirty for Jesse Johnson in St Louis, and that's how it come about.

He got good material

Roosevelt Sykes

So I got this feller St Louis Jimmy – I listened to St Louis for quite a while 'fore he got well known for his singin', and I knowed he got good material so I mentioned him to this feller Lester Melrose. Melrose had different materials with different companies such as Victor, Deccas and so on, Columbias and what not, so Jimmy was O.K. So he recorded a tune he called *Goin' Down Slow* and I played the piano on that for Jimmy. *Monkeyfaced Woman* – many good blues he had. St Louis Jimmy and I worked together for some years, we traveled on a lot of one-nighters throughout the country, north, south – traveled through different towns, playin' one nighters for different night clubs and theaters. Now this tune *Night Time Is the Right Time* – St Louis Jimmy wrote that. But he didn't give it to me, he gave it to my brother. My brother wasn't a recordin' man, but Jimmy thought he wanted to record some tunes so he gave him this. And I asked my brother to give it to me. So I tried to fit a tune of Leroy's to it:

Gonna warn you baby, just before you begin,
You stays out all night long darlin', I declare that'll be the end,
Night time is the right time to be with the one you love,
– with the one you love.

There's one thing baby that I want you to do,
Love me in a way darlin' that will make me think you love
    me too,
Night time is the right time to be with the one you love,
– with the one you love.

Well then there was another guy in St Louis name of Charlie McFadden, used to sing. We called him Specks – he had them on his nose, you know, ole four eyes. So he used to sing a thing 'My name is Piggly Wiggly, I got groceries on my shelf' – oh there were so many fellers. We had another guy they called Cranstone. He come up with me out of West Helena, he was a good pianner player. And another feller come out of there, don't know if you heard of him, Floyd Campbell, only he played drums. He's livin' in Chicago now, workin' at the courthouse. He left West Helena and come up to St Louis and he had a great band Floyd Campbell did. He and Cranstone was with this feller Charlie Creath. They had a tune was made by Charlie Creath, *Cold in Hand Blues*. Campbell was the drummer and Cranstone – Cranstone Hamilton his name was, he played the piano. Everybody called him Ham.

I Had It Pretty Hard
St Louis Jimmy was badly injured
in an automobile accident

'Screenin' the blues'

Henry Brown

St Louis Jimmy there, boy . . . long time I don't see you ole man. Let these blues speak for you . . . . We get over to ole Katy Red's over there in East St Louis, break 'em down over there in those days. And ole Sykes was there, you know, ole Keg. We used to call him Keg 'cause he likes to gettin' so fat – he'd order all those chittlin's – man we had a good time then, I'm tellin' you. That was old time . . . we'd really break it up then, when it get late, past 'bout one, two, three o'clock, that's the time to soften down on the pedal. That's when the polices come through with their gang. But we play it soft and low, we don't get raided. Yeah, ole Roosevelt . . . Blind Darby, he was Roosevelt too you know – Teddy Roosevelt Darby, used to play guitar. He got blind years ago; we used to call him Blind Darby, and we'd call him Preacher Darby. He become what we call preacher; Lord, he'd preach all night, but he'd sing the blues too. He's preachin' now, out in Missouri some place. We had lots o' names – Papa Slick Head, he was good too, played

guitar. Yeah, Lawrence Casey, that was his real name but we call him Slick Head and Papa Egg Shell too, 'cause his head was bald, clean as an eight-ball. He's still around I guess but I ain't seen him in years yet. And Ike, my old buddy Ike. Him and me was partners you know for years roun' St Louis. Back in 'twenty – I was workin' in a dairy then. I worked in the dairy four to five years and Ike and me would play, nights. Ike was a great player with the mutes you know, used to use ice-buckets, tin cans, liquor glasses, anything he could lay hands on, used to blow that horn right in it. And he could make more sounds out of them than you could think of. Him and me made that *Screenin' the Blues*. When we got in that recording studio there'd been some band there some time; dunno when. So the drummer left his drums around and Ike got hold of the snare drum. He had the idea of loosenin' them snares and holdin' up the drum and playin' into it. That's how we made the record and that's how Ike got the idea of the tune. See, he thought it

looked like a screen, you know, so he calls it *Screenin' the Blues* playin' through a snare drum like that. Oh, man . . . . Those days after I was workin' in the dairy I got me a job as a clothes presser; steamin' and pressin'. Got laid off in the Depression. Ike and me worked on that W. P. A. in the rock quarry – yeah, breakin' rocks! Aw, we had a tough time then! Went right on and did road construction, Ike and me; go over to Katy Red's and make a little spending change; go on to the 9–0–5 at nights. Got me a li'l band together sometimes . . . had Earl Bindley on drums, you heard of him? And Ike. Henry – Henry Townsend play guitar and Little Alice sang. We'd play joints on Franklin . . . Delmar. . . Easton . . . spots in East St Louis – like the Blue Flame Club. Come on up I got a job workin' at the Edwin Brothers Shoe Company on Washington Avenue. I had a piano in the back of the warehouse there; when I knock off I could kick 'em on down again.

Still Kickin' 'Em Down
Henry Brown had a distinctive style of playing 'soft and low' blues.

I Got Me A Job
Pianist Henry Brown on Easton Avenue, St Louis

Real things in life

Henry Townsend

There was Robert Nighthawk – er, Robert McCoy I think his name is – he and I used to work together for quite some time. But Nighthawk is always goin' off some place and right now I think he's down in Mexico. He and I did some recordin' with the original Sonny Boy Williams you know, you heard he was killed or somethin'? Course I played with this other Sonny Boy – I believe his name is Rice Miller, quite a bit when he was in the city of St Louis recently. So of course I've worked a lot with Sykes, and Ike Rodgers and I've played for quite a few women. Like Alice Moore – she was a real nice girl. She was real devoted to her blues singing. From my point of it she was pretty well a nice mixer with the public and a fairly intelligent girl. They used to call her Little Alice – well she *was* quite small I think at the time they adopted the name to her as Little Alice but later, I think she defeated that name, by getting quite some size – she got extra size before she died about ten or twelve years ago. Henry Brown has played for Alice Moore, for a fact I think he started her out, and she was a devoted blues singer. Well I feel that blues has its own to do with you. You have to have a inspiration, you have to have a feelin' to dish this thing out. You got to foller that feelin' otherwise you just cain't do it. It's got to be a part of you to make you issue this thing out. When I made *Poor Man Blues* I was very poor – well the things that I have sung about are the real things in life. See I heard about some recordin' was gonna be soon and a feller by the name of Sam Woolf on 15th and Biddle was handlin' it so I went down and had a test with him and he selected I and Sylvester Palmer. We were fortunate enough to go on a recording trip to Chicago and we recorded over there – I think I did four numbers, *Mean Mistreater* and *Henry's Worried Blues* and *Poor Man Blues* – something like that. I had been broke down and I had been very poor at that time and I remember I sang:

It's never mind, never mind baby, I got my dog-gone eyes
   on you,
And it's never mind baby, I got my eyes on you,
And some ole day baby, do like I want you to do.

When I was sick and down you drove me from your door,
When I was sick and down babe, you drove me from your door,
Now you knowed I was a poor man, sleepin' out in the ice
   and snow.

That's all right for you baby, I m gonna pawn my watch
   and ring,
That's all right babe, pawn my watch and ring,
I done give you all my money and give you most everything.

Maybe it wasn't exactly then but I had the experience of these things. You find that it's easier to tell the truth about your life so you sing about it. That's the way I see the things you know. So anyway, they sold pretty good so I got a little fame and so from time to time I went to play in night clubs. Then I joined up with Roosevelt Sykes and started playin' with his organization and from that to Walter Davis and I follered him through the entire course of his musical career. And then I was on my own again. So I work in these places in St Louis like at 14th and Cass. It's a fairly decent tavern, and I guess the capacity is about two-three hundred people – not to be seated of course, that's standin' room. And they have a small band in there and they have every week-end, Friday, Saturday and they do have Sundays, and it's I could say a Grade 1 place. It's not A1 but Grade 1. And now they have a decent crowd there, each week-end. Of course through the week you know how it go, people is workin' so they don't have too much of a crowd. And other places that I worked such as the Bolo Club and so on – that's a rental hall: it's for different organizations that have clubs and so forth and I have been booked by Masonics and other local organizations and well one or two times I was at the Western Waiters Club. An A1 place it is. It's fireproof and everything, well – it's one of the outstanding clubs for Colored in the city of St Louis.

You could change around
Roosevelt Sykes

There was a feller by the name of Jesse Johnson in St Louis in 1929. I was living in East St Louis at the time. And he learned that I played pianner and he asked me to come over to his music shop and let him hear a few of the tunes I had. He had a record shop there and he was looking for different artists and to take 'em to different places to record. So I did go over to his shop and I done a few tunes over for him so he seemed to like this tune – the *44 Blues*. And I had another tune by the name of *The Way I Feel Blues* and another tune, *Boot That Thing* and the *Henry Ford Blues*. So he decided that the numbers were all right and that they would go. So he asked me would I go over to New York with him, see, from St Louis. So we goes to New York to 11 Union Square, that's at where the Okeh Record Company was, and that's where we recorded the *44 Blues* and these others on the 14th day of June in 1929 and my first release was 8702 which was the number of it. And after that I made records for different companies and at that time you could change around, sort of change your name, and have a different tune. Why, you could make records for different people. So I had a contract with Okeh and I did recordings for other companies under different names. One of my names when I was a kid was Dobby. They always called me Dobby, so my mother's name was Bragg so I used the name Dobby Bragg. Then I had a brother who was a half-brother. His father was a Kelly and his name was Willie. Actually his name was Willie Sykes but his brother married another girl by the name of Kelly so I used the name of Willie Kelly – was my half-brother's name. So that's how I used the names on these other labels. So in little later years as I had been round the studios like R.C. A. Victor and Decca and I seemed to be popular with the fellers that was runnin' the record business such as J. Mayo Williams and Jack Kapp. Those fellers figgered I knowed pretty well about blues singers and that I knowed pretty good materials when I heard it, so they ask me would I go out and find some new artists for them. So I listened to Walter Davis's songs and I thought they were very nice so I took him over to this feller Jesse Johnson who had taken me to New York and he listened to him and he liked him so they put Walter Davis out.

I knew he meant business
Walter Davis

After I left home and come to St Louis I began to playin' at places. And I was playin' over there for J. C.'s night club in East St Louis. And after I started playing for J. C.'s over there, Jesse Johnson and Jack Kapp came over and they heard me play and then they asked me about making some recordings for R.C. A. Victor. Well, I didn't think I was good enough to play for a big outfit like that but they told me I was doing fine. And they ask me to play some more blues, so they can hear them. Well, naturally, blues was something that was just talent to me somehow or other and I played a couple more blues for them. And so Mr Kapp signed me up; gave me a contract. Well I didn't think too much about it till he gave me fifty dollars. So after he gave me fifty dollars I knew he meant business, because he wasn't just giving away fifty dollars. Then I got ready to go to New York. Why I was a little frightened, but after they got me in that studio they had taken me up and I was sittin' there lookin' out of the window – I think on the thirty-fifth floor of Victor's building – just touching the piano along. So after a while a different kind of feelin' come over me. So I told the engineers I was ready and they turned me on. But Roosevelt Sykes accompanied me on my first recordin' – *M and O Blues*, my *first* one, because I was kinda a frightened feller. I couldn't play – I was tremblin' too much! So after he accompanied me, why he seems like he was doin' pretty good so I started feelin' all right myself. So I played for myself from then. My first recording was *M and O Blues* and *My Baby's Gone* and a few months later why it came out and it was a success, it was a great hit. I had my picture put in the *Chicago Defender*, the *Pittsburgh Courier* and other local papers and naturally I became pretty famous. Roosevelt Sykes, he was just one of those brainy fellers, he's just a regular feller after all. He was a good friend of mine and another cause of my gettin' in the record business. Because the first time I heard him I went down again to the Southern states. I had been there and told the people I knew him and nobody believed that I did. So when I came back I finally got a break to make these recordings for Victor and they didn't believe it was *me* until *I* went back. I went back and showed them my picture and contract and everything . . . next thing that convinced them it was me I had that long Cadillac! Then they were convinced that I had to do somethin' to get it, and that I got it by makin' those recordin's.

Well after that I made a number of others and I enjoyed it very much and the company was very nice to me. Any time I wanted something all I had to do was to write them a letter; they'd send it right away. And those blues just come to me. Blues feelin' . . . I don't know if one could even describe it. Something that gets over you, comes over you that you feel. You sit down at the pianner, you start touchin' the keys, softly. Next thing you can practically see yourself in some place you never been before. And that's what make that blues feelin' come over you. That's the way it appeared to me. You think about some days you didn't have anything, you didn't have no shoes; some days when you wanted to help your mother and you just wasn't able to. I guess all boys feel like that some days when they just want a chance to do somethin' for their mother, so naturally I had the same feelin'. Finally I had the chance to make some recordin's for Victor and then I had the chance to help her out a lot. Well, that's what make me homesick when I sit down at the piano, thinkin' about those days in Grenada, Mississippi.

Blues Just Come to Me
A partial stroke ended Walter Davis's career as a blues pianist and he took a job as a hotel switchboard operator

114

A little ditty I made

James Stump Johnson

My brother Jesse Johnson had a music shop which was on Market Street which was a very prominent street for the coloured people. He had a piano in there and I come to sittin' aroun' and picked on the piano and learned how to play a few little blues – without notes of course. I was sittin' in this place close to Christmas day and I was broke and didn't have any money. And a scout came here from Chicago lookin' for someone to make recordin's. Well he heard me play a little ditty I made on the piano which I later gave the name of the *Duck's Yas Yas Yas*. It was somethin' like:

Mmmmm . . . mmm . . . mmmm . . . .
Mama bought a rooster, she thought it was a duck,
Bring it to the table with its legs straight up,
In come the children with the cup and the glass
To catch the liquor from his yas yas yas.

Me and my girl goin' down the street,
She caught the rheumatism in her feet,
She falled over to pull some grass,
And the same thing struck her in the yas yas yas.

I'm goin' down on Market Street,
Where the men and the women all do meet;
That's where the men do the Georgia rub,
And the women fall in line with that big washtub.

You shake your shoulders, you shake 'em fast,
If you can't shake your shoulders shake your yas yas yas,
Drink some rukus juice before goin' to bed,
Wake up in the mornin' find your own self dead.

Down on Morgan there's a good location,
Right next to the gasoline station,
That's where you cin get girls all the week,
All the women cryin', 'Honey, won't you come in quick?'

He asked me if I had ever taken music or had I ever made recordin's and I told him no. And did I make it up? Well I made it up right then at the pianner and I was pickin' it out. And he asked me would I go to record and would I go that night, so I told him I would, but my sister-in-law told me that I couldn't go unless she went too. Well by bein' a scout he had to make arrangements because he didn't know if she could go

or not. So he left and went on down to Memphis. I was very disappointed. I was mad at my sister-in-law from the time he left! But the followin' Thursday he come back and had made arrangements for me to go to New York with her unbeknowin's to me. So they told me I was goin' to New York. The only overcoat I had that was worth a nickel was in the pawnshop and I'd got about four dollars on it in pawn. I had a girl I was goin' with and I wanted to give her a Christmas present and I wasn't goin' to be able to give her anythin' so now I was thrilled to be goin' to New York and to get some money. I did have an old raggety overcoat to put on and we started out for New York and we were supposed to prepare our material for naming the records but we didn't 'cause we were too enjoyin' ourselves seein' the sights of New York and we forgot our material. So we slept in the open air that night and next day I was hoarse and couldn't talk and couldn't sing and we got lost. We were goin' to the studio and the cab driver charged us three dollars and seventy-five cents for takin' us over there, and when we got out we saw the Grand Central Station where we come in and it was only half a block from the studio! So they put us on. I never drank anything in my life and they thought that all blues singers liked to drink which I was one that never did, and they gave us two or three fifths of whisky – quarts of whisky at that time – and so my sister-in-law enticed me to take a drink. I taken a drink and with that the drink went to my head and I was high. So when we got through the recordin' I was so excited I said, 'Well give me another drink of that whisky then!' which they recorded on their outfit before switchin' it off – which became a nach'al hit all over the country. I signed a contract with just about every big recordin' company there was and that's how I started to makin' records. And then overnight I become a star – an artist I guess – and I recorded under about ten different names – James Stump Johnson, Shorty George, Snitcher Roberts, The Little Man and any number of fictitious names. At that time if you had an idea in your mind you could record it if you could find somebody to put it on.

Without Notes of Course
James Stump Johnson was a
popular recording blues pianist
in the 'twenties

Better Than Some
The widow of promoter
Jesse Johnson, Edith Johnson
was a fine singer

'Nickel's worth of liver'

Edith Johnson

My husband was in the talent business and he always would let somebody else go – he would never take me. And of course I thought I could sing as well as the rest of them and I thought I could sing better than some of them. So he had taken James – that's Stump – and he had some good blues. So I kind of blackmailed Stump. I said, 'Jesse, he cain't go unless you let me go along with him.' So they let me go and I did some recording then. It wasn't too good but at any rate after I had gotten paid for the recordin' I had some real money! I came back home and Jesse seriously considered lettin' me do some recordin'. So I was thinkin' up words and tryin' to think of titles that no one had used. Well I thought of one . . . but I couldn't use that! So instead of usin' the right words I changed it to *Honey Dripper*. And then I tried to sit down and think of some right words that would fit it! So anyway I did, and Baby James and Roosevelt Sykes and Ike Rodgers were accompanying me on this visit. We went to Indianapolis. Well the first time I recorded I saw that people were drinkin' and I thought you had to drink to record. But this time I didn't want to drink because I wanted to see how it would sound myself. And boy, guess what! It was a good record, and I made the company a lot of money. I played the piano myself on *Nickel's Worth of Liver* – but that's no piano playing, I was just goin' plunkety- plunkety-plunk whilst I was singin', somethin' to fill up the record you know:

Bring me a nickel's worth of liver, dime's worth of stew,
Feed everybody on Lucas Avenue,
  Won't you be kind to me, I'll be so nice to you,
  Won't you be good baby, I'll be so good to you,
  Don't ever leave me, don't know what I'll do.

Bring me a nickel's worth of liver, dime's worth of grease,
Whipped my man – he called all the police,
  Won't you be kind to me, I'll be so nice to you,
  Baby, I won't care what you do,
  Don't ever leave me, don't know what I'll do.

Listen Papa, don't give me none of your head,
Keep on foolin' you'll be filled full of lead,
  Please be nice to me,
  Please be kind to me, I won't care what you do,
  Don't ever leave me, I won't care what you do.

When you see me worried I'm thinkin' bout my boiled liver,
I'll tell you 'bout him and my hand won't even quiver,
  Babe be nice, don't care what you do, Don't ever leave me,
  don't know what I'll do.

But after that he still didn't want me go too much – I don't think he wanted me to make too much money you know? Well, looking for talent naturally kept my husband away from home a lot: two or three or five in the mornin' he's comin' home. 'Is that you?' I'd say, 'Where you been?' 'Oh, I had to go get Mr Kapp and get up talent for him.' And they're off having a good time where they be playin' music and singin' the blues and all that, and I'm home asleep, never havin' fun. But anyway, it was interesting when they used to have recording dates. I don't remember too much about the talent my husband got up. Primarily he was doin' a job you know. He'd bring them to the music shop and we had a player-piano there. Naturally during those years we had piano rolls. But he'd bring them down to the place and they'd sing – I thought they sounded pretty good and Jesse usually let me decide. However, he had a very good opinion himself about how the blues should sound. And of the many people that he did bring down here I particularly remember Victoria Spivey. I remember I was putting magazines out in the magazine rack right in front of the store and she came in and Jesse wasn't down yet. She was a li'l skinny girl, dark brownskin, and she had on an old blue coat and she said, 'Can you tell me where I can find Mr Jesse Johnson?'

I said, ' Honey you're at the right place and he'll be here shortly.' So we go in and she sits down at the piano and starts playin'! And oh, boy, I ate that up! *Black Snake Blues* – it was a different kind of blues you know. And Victoria went a long way after that first record but there never was another like *Black Snake*. She made many others – one of them was *T.B. Blues* and any times when I'm at home right now and I get to coughin' I say, 'Oooh, T.B.'s killin' me!' – that was part of the words of the record you know. I don't know where in the world Jesse heard about her but she did have a good blues.

I commence to whippin'

Victoria Spivey

My brothers said to my mother, 'Well, if Sippie Wallace can go and sing, and I know that my sister can sing as well as she can, we'll send her to St Louis.' And well, they got together and they sent me to St Louis, Missouri, and I was just about fifteen years old. Well I walked in that mornin' – I walked into that Central Station that was on Market Street and I was frightened, I was afraid but I wouldn't let anybody know it. And I walked into this De Luxe music shop that Mr Jesse Johnson owned at the time. And I spoke to the girl behind the desk, I says, 'Is the manager here?' And she says, 'No, he's gone to Chicago.' So I says, 'When will he be here?' and she says, 'He's due back tomorrow. What you want with him? I'm the manager here,' she says, 'when he's absent.' Well I say, 'I'm a singer and I wanna make a record!' Just that simple – that's true. She says, 'Girl, you better go home!' I says, 'What's home? I live in Houston, Texas, and I'm not goin' home. I come here to make a record.' She says, 'Well, there's a piano over there; can you play the piano?' I says, ' I certainly can!' 'I was darin' you know. So I just sit there and commence to whippin' on them ole *Black Snake Blues*!

Some mean black snake bin suckin' my rider –
   hear me cryin', Lawd I mean it,
Some mean black snake bin suckin' my rider's tongue,
You can tell by that I ain't gonna stay here long.

Cause my left side jumps and my flesh begin to crawl,
My left side jumps, my flesh begin to crawl,
Bet you my las' dollar, 'nother woman kicking in my stall.

I'd rather be a catfish swimmin' in that deep blue –
   Lawd beneath a submarine behind a floatin' boat,
I'd rather be a catfish swimmin' in that deep blue sea,
Than to stay in Texas, feel like they wanna do poor me.

Well she was just dumbfounded at that! And the same day I went over to my sister's in Moberly, Missouri, and two days later Mr Jesse Johnson rolled up in a blue phaeton – Packard – and signed a contract with me. And in about five more days the *Black Snake Blues* was in Brooklyn being pressed and a hundred and fifty thousand of those records was sold in thirty days! And then they couldn't get none – they couldn't press them fast enough. But *Black Snake Blues* was just a joke; my

sister used to go with a guy and they called him Snake – he was a pianner player: he taught me to play pianner. And he was the one that inspired me to play this. And my sister was angry; she says, 'You ole black snake you!' So I just looks at her and I thinks 'Uh-huh . . . .' So when I gets my ideas of it, as he was the one that taught me to play pianner, so I tho't I would make the *Black Snake Blues*. And I wrote the thing myself. He had always shown me the melody, but I got the first rhythm – of blues with rhythm. Now *Garter Snake Blues* is just a steal from the *Black Snake Blues*, and *T.B. Blues* is another steal from it. Just different lyrics and brought the rhythm down. I'll never know what made me make that record. 'Cause my mother heard it and when she heard it she dialled Tommy Rockwell who at that time was handlin' me and ask if I was sick, if I had the T.B. And then I got afraid I *might* catch the T.B. and every time I hear it I'd shake. I don't know why I said it. But at that time I had been lookin' at people who had the T.B. in part of the country and at that time, if you had the T.B. nobody would have no part with you; they put you away in hospital and you was just doomed then, you gonna die. So I figgered it was a nice thing to write about.

I was Daring
Victoria Spivey was only fifteen years old when she determined to get a recording date

Right good on the first out

Mary Johnson

A scout came from Chicago down to here and they heard me singin' in a night club and they interviewed me and had me to sing for them and they liked it very much and they taken me to Chicago. And I made right good there and I made right good on the first out. They gave me a contrack at the store. I made six numbers without the paper. I had lost the paper and didn't have nothin' to go by and I remembered every word. And I was so thrilled – they give me fifty dollars a side and later on they called me back again and I made six numbers, second trip, twenty-five dollars a side of each record which was fifty dollars and they give me three hundred dollars and was I thrilled! Poor as I was, oh I could hardly eat. And my mother was poor and got nobody, no husband and she was workin'. So my first number was a hit – the *Black Man Blues*. I don't know where I got the idea of 'A man in Atlanta, and one in St Louis too', – I didn't have all of them! So I made very good on that and I used to go around night clubs which I was already in and I made good and was able to help my mother. I got some of my ideas from my husband, Lonnie Johnson. He didn't give me the ideas exactly; I think you know you just have a talent for some things. I used to help him a bit. We were sittin' there and I give him a few ideas on the *Tornado Blues*, that's when the tornado hit St Louis. And he says, 'Sweetheart, why don't you compose your own numbers and we'll play 'em for you and you make good yourself.' And so we did. So I had many blues like *Black Gal Blues* and *Prison Cell Blues* and *Barrel House Flat Blues*. That sold real good, *Barrel House Flat Blues*:

> I'm gonna build me li'l barrelhouse flat way out in Dago Hill,
> I'm gonna build me a barrelhouse flat way out on Dago Hill,
> Where I can get my good whisky fresh from the still.

> Those babies like my whisky and they drink my good sherry
>   wine,
> Those good babies like my whisky and they drink my good
>   sherry wine,
> So if you want a good time try this barrelhouse flat of mine.

Colored folks don't live on Dago Hill. You know that's an Eyetalian place And they had all the bootleg at that time so I thought that would be the best place to have a barrelhouse flat, right where they were makin' that boot whisky. I had all sorts of other numbers I've forgotten if I ever recorded. I write my own numbers at the time; I composed my own blues and I would just write them down and then throw them away and I wouldn't think no more about them.

A whole lot of numbers

Lonnie Johnson

They had a blues singing contest at the Booker Washington Theater in St Louis. It was mostly a talent scout contest. See the scouts for Okeh Records started that off. Whoever win the contest that week got a contract – three weeks in the theater or got a recording contract. I win first prize for eighteen weeks. I win every week for eighteen weeks and I got an eleven year contract with Okeh and that started me in business. Made some fine recordings for Okeh. Yes, sure, and won that lovely contract. And that's the way it started and from then on I've been singing blues and I've wrote a whole lot of numbers in my life. I'm drawing royalties from a lot of songs. My first one was published in '48 and I remember the name of it sure, *I Found a Dream*. Rest of them mostly I just copyrighted that's all; not published. Such as *Jelly Roll Baker*, *Feeling Lowdown*, *Rocks in My Bed* . . . I recorded so many numbers . . . it takes a lifetime to figger them all, but yes, I know how many. 572. I know, I got copies.

Pretty good material

Roosevelt Sykes

In little later years as I had been around the studios like R.C.A. Victor, Decca and so forth and I seemed to be popular with the fellers that was runnin' the record business such as J. Mayo Williams and Jack Kapp – those fellers knowed pretty well about blues singers and that I knowed pretty good material when I heard it, so they asked would I go out and find some new artists for them? So I agreed and they wrote me a letter of introduction to different places that I would go to out in the countries. I had to have the letter because certain places we'd go fellers be workin' in – you go in and ask them for an audition and the boss would think you come to steal the guy away. And you had to show them what you was up to; that you didn't come to steal the guy away and to show them what you was up to in that you be there for makin' records, and you didn't come to take nobody off their job and they'd return right back and carry on with whatever they were doin'. I'd went down to Mississippi and listen to an artist and they tol' me that a feller out in the country was pretty good and the feller, white feller, wanted to know what I wanted with him. This feller was workin' on a farm didn't want nobody takin' his staff away. See he was farmin', ploughin' and choppin' cotton and this blues singer was a hand on his place plowin' cotton and choppin' and this feller didn't want to lose him. He wasn't satisfied, he said, 'You goin' to tell him a long story and take him away from me.' It was kinda difficult at times and different places you go, you don't know what kind of guy he is you goin' to meet. But still I found some good talent.

Their own originals
Sam Ayo

Everybody was trying to get on record
Edwin Buster Pickens

Usually I've gone out and found the talent myself. There's an awful lot of talent in the field if a feller can just go on out and discover it. And Race talent – a lot of times you be talking to someone, ask them if they know of some good singers and usually you go out and contact them, try to find them, have a little rehearsal and find out if they do have pretty good talent. At other times a lot of it is not worth listening to, though actually I believe a feller should really get out and scout talent. Or if he has an office and does a little advertising you'd be surprised at the number of people that would come to your office and want to discuss recording with you. Years ago, the major companies I would take them to was Columbia and R.C.A. Then of course, after that, well, I started my own label and ordinarily farmed the talent out to other companies. Most of them were employed here in Houston but years ago, when the portable stations come through, it would be Dallas or San Antonio or some such place like it. A portable station was actually the old wax deals. Of course I'd get the hotel rooms and drape them up to make them soundproof, and actually arranged to record in the various hotel rooms. At that time the instruments the blues artists used mostly consisted of pianos and guitars and drums and that sort. They all had their own material – in other words we wouldn't record anyone else's tunes – they'd have their own originals. You have better luck recording a person's own originals than by recording someone else's tunes. Blues – mostly blues, and it was all original stuff.

We left Corpus Christi, me and a guitar player by the name of Otis Cook. Otis never did any recording but he played guitar and he and I decided we would travel a li'l bit, and left, and got on the wrong train. Supposed to take the Southern Pacific out of there for San Antony, but seein' we was on we decided we'd go on round through Laredo. So we made it for Laredo and into Old Mexico and we spent a day or two over there and come back, and we decided we would make for Robstown and hit for San Antony and take the train from there. In those days everybody was trying to get on record you know, and that was right after Coney Burks and Black Boy Shine and them made their recordin's so we thought we'd try. So we got on this freight – ran into the freight yard at night – round about eleven, not thinkin' the train was already made up and everything 'cause the engine hadn't come down. So we got onto a gondola car to sleep, take a li'l nap. Well they found us sleepin' there, and we couldn't get out of the yard. And so we got arrested that night, got ten days in jail. And so we never did get to make no recordin's.

A feller ask me
Oscar Kelly

The boys all tell me I ought to make a recordin'. They tol'
me about this feller in Crowley, said I ought to go see him. I
dunno though, you cain't never tell . . . . It's like I say, people
get jealous of you. And maybe you don't know nothin' about
what they call the contrack. I heard about it, I heard about
from guys I be workin' with that you know, do recordin'. Well
I play git-tar aroun' Baton Rouge; cross the River . . . go up to
Greenville sometimes . . . played in Arkansas. And a lots of
these fellers they do recordin' and they tol' me about it and
they tol' me I ought to make a record. A feller ask me once;
come up here, ask me if I'd like to do some recordin'. I dunno
where he's from, so I guess I just didn't feel like it. Maybe I
will do some recordin' . . . one day . . . get myself together.
Right now I got a job needs fixin' . . . .

Feed Everybody
'Recreation Parlour' on
Lucas Avenue, St Louis

This is a very, very hard field
J. D. Miller

I'll listen to everybody. Cause it's my way of determining this;
that's the only way you gonna find or discover someone. So
I'll listen to anyone that will come to my studio, because I say,
ninety-five per cent of the time maybe, I'm not interested but
that other five per cent of the time I find something good –
and that's to my benefit of course and it is to theirs too. You
got to treat 'em right you know, for them to give of their best
for you. And you never know how you may get these boys: you
can't look at them and tell if they're gonna be good musicianers.
Least you can with your higher class musician you can get a
good idea but not these blues boys. If you see an ole country
boy, that's your blues man; not the other guy that knows his
music on a higher level – because he's not a blues man no
more. I never do go out, not for the blues type of singer. And
the reason is this: I want them to be sold on the idea – wanting
to do something. Because this is a very, very hard field. Some
singers don't turn out to be good blues singers and as far as this
is concerned it's like this. If they don't feel the material they're
singin' – that's it. People can distinguish whether they're
authentic or not or whether it's just a synthetic singer and
that's all. But I've had boys come in here and sing and actually
they had the blues so bad they were cryin' when they got
through. They really had their heart and soul in it. And to my
way of thinking, that's a good blues man. Now Lightnin' Slim,
of course as far as knowledge of music I would say he knows
less about knowledge of music than anyone else that I record,
but for all that he's one of my best sellers for the simple reason
that what he does, he does feelin' it. His father was a tenant
farmer and they lived out there in the country and after the
men would get through work they used to sit out and they'd
start playin' and singin' you know. And they'd sing these ole
blues and the blues was generally bad luck and the troubles
they have had. That actually is the thing; Slim seems to give
out more of something real when he's talkin' about either his
girl or his wife has quit him or he's lost his money . . . and they
sing about fishing and wild life and different things like that –
in a blues slant.

They Come to Your Office
Headquarters of a blues
label – Fortune Records,
Detroit, Michigan

Their Own Material
Fortune Recording studio
after a session. Blues singers
have no use for sheet music
and music stands

How could he tell me?

Bo Carter

Tell ya, we was the Mississippi Sheiks and when we went to make the records in Jackson, Mississippi, the feller wanted to show us how to stop and start the records. Try to tell us when we got to begin and how we got to end. And you know, I started not to make 'em! I started not to make 'em 'cause he wasn't no musicianer, so how could he tell me how to stop and start the song? We was the Sheiks, Mississippi Sheiks and you know we was famous. And we traveled all over and we made records and we played just about anywhere you could name. San Antony, Texas . . . Jackson, Mississippi; Chicago, Ill'nois; Atlanty, Georgia. When we made the records for Mr Miller in Atlanty he come down to the Delta to see us and he ask us to go to Atlanty to record for him. My brother Lonnie, and Walter. So they say, 'Mr Miller, we want to see some money tonight.' He say, 'Well, you'll have to see Bo Carter, have to see him. How much do you want? He'll give it to you.' So they says, 'Oh, we want a hundred dollars apiece.' So he gives me the money and I puts it in the can. 'Cause all them recordmakers hand it to me at that time, 'cause I didn't get drunk you see. So I gives them a little and those boys went right out and spend it like I knew they would. And Mr Miller give me the money for the gas for to take me and Lonnie and all of them. Well we got to Atlanty and we did all the drinkin' that day we were recordin'. We could have had ten gallons of whisky if we wanted. I say, 'No . . . I don't mind,' when the bottle comes roun'. I passed him up three times. Then we been singin' and I'm gettin' kinda thisty then I say, 'Oh, boy, I think I will.' Those boys say, 'Man, you comin' on the Lord's side . . . give 'im a drink!' So I takes a drink and a few more and I say, 'You dawg, you. You put a shot in that las' one!' Got so drunk I couldn't hardly make it. So I gets the gang together and come along in the car at a service station and I was a long way over, 'cause the lights was burnin' down. And the police ran over. They backed up they did, and they come across the street and runned by me. One says, 'Git in the kerb!' I says, 'I'm in there!' 'Whatcha got in yer git-tar box?' Says, 'Git-tar!' Feller says ,'Whatcha bin drinkin'?' I says, 'Ice-water!' So the police gets kinda ugly then but the other feller knowed me and he says, 'That's ole Bo-Weevil – he don't never git drunk!' So if it hadn't a bin for the older feller the younger one would've carried us to the jail. Aw . . . I've had my fun.

Treated me so royal

Walter Davis

Most of playin' was tourin', bein' a recordin' artist. Places I played at in St Louis – oh well, I was the pianist at a night club on South Broadway for an Eyetalian feller called Nick. And I played in Baden for another Eyetalian feller, name was Gus. But most of my playin' was tourin', when I was makin' those tours. And of course, locally playin' I never did too much of that because after I git with R.C.A. Victor and they was so nice to me, and was so royal to me – treated me so royal – I figgered I was in demand, I didn't fool with those local places too much. But on tour I had Henry Townsend playin' guitar, and a boy we called Brother Fox, he was the drummer. And another boy played saxophone – and myself. Four or five fellers. We went all round Dallas, Texas and Poplar Bluff, Missouri . . . and Memphis, Tennessee. Right down through Mississippi – went back to Grenada with my long Cadillac, I always had me a long Cadillac. Well, we was in charge of South Carolina one time, that was in the 'thirties. And then there was, well down in Galveston, Texas and different places on the way . . . tourin', one-night stands and so forth, all the time. Like I had heard them in Mississippi – Ida Cox and Bessie Smith and this feller Will Ezell, was playin' for Bessie Smith then.

She had a piece of land

Brother John Sellers

Just about the earliest thing I can remember was my mother crying and moaning when the backwaters came and took our home. I had been born in Clarksdale but we were living in a little place, Burdett, Mississippi – it wasn't nothing more than a saw-mill and shacks around, and box-cars that they had made houses out of. And the river was about ten or twelve miles away but we'd heard that mighty rumblin' all day and all the hogs and horses screamin' – it was awful. Terrible. Of course I was too young to know much about it but I do remember that they pushed us into freight cars to get us away and I do remember my mother crying. It was the most terrible thing. And after that she had to get a job somewhere so she went down to New Orleans and left me with my godmother in Greenville, when the waters had gone back you know. And my godmother she had a house there on the edge of town and a big piece of land in back of it. She used to rent out the lot to the traveling shows. See, they had shows comin' through the town all the time but 'specially in the fall and they would pitch their tents behind the house. I used to help in the kitchen because my godmother used to fix them food. And there was always a lots of women be in the back, fixing their hair and so forth. Well, I didn't know it right away because I was too young you understand, but it was really a sportin' house my godmother had. So there was always people comin' and goin' and I was kep' busy runnin' messages and to buy things and so forth. And sometimes they'd have these blues players come in and when I was even very young I used to hear them at the barrelhouses and that give me the idea to sing too. Then when they put up the big tent I used to slip on out and watch the show – lift up the edge of the canvas. Then they used to have talent competitions sometimes and I was just a kid but I would sing too and I got quite a few prizes that way. And then I could see the show from the inside. It wasn't only blues you know, they'd have comedians and dancers and so forth like that but I always did remember the blues singers best. That's how I first heard Ma Rainey and Ida Cox. They had a stage up there with curtains and everything and then these would open and some big woman would be hollerin' there. This was with the old Rabbit Foot and Silas Green's from New Orleans – minstrel shows. And of course these singers would be famous from their recordings and they'd get a big crowd – big crowd, they be packed in there like rice in a bowl. So I used to hear them and I'd hear the blues singers in the beer tavern near where we lived – Leroy Carr came and played there once or twice and we'd always have these blues on phonograph records. We had a Victrola at the house and though I didn't hear Bessie Smith in person I did hear many of her records.

Pretty talented people

Norman Mason

Minstrel shows was very interesting and I played with the Rabbit Foot Minstrels for quite a few years. I could properly start to talk about the Rabbit Foot with the band. This feller Joe White was the drummer and Real Mark Chainey was the violinist in the orchestra and Archie Blue was the bass drummer and I played trumpet. Now for the blues singers we had Ida Cox sing, we had Lizzie Miles. Also Mamie – Mamie Smith, and speakin' of Chippie Hill and of course, Ma Rainey. And acts too and some pretty talented people in that they were able to compose songs – like T. H. Dumas, he was once a star comedian and he played in that part of the show that was known as Skeeter and his wife was Lil Liz. We had another man was outstandin' by the name of John Pamplin, he did that Devil Act, that Faust; raffled that big iron ball and did a lot of juggling. And then we had another very outstanding person in the show was Delamon Miles, a contortionist who could turn himself around completely and he was quite baffling to the people in that he was able to move around and walk backwards with his feet turned in opposite directions. And we had two other acts that were really great, those acrobats from down in New Orleans called the Watts Brothers, and also the Miles who had an ariel act. We had a girl down there, the super act of our show by the name of Mary Brown – she was good at blues singing but she could sing some of the other too. The show traveled around on a car; we had a Pullman car – one side we used for keepin' the members of the show and the other side for the canvas. We had the canvasmen to put up the tents and we ate on the car and we traveled by railroad. We made short jumps mostly during the week because of the fact that we played quite a few small towns. Caught the cotton crop down in Mississippi in the fall and we'd go out and catch the tobacco crop in North and South Carolina in the spring you see. We also traveled out in West Virginia where we played the coal mines, up in the hollers there. Of course the people lived way back in the mountains and you wouldn't see them in the daytimes. Sometimes we played a concert to advertise the show; we'd play in front of the Commissary and of course when the people back in the mountains hear the music, hear the type of music, why they'd know the show was in town. Out in North Carolina too and even to the Sea Islands; we'd made several trips out on a launch. Go out on a launch to those islands and settlements from the mainland and attract the people to come to town at night to enjoy the show. The Rabbit Foot Minstrels Show of course toured Florida in the winter and the following year we'd go out to Texas, Oklahoma, and the borders of New Mexico. And we did get a chance to get down to Old Mexico too, down to Laredo. These things were very intriguing because you seemed to be doing something that people got quite a bit of enjoyment out of. And it was really something to be playin' behind those blues singers. I like the blues because it do express the feelings of people and when we used to play around through Mississippi in those cotton sections of the country we had the people *with* us! They hadn't much outlet for their enjoyment and they get together in those honkytonks and you should hear them. That's where they let out their suppressed desires, and the more suppressed they are the better the blues they put out, seems to me.

Sleepin' Room Black Hotel in Terrell, Texas: 'Ole Rabbit Foot' under
the porch; circus posters compete with West Side Story on the side wall

Florida cotton blossoms

Charles Love

Feller by the name of Bob Nelson knowed what kind of musicianer I was and hired me right away for the Florida Cotton Blossoms Show. I left Texakarna and just got over there and we had about seventeen pieces in the brass band. The first show was in 1930 and so in 1931 they kinda liked my playin' so they turned the band over to me. Sergeant Cain was the leader of the band and I was first bandsman and responsible for all the mistakes and everything. I was the solo cornet player – they had about four or five cornet players but I was responsible for all their mistakes because I had to take care of the brass section and he used to take care of the whole business. Sergeant Cain – he was a very nice man and a good musician. We were called the Florida Cotton Blossoms but we had never been to Florida you know. So we went down to Pensacola, Florida, but business wasn't like we expected, so we had to cut the show, cut some of the people out. So we turned round and brought the show back again. We used to parade the brass band at twelve o'clock and go to the business part of the town and have a little show. Some feller'd sing and dance and the whole band would play. The banjolier would play a solo and he was a great singer – Jesse Davis. He used his own tenor guitar too. Then we had another feller used to clown – you know, he'd do eccentric dancing and then we'd play and march back to the tent. It was a regular minstrel show under canvas; had its own wagons, big trucks – used to have a side that opened up and had a cart there just decorated and a regular stage that come down right on the wheels. Foots Robinson was one of the comedians; a feller named Perry was another and a feller by the name of Sapp used to dance and tell tall tales. That's about six comedians and the rest was ballad singers and blues singers; three or four of them was ladies, they would sing. I remember they had two from New Orleans, one was Eva Gonzales and one was Henrietta Leggitt; and there was Mary Louise from Atlanta. Well then, I joined up with the Rabbit Foot Minstrels 1937 – was the last year I can remember they was out. They had a show after that but I wasn't there. Well, I went to Port Gibson, Mississippi, that's where I joined the show. F. S. Wolcott's Rabbit Foot it was and Wolcott had a nice house in Port Gibson. Wolcott was a fine feller; a little short feller but he was an old minstrel man. He used to be in the Big Top with the Ringling Brothers Number Four troupe – that's what he told me. Said he used to be a peckhorn player with the band, and at the time I believe Harry James's father was the leader of that band and Harry was born on that show. And when he was big enough he used to be the bass drummer. He used to catch all the other fellers on the trapeze you know. Started out music playing on drums but I guess he took after his father and wanted to play cornet so he did. And now he's tops. So the Rabbit Foot was just about the same kind of show as the Florida Cotton Blossoms – minstrel show under canvas. And we used to travel in buses, the only difference being that when the show get to the place where they goin' to play everybody had to get out and get theyselves a room, sleepin' room. Next mornin' they be in the next town. One-night stands . . . look like the Blossoms had about eight buses divided in two just like on the Pullman trains and the musicianers would have each feller a bunk; two up and two down. And they had a little space right behind the driver where you could sight-see; where he was drivin'. Wolcott didn't have that. You had to go out and get a room and get back on that bus. Something like a Greyhound bus. But we used to open up just as the Blossoms did and the Rabbit Foot had just about the same territory. We didn't work in Louisiana tho' because Louisiana always been a bad state. We'd be in a country town like on a Saturday night. They have to work that Monday so Saturday night they'd bring their girls and Monday nights they'd rest you see. So on Sunday, we'd walk around and see the sights; then move on. Next place, Monday, they'd put the tent up.

A rough neck

Blind Arvella Gray

I cut out and joined up with the Ringling Brothers Circus. I wasn't entertaining or nothing. That's when they had wagons to put the tents in and carry the show, so they had wagon trains when they used to move from town to town. Also they had transportation by rail too, but they could use the highway quite a bit in those days for moving from town to town. So they had singers and comedians and acrobats and all those kinds of people with the show and they used to have the show under canvas, what you call a tent show. So I was workin' in the crew that put the tent up, what they call them on a circus – they just say a 'roughneck'. I was a roughneck – you know, just put the tent up and the seats and things. There was a whole gang of us and we'd be singin' as we workin' like when I was workin' on the railroad. Because you have to do those things together and there's a certain way you have of puttin' up the tent.

It was really something

Norman Mason

The way of it was this: we'd get into the town and find our plot you see. And the first thing they would do would be to get the canvas out. The canvasmen did that. They get the canvas out and get the centre poles out and start to put them up, because the tent had several centre poles and they had to get those up first. And the canvasmen sang when they were putting up the tent – they had a head canvasman and a gang of roughnecks, they call them, and they would sing – well one they sang quite a bit was:

> That's my gal, leave her alone, before I cut your head,
> That's my gal, leave her alone or you'll find your own self
>   dead,
> Cause a dollar rolls from a hand to a hand,
> And a woman just goes from a man to a man
> But that's my gal, better leave her alone, before I cut your
>   head.

And they had another song they sang was *He Who Sits on a Red-hot Stove Will Surely Rise Again*, and we had a comedian on the show who used to use that one. But it's been so long I don't remember the words. Of course, if you ever had the chance to be in a tent show when a storm come up and see the tent start to blow down you'd understand how dangerous it was. I was in a place in Kentucky they call Dawson Springs, when a cyclone come through and the tent blew down and it was really somethin' trying to get out of the tent you know, with those poles and the trees fallin' down and you could hardly see your way through because it was so dark out there, and the wind throwing you about. Of course they would put those tents up and get them down real quick and you know it's a funny thing, but by the time we had changed out of our uniforms they have the tent down and the whole place would look so different we couldn't find our way around.

Putting in the stobbs

Charles Love

Fellers puttin' up the tents they had their own little songs you know – they used to sing when they were pulling them ropes and using them sledgehammers and driving those stobbs down. They used to sing such a song as:

I loves Sally, she's a fine girl . . .

She got good cabbage and good pigmeat . . .

I like Sally, she's a sweet lookin' woman . . .

Got them big bow legs, got them big bow legs. . . .

That's the kind of stunt they'd pull. They'd be singing and we'd be laughing, looking at them putting them stobbs down. They had fifteen or twenty of them, some putting in the stobbs and some nailing them down. And they had a boss canvasman and he'd stand up and tell them what to do. Then they'd pull that ring up and they'd put the side on. The sides of the tent. And they would sing a song as they pulled the ropes and got the tent up – they were the same like railroad songs and the way them roustabouts on the steamboats, they sing a lot of that stuff too. So by the time they had the sides on all the way round and got that in good, the band would go in and if they had to practise anything they would do it in the tent. Then we would parade about twelve o'clock and then back to the tent for a shower and then walk aroun' a bit. Back again at seven o'clock because we had to be in the busiest part of town to play a short concert – 'bout three pieces and then hit a little march and play it all the way back to the tent. And the people would fall in line right behind the band and stomp right into the show. We'd stop outside the tent and they would buy their tickets and go in. Then they put the chain out and we know the show was loaded. Then we be ready and come on into the pit. On the stage they had what you call the Grand Opening. Three on this side and three on the other and the ladies. And the feller in the middle he would be the interlocutor – ask questions and funny fellers would muddle him all up. And the people be laughing and the band take up a tune. Well, after each feller had done something and the ladies had sung a song or blues or something, we'd do a great number and they all get up and dance and the curtain would come down. Then would come the Olio. The band would play a short fanfare and a feller would come down to the front of the stage and tell a tale – monologuist they call it – while the rest of the people behind the stage be dressin'. Then he would leave the crowd laughin' and the curtain would go down. We'd get a wink from the footlights and that means we's ready; man, we'd hit it!

Rough going

Jesse Crump

I heard blues when I was a kid; I used to go in the country in the South and hear guys with their guitars on Saturday nights, at church suppers and things . . . playing the *Wearied Blues* and those things you know. So these got buried in my brain and I said when I learned to play the piano I was going to write some of those things. I got started when I was a kid, I was foolin' around with the piano, so I started to take a few lessons and studied for myself and went round and got in little carnivals. Little carnivals and 'gillie' shows. Aw . . . rough going *that* was! But they say you never get anywhere in show business unless you have had rough times – so I had them! I started in carnivals and then I got from carnivals to tent shows. Nice – well, pretty good tent shows we'd call them, when you get a salary for playing! When I first got in show business I seen some very bad days. Cause those were little tabloid shows you know. They be up today and down tomorrow and you play to all kind of little towns in the South – sometimes you have to borrow a garage to play out there. Then from there on I hit the road with these shows, with the TOBA shows and things. Well it was very good and the pay was good in those days on the TOBA. So after I grown up well, naturally music was still in my mind so I tried to compose some blues and to find out if they was any good and if people liked them. So from then on I just continued to write blues numbers and then I went to Indianapolis, Indiana, and I met a girl there called Nina Reeves and I wrote for her *Indiana Avenue Blues*. We did some recording there for the Gennett Company in Richmond, Indiana. She was away ahead of her time, she was a great singer. So it was from there on up to the 'big time' – we used to call it the big time when you played in theaters. I was in vaudeville at the time I used to sing and dance, play clarinet – well I was versatile you know. And I played comedian at one time; I was supposed to be one of the funniest guys in the business but I quit that and just kept up with my music, and so that was the thing that put me over. I knowed it from A to Z; from the bottom and worked to the top.

Uncrowned queen of the blues
Sam Price

Ella B. Moore put me in show business because I used to hang around her Park Theater all the time. And I had an opportunity to hear Bessie Smith and Trixie Smith, Mamie Smith and the greatest blues singer that I ever knew, Ida Cox. And of course with Jesse Crump playing the piano. And it was Jesse Crump whose records I learned to play – by listening to his records and watching the piano rolls to know the different keys. This is how I learned to play watching the piano rolls. You put the piano roll on and release the catch that would lock the keys; watch these keys go down and that's how I learned to play piano. But one night in Dallas that was the beginning of my going into show business. I was a dancer – a Charleston dancer – in the front row. And Ida Cox knew that I loved Jesse Crump's playing so she introduced me – the theater was full of people – and she said I want you to meet a fine piano player one of the local blues pianists. And she introduced me, called me on the stage and that was the first opportunity I had to play with a professional blues singer – and that was Ida Cox. She was the greatest blues singer of all time. She was actually the Uncrowned Queen of the Blues. That's what she was known as and she was just that. Hers was a good blues style. When you hear my playing and someone singing the blues with me,

To Catch the Cotton Crop In such barns and warehouses travelling shows played. Outside, Cola sells on work incentive. Terrell, Texas

that would be her style because I play exactly like Jesse Crump. So then I went on the road. I left home in 1926 and traveled through Oklahoma with a road show and in 1927 I started traveling and I left Dallas and I went all the way up to Philadelphia on the TOBA circuit. Well you didn't get no money and you didn't want any. You joined the show and in one week s time you friendly with everybody and you're like one big happy family. We were traveling with one week stands. We played theaters – we left Dallas went to Houston. Houston to Galveston; Galveston to Shreveport; Shreveport to Pensacola, Florida; Pensacola to Lynchburg, Virginia and

all the way up to Baltimore, Maryland. We didn't play the Howard in Washington because these theaters we played were the smaller theaters on the TOBA. Milton Starr was one of the members of this – see S. H. Dudley, Milton Starr and Ella B. Moore and several others had this circuit. They had certain theaters and areas which they controlled or had something to do with. But the TOBA went out of existence and unfortunately so because it was a good training ground. TOBA meant Theater Owners Booking Agency but they used to call it Tough on Black Artists. Well it could be tough but there were good times too.

Some of the Theatres Were Very Small The Rainbow Theatre in Houston, Texas, is typical

Standing in line
Jesse Crump

After I got with Ida Cox the goings was very easy because she made a lot of money and she paid me a real good salary. The Paramount recording manager heard about me – fact she told him about me but he had heard me at the Golden Rest Cabaret in Indianapolis. So he sent me a telegram inviting me to go on a tour with Ida Cox so I did. I went to Chicago then I did a few recordings with her and wrote all of her numbers and went onto the TOBA time – only we called it Toby Time. We traveled all through the South and the Middle West and we just turned them away. She was a topnotcher in those days and the people was all standin' in line two and three blocks long to hear her. That was a great thrill for me just to say that I played with one of the great blues singers and was writing all of her tunes. You don't know what a thrill I got out of that. I was proud to accompany one of the Uncrowned Queens of the Blues through the twenties and the thirties. She was a blues singer – a very, very good blues singer. Then so by me playing bit solos on the stage whilst she was changing costumes I went over big too. Because I did a lot of comedy at the piano and swinging the tunes – the people just went wild. So that continued about ten years. Some of the tunes I wrote for her did very well were real hits and some not so well but mostly – two-thirds of them – were hits which is *Death Letter Blues* and *Black Crepe Blues* and *Cherry Picking Blues* and so on. So, well, she decided she wanted a big show so I had a twelve-piece band and a presentation show you know – chorus girls and what have you; comedians and everything. So we traveled and traveled to 1936 and then I gave up; was tired of traveling you know. But Ida Cox, I think, was one of the great blues singers of her times and I must say I wrote some very good numbers for her. So those are the things that gets next to you.

Like the gay nineties
Norman Mason

Of course on the Rabbit Foots we had some really famous blues singers and entertainers that had been in the big time on the TOBA and so forth. Like Butterbeans and Susie – and because of the originality of them, he and his wife are still rather popular with the people now, even though the act is almost fifty years old. But I think the thing that was most intriguing about him to the people was how he could get into those tight pants! And nobody ever figgered out how he could do it. However he had a zipper on those things and just zipped them up – I mean before they become popular. They toured with us a lot. And Ida Cox of course. Her husband also came to the Foots and played a while with the band, but Ida, she was really what they call a 'coon shouter'. Oh, she could really sing the blues you know. Of course she left the show and went into Tom Anderson's out in New Orleans and sang there for several years before she went out on the vaudeville circuit. I guess Ma Rainey was the most famous. Because Ma Rainey was quite a character or legend in America here, in that she had such an outstanding voice for the blues, and she sang songs like the *Florida Blues* and the *Kansas City Blues* and the *Jelly Roll Blues*. She sang songs then that would sound as up-to-date as if it were played right now. During that time people didn't dress like they do now. In that people then used to have more clothes on and she used to have those real long dresses sometimes with a high neck, well, like you would call it – like the Gay 'Nineties. But she had one of those voices you never forget – particularly for singing the blues.

Dying for red beans

Charles Love

At the Star Theater in Shreveport on Texas Avenue we had all the TOBA circuit used to come in with different shows like Drake and Walker, and Luke Scott. That was reguly theater you know, reguly vaudeville. Drake had a good show and he had his own piano player, feller by the name of Udell Wilson who went to Kansas City later, a very good piano player. Udell and Willie Jackson and Ida Cox and I used to work together for Tom Anderson at the time I was playing for him in New Orleans. Willie Jackson was a nice entertainer – he used to sing *Il Traviatore* – at least he had a burlesque about that. Well, the words were about he's dying for red beans and macaroni and he really used the real *Il Traviatore* music. We'd play it and he'd sing it and man, he was a knock-out! He'd get plenty of money for doing that! Feller from New York picked him up and asked him would he like to go. He went to New York but he came back again. Lucky Thomas, he and Willie used to work together, oh they were good entertainers and they'd sing blues too. He had a son, and they also worked together and his son was a great singer. So when we were all together with Ida Cox it was a great act. Ida Cox, I don't know where she is now. She was workin' at Tom Anderson's when I first come up from Mexico. She left New Orleans here with her own show, got her own show together and I don't know where she went. She was a nice singer, what we call a 'coon shouter' – sing blues and everything.

Lots of pep

Billie Pierce

In my teenage I was with Joe Jesse's Orchestry in Pensacola, Florida, and the first job we played was at the San Carlos Hotel and that's the biggest hotel there. And then from there to different spots at the Bay View Park in Pensacola and then points all round the Gulf we worked. So after I got through workin' with Joe Jesse – he passed – I started with Billy Mack and his traveling show out of New Orleans. That was Mack's Merry Makers. We traveled and worked lots of places and little towns in Florida and Louisiana. I worked two weeks for Bessie Smith before that, at the Belmont Theater in Pensacola, that's when Clarence Williams, her pianist, was taken sick. Bessie Smith was good too – she was a good entertainer. She wanted me to go but I didn't care to travel then. I was too young to hit the road. Then I worked with Mama Rainey as a chorus girl – I was just a chorus girl with Mama Rainey, I didn't play piano for her or nothin'. Only thing I can tell you about Mama Rainey was – she had a real good voice; a heavy gross voice for the blues and everybody liked her singing. Ida Cox had a show in my home town at the Belmont Theater so I was quite a kid but I taken over to play piano for her too. That's where I got my start with Ida Cox; playing blues mostly. Her style was the same style as my singing is. She had lots of pep on the stage – lots of pep behind her singing; she was a great entertainer. Well after I married Dédé we had our little band together and him and I started traveling. The first job Dédé and I traveled with was with Ida Cox and we traveled from New Orleans clean to Miami, Florida, and back to New Orleans. Then I got taken sick and Dédé by then had lost his sight too, so I just didn't care much about playin' you know, not like I used to.

Her heart was so big

Al Wynn

I was asked to join the Ma Rainey organization just as she was forming a new group in about '23 or '24. She was coming out of retirement – she had retired to Mexico for some time and was on her way for a comeback. After several rehearsals we opened up at the Grand Theater – the band included Thomas Dorsey piano, Henderson on trumpet, Gabriel Washington on drums, Pollack on saxophone and clarinet and myself on trombone. We opened up at the Grand Theater and made a tour of the TOBA circuit playing most of the prominent theaters throughout the South and Middle West and doing quite a few dates in schoolhouses and so forth, dance halls and what have you. The tour was very successful. Ma was a wonderful person to work with – very lovable disposition. She was always doing nice things and taking everyone as if they were her own kids because at that time we were very young. And contrary to what most people believe – Mother – Ma Rainey wasn't old at that time although she was well known and well established because she started so young, she was a child prodigy in her time. She enjoyed doing pleasant things and the people were very nice to her all over the country and we were making nice salary for the time. She had started as a young girl and I had the pleasure of meeting her mother and her grandmother who were still living at the time and going to her home in Columbus, Georgia. They were very active and remarkable people. Ma Rainey was rather heavy – she wasn't attractive at all, but what she lacked in looks she made up in personality and sweetness – her heart was so big it made her beautiful in the eyesight of everyone that got to know her. Her gowns were very elaborate for the gowns of the day. They had rhinestone bits and jewellery – oh she was a fanatic for jewellery – all kinds of diamonds and gold pieces were still in vogue and she had any number of necklaces made up of twenty and fifty dollar gold pieces. She had a fabulous collection of diamonds and jewellery most of which she couldn't afford to wear in the streets but she would wear them in the theater. I remember one incident very clearly – in Nashville, Tennessee where the authorities got on her and gave her a hard way to go until she could prove that everything was bought legitimate – I don't know how she acquired them – some place in Mexico or somewhere but they were bought right and she proved it. In most of the places the theaters had large bands in the pit who played the overtures before the curtain would go up and we being the main attraction we would be crowded on the stage with along about four pieces. But when she would come out to sing she would prove herself to be the real star of the whole evening. Her entrance was – she would come out of a large Victrola – it was made just like a old-style phonograph and she would walk out of that singing the *Moonshine Blues* which was her big hit at the time:

> I was drinkin' all night babe and the night before,
> When I get sober ain't gonna drink no more,
> Because my friend is standin' in my door.
>
> My head's goin' round and around babe since my daddy
>   left town,
> I don't know if the river is runnin' up or down,
> But one thing's certain mama's gonna leave this town . . . .

People enjoy it

Edith Johnson

During the early part of the twenties my husband being a promoter, in order to advertise something – other than handbills or newspapers we had no means of doing it. However he'd rent a truck and have cloth sides made and put on the outside and get Baby James or Oliver Cobb or some trumpet player here and go up and down the neighbourhood where we hoped to get our customers for the night. And they'd blow up a storm! And every time if I hear a trumpet blowin' the blues down the street I'd run to the door to see what was goin' that night. When Louis Armstrong made his first big hit record my husband went up to Chicago to see if he could get him down here and he would really break 'em down! Front him before a local band and everybody'd die when he began to blow! Jesse would do that with Bennie Moten here – that was his first out of town promotion. And when Cab Calloway was here we had thirteen hundred people and my husband went up in an airplane and I went up and Stump and we threw down tickets and leaflets and oh, it was a big thing. We had a parade . . . and too we had a music shop which was just behind the Booker Washington Theater and that made it convenient for me to see all the actresses and the blues singers – and it made it convenient for them too. Years ago at that time blues singers on the stage were real new around here and each week at the Booker Washington they would feature some blues singer like Ida Cox or Clara Smith or Bessie Smith, Ma Rainey, Blind Lemon and . . . oh my, Ethyl Waters. Now she's real famous and real fat but when she was young she was really attractive, slender and sang in such an expressive way. I always thought she was one of the better singers that we had because she knew what to emphasize and what not to emphasize. I just thought when she sang, 'Go back to where you stayed last night!' She meant, 'Go on back there! Everything is over! Go on back there where you were stayin' las' night! Git back there, go on!' – I thought she was real good. If you sing, well that's all right and people enjoy it. But if you don't have no personality with your singing, your singing is enjoyed but you are soon forgotten. Now for instance, take Bessie Smith and Clara Smith. Clara Smith made wonderful records and we sold many of them, but there was no comparison between the two women. Once you'd seen Bessie – her great big eyes, and stout – oh, she had the look of a blues singer. While Clara – well, she looked like a blues singer in a way, but she didn't have the personality, so it didn't come through and I can truthfully say I can't hardly remember what she looked like, but I can vividly remember Bessie. But Ma Rainey . . . what about Ma Rainey? She was just a – well Ma Rainey was just a great big – well, she was the worst lookin! – oh, I won't say that – she was the worst lookin' person I ever seen! But she sang. And how she sold a record I'll never know! But we used to have the music shop at that time and surprisingly enough we sold quite a lot of her records. But I never could see her . . . . No, no sort of way, she didn't move me. Lonnie Johnson though – well, Lonnie was a St Louis product and everything Lonnie made seemed to go. I personally liked his blues – however they got a little monotonous after three or four years because everything was in the same tone. But Lonnie was a very fine person and a good blues singer I thought. And the way he sang *Mister Johnson Blues* and *Falling Rain Blues* – and I can't remember the many records he made, but most of them were very good records. Then, of course, blues is just blues and if you got a good blues singer she moans – or he does – she moans, and she groans and she carries on just like we're supposed to do, and you feel it; you feel an answerin' in your heart from what she did – then you know she's a pretty good blues singer. And then, sometimes some of them just shout – and sometimes you're in a shouting mood and you listen to the shoutin' and you enjoy the shoutin' – it all depends primarily on what mood you're in. If you go feelin' down-hearted and they sing some old lonesome blues and it just hits you right and you go with the singer. But if you're in a happy mood and they come out shoutin', then you're in a mood when you're still with the singer. Blues are mostly a mood, and we enjoy – at least I enjoy – all kinds of them, I really do.

From end to end
Lonnie Johnson

Cravin' new experiences
Al Wynn

Well, I played on the TOBA and I played on the RKO circuit too. I worked from Coast to Coast on the RKO circuit and I played in everything that was playable. Every theater there was and every place they could make into a theater or call a theater. I was with the team of Glenn and Jenkins and I was with them for four years. But the TOBA . . . God, I played the TOBA from end to end. Just every place they had from New York to Texas . . . . TOBA's like any other business, you're on the stage and you do so many shows. At that time on TOBA you work – you do five, six shows a day; you got little money, but everybody was happy. I started on TOBA in Philadelphia – that's where I started from, the old Standard Theater. I first had the band in the theater. Then after they put all the live shows out, then I went on the road, traveling, and I went as far as TOBA can carry you, from Phildelphy to New Orleans. I played the Lyric Theater there – oh God – with Clara Smith and with Mamie Smith – yeah, Clara and Mamie both. I knew Clara real well, she were a lovely piano player and a lovely singer. She played piano and she sure could sing. And worked right back . . . and back again. Played in Atlanty, Georgia at the old 81 Theater. I played there about fifteen times, and at that time Tom Bailey was the head of that city. If you got to be out after nine o'clock you had to get a pass from him or you couldn't walk the streets. That's a fact – they put you in jail. Even if you worked the theater. That's right – not only Negroes – everybody. Off the street at nine o'clock. That's right, after nine o' clock at night if they catch you out they want to know what you're doin'. And you had to have a slip if you wanted to go down town to get shoes or clothes or anything. He had to write a slip – that the only way you could get anything from the city. So that's what they mean when they say that ole TOBA means Take Old Bailey's Advice. That's right, that was Bailey and his 81. But he's dead years ago. So after I left from there I headed back East and came on to Chicago. And that's where I started really – in the night club business; I started in Chicago.

We made a complete tour of theaters – TOBA theaters mostly – one-week stands. Occasionally we would be held over for a second week which was very rare in those times and we also played quite a few split weeks in the smaller towns in Ohio and different places. Sometimes we would play in the schoolhouse for three nights in one town and then perform the rest of the week in another town. After Ma had taken numerous encores the band would demonstrate their ability alone. One of our feature numbers was Old Joe Oliver's tune – the *Dippermouth Blues*; we used to do that and then we'd do a slow blues similar to the general blues that folks used to sing. And then Ma would come on and finish the programme. She always carried a unit with her – the unit included such stage stars as Evelyn Pryor and Jack Wiggins who at that time was considered the world's champion tap-dancer. All in all it was a very good show and very successful at every place we played. Some of the theaters was very small. And others were not such small theaters but as far as dressing-rooms and quarters for the performers they were very small. Most times we would have for a dressing-room just something like a chubby hole where you

Living in Chicago
Looking up West Lake towards
Desplaines and Halsted

could just slip on your main garments in and do the rest outside. They were very small and one of the worst theaters on the circuit was the Monogram on State Street, Chicago which was very bad: I mean two people couldn't hardly pass one another backstage. But then there were – well fairly nice theaters on the circuit, like the Lyric in New Orleans which was a very nice theater. All in all the conditions as far as dressing-rooms and so on was concerned wasn't too bad and the working conditions were good – we traveled by train and had a very happy time and a wonderful relationship. The audiences were run-of-the-mill audiences. Everybody really enjoyin' live entertainment and especially blues singers. And of course Ma was very popular after having made a very big hit like *Moonshine Blues* – I don't know how many records of that were sold at the time. Blues was in vogue and Ma Rainey was known as the Mother of the Blues. And there was Bessie Smith and Clara Smith. I enjoyed Clara Smith's singing very much and she was definitely one of the top fives. She was very attractive and a nice person. And there was all them Trixies and all the other Smiths – all blues singers were popular and we would draw tremendous

crowds every place we were at. That tour was my first professional job away from home and I was cravin' for new experiences and so after about three years I made a deal to exchange places with a friend of mine in Chicago, a trombonist. See we had replacement musicians from time to time. Cedric Odum he replaced Gabriel Washington in the Ma Rainey band and he was a very nice drummer and a wonderful sign painter too! In his last years he strictly painted signs. He passed I guess six or seven years ago now. He was with me on some of my records under my own name and so was his partner Lil Hardaway; she used to play with Joe Oliver too. She'd sing blues and she was a very fine pianist – very great pianist to my ideas; real jolly and a wonderful personality but she passed some time during '35. Well, so I changed with this particular trombonist Taylor who was working with a large band of about ten pieces a band which included Les Hite, George Dalton and a number of the greats of that time. So I wanted that experience and Taylor, he had never been any place so we just switched jobs by mutual consent, and it was very satisfactory with everybody and I commenced playing regularly in Chicago.

I wasn't broke
Blind Arvella Gray

After I quit the circus I did all kind of jobs and so then, I hitched to Chicago, Illinois. I got off at 92nd and Commercial Avenue, that's South Chicago there, and I was walking down the street in the main town and I met a fella who owned two restaurants – an Eyetalian fella – and he asked me did I want a job? And I told him 'Sure'. So I went there and I started working at this restaurant and he gave me eight dollars a week and my board and I peeled potatoes and washed dishes. But I quit that job after a couple of weeks because he had three waitresses – girls – and they found out I was from the South and real backwoods and no education and nothing so they started picking at me and they just scared me to death. Because I had seen certain things happen in Texas that wasn't so nice – and I didn't want them to do to me what they did in Texas. I didn't know that Chicago was different from what it was in the South at that time and so these Eyetalian girls picked at me until I was so scared I left there. So then I went to Detroit, Michigan and I got a job as a mechanic. And in my getting around I met wrongdoers, I learned how to peddle dope in all forms and I have used it to a certain degree, but I didn't get a habit but I did use some of it. But it didn't affect me because I know one time I had used some and it give me a haemorrhage at the nose and I got scared like, because I thought I was going to die so I put it down. But peddling I did. And I was gamblin', and runnin' my gamblin' joint and I got used to handlin' money, somethin' I was never trained to have. See a person has to be trained to handle money, to know what it's all about. So I was just gamblin' and so when I got broke, I wasn't broke because then I'd go out on stick-up jobs such as fillin' stations, banks – I was goin' to say a whole lot of banks but I stuck up one bank in 1930, 7 January in Detroit, Michigan, I stuck up this particular bank and then I was on the run again. It was on Brewster and Hastings Street from which I got six thousand dollars. But when I got the six thousand dollars I managed to escape from there and I went to such places as Fort Wayne, Indiana, and from there to St Louis, Missouri, and then I doubled back to Kansas City, Missouri, and right there on 18th and Vine, in a basement we used to gamble in, I lost every penny of that, and then next day I was broke and asking for a handout.

Now I believe I go 'cause I don't feel welcome here,
Now I believe I'll go 'cause I don't feel welcome here,
Says it ain't my home – I sure don't have to stay.

Say meet me in the bottom, bring my boots and shoes,
Meet me in the bottom, bring my boots and shoes,
I'm gonna leave Chicago, 'cause I got no time to lose.

Joints along Hastings Street
Hastings near Brown's Club where Big Maceo worked has been destroyed to make room for an expressway

Big instruments

Floyd Taylor

My parents come up from Tennessee in World War I because there was plenty of work up here then. Mostly people were goin' to Detroit or Chicago, Illinois, and they come here to Detroit. I guess I must have been about nine years old at the time because I was born in 1909. So I started to play piano quite young because my parents were musical and they learned me how to play. Then I heard a lot of the fellers that were playing in the joints along Hastings Street. There were lots of Willies I remember, Pinetop Willie and of course Willie Ezell and several others. Will Ezell was real good; he came from Texas I heard and he played that low-down barrelhouse blues. Charlie Davenport, which we used to call Cow Cow, was another feller that was well known in this part, he was always coming and going, didn't stay too long at any one time. That puts me in mind of another Charlie – Charlie Spand, played that *Soon This Mornin'* which was a special number of his. And I particularly remember Tupelo Slim out of Mississippi because he really was a big influence on my playin' you know. Tupelo Slim – I don't think he ever made a record and he passed many years ago, but he was real famous in Detroit. Most of the fellers had their own style of playing but they used to learn from each other too. Sometimes you could tell where a piano player came from by the way he played the blues. This type of music was played say about 1928–27, when mostly the piano players were floatin' from town to town. The piano was a big instrument then; matter-of-fact it still is – right? But this is the type of parlour blues that were played during the day – especially by one Pinetop Smith, which they called *Pinetop's Boogie Woogie*. Then the type of music that came out of St Louis was more of a shuffle rhythm they call it. Then I remember a little later on, say aroun' the last of '28 a piece that became very popular which Charlie Davenport used to play and we called it the *Cow Cow Blues* from him. And from this piece there derived another popular run-of-the-mind tune around 1929 among these hot piano players as we called them, which we called *Doodlin'*, which had a sort of a walkin' bass. Then a couple of years later there was another blues that was very popular in Detroit they called *Dupree*. So this was the kind of blues that we played in these joints. They were – well, some of them was what you might call night clubs, but mostly they were show clubs you know and strip joints. Show clubs had these freakish fellers – what they call female impersonators and some of them was very funny. And there were plain strip-and-clip joints but they all had we blues players.

Different parties around
Little Brother Montgomery

35th and State
Brother John Sellers
standing at the derelict
front of the States Theater,
Chicago. On the upper floor
was the De Luxe Café

When I got to Chicago in 1928 they mostly had jazz around. But I met quite a few piano players at that time comin' into Chicago like I was, and some of them were already livin' there of course. Well there was fellers like Jerome Carrington, Jimmy Papa Yancey, Albert Ammons, Pinetop Smith, Robert Alexander, Clarence Jones – Ole Man Clarence we used to call him – and such fellers. Later on in years I ran up against Bob Montgomery, another great piano player – I think he was some kin to Jump Jackson. So when I got to Chicago I started makin' a few records, and I recorded with Irene Scruggs at Grafton, Wisconsin for Paramount. I was livin' in Chicago but we were recordin' in Grafton out on the other side from Milwaukee. I made a lot of numbers with her – *Good Meat Grinder*, *Got to Get Mine in Front*, *Sweet Patuni* – and all different numbers like that but I disremember how many. Then I come back to Chicago after that, but that was when I made the first *Vicksburg Blues* and *No Special Rider*. At that time I was a singer. I used to sing pretty good I reckon but I don't like it no more like I did then:

Now rider, rider, rider, Mama tell me where you been so long,
Now rider, rider, rider, tell me where you been so long,
I ain't had no lovin' baby since you been gone.

Now I hate to hear the little *Katy* when she blows,
Now when I hate to hear the l'il *Katy Adams* when it blows,
It makes me wonder, Mama, makes me wanna go.

Lord I ain't got me no special rider now,
Lord I ain't got me no plumb good rider now,
It seems like my rider she tryin' to quit me now.

Now the big bell keep ringin' and the li'l bell she sadly tones,
Well, the big bell ringin' and the little bell sadly tones,
And I'm lonely, lonely, lonely, and a long long way from home.

Lord I wonder, do she ever call my name?
Lord and I wonder, do she ever call my name?
Now if you ever felt like me I swear you'd say the same.

No more coloured

Lonnie Johnson

We used to play at house parties in those days – I used to play them at the old Angeles Building and round at the Grand Hotel on 31st and State. Different parties around – house parties and rent parties we had at 4048 Indiana, 5758 South State, 5009 Vincennes . . . different other places we played and we played blues and boogies only at those parties. We had a guy named Forty-Five and he used to play parties all the time.

At that time 1929 it was hard to get a job anywhere and I didn't start in with that night club work right away, least, not in Chicago. I was with Putney Dandridge for a long time and we had thirty-three dollars between us and we were makin' for Chicago but we couldn't make it so that's what run us into Cleveland, Ohio round on the Lake there. And we were lucky enough to go into the Heatwave there – and it's *still* going, it's a big club, one of the biggest there is there, it's in the Majestic Hotel. So we were playing blues there 'cause that's all go in any place, that's blues. If you don't know some blues you might just as well forget it. You can play popular songs, anything, all night – but somebody's going to ask you, 'Play me some blues.' I don't care what they bring out, it'll live for a while but it finally disappears and they're right back to the normal, basic blues. So we played a couple of numbers at the Heatwave and Miss Ruth, she went to the head of the broadcasting station and she gave us a contract. So that's where we started, in 1929, WATM. And we had everything sewed up, but Putney broke it up. We were there four months . . . then, so he seemed to have female troubles . . . as usual – a lady. She kep' on writin' to him, she was so lonesome; so he wrote back to her in Albany, New Jersey. Then when he went to her and he got there he didn't find her, she had gone off with somebody else then. He didn't come back because he had broken the contract. And Miss Ruth, she never did hire anybody else: no more Colored on that broadcasting station. We were the only two in all the years she had. And we were making nice money at $400 a week! And we only did fifteen minutes, twice a week! That's good. So I was back on my own again. So I tried to make it in Chicago but I had to quit the music business. I worked for a firm makin' railroad ties in Galesburg, Illinois – that's right! Those ties weigh as much as me – 180 lbs! So then I went to Peoria, Illinois, that's about sixty miles from Galesburg, and I work' in a steel foundry there. Play the blues at nights. . . . That's true – I've done all kinds of work, even been a coal miner – oh, God yes, I done everything! So right now I'm a janitor at the Ben Franklin Hotel. So, after that – I hit out for Chicago again.

The way I got blinded

Blind Arvella Gray

I went back to Peoria, Illinois, where I got shot at on 13th day of September 1930. See I got in an argument with a feller over a girl, her name was Ardella, and he said, 'I won't fight you, but I'll shoot you.' See by me gamblin' I went away from home and when I got back this feller Lamar Kilgore was in the house and they had the door locked. Part of it was glass and part was wood. Well I tried to put the key in the lock and it wouldn't unlock so then I knocked on the door and Ardella say, 'Just a moment!' So whilst I was waitin' I struck a match on the door facin' and was lightin' a cigarette. And when I put the match up to my face they could see the flash of the match through the glass and they just blasted away at me, Lamar did. And then, when he did shoot me he said, 'Get on away from the door or I'm gonna shoot out there.' So I said, 'What the devil do you mean, you gonna shoot? You done shot half of my face off now!' – and not realizin' I was blind. So then I stepped off the porch and walked a block and a half to the police station and I told the police, 'Lamar Kilgore done shot me.' So he said, 'Well, you stay right here,' and told one of the citizens come from Chillicothe to stay with me. And I told him whilst the police was gone to get the doctors and the ambulance to carry me down to the river which was a block from the police station, so I could wash my face. So he carried me down by the arm and I'm mad now all the time because the guy done shot me, and I might have been more mad about the man being with my woman. I don't know now, but I was pretty tore up. So when I got there I just decided, 'I'm gonna commit suicide,' and I jumped in the water and the water was only about three feet deep and about that time the police had got back with the doctors and everything and pulled me out. So the citizen that carried me there he was locked up in jail for about three weeks because they say he was tryin' to drown me to get rid of me so I wouldn't talk against the other feller. But I was tryin' to drown myself on my own. So Lamar got fourteen years for shootin' me, and that's the way I got blinded and that's the way my fingers got shot off. And after that I been a street singer ever since. I had it pretty rough when I started but I said, 'I'm not gonna let nothin' beat me down.' After me bein' blinded it was somethin' new to me and I were tryin' to find my place and how to manage myself. And I went to church a few months and that kinda bowled me and the people would kinda say, 'Well, here's a blind man, sit him in the corner so he won't get in the way,' so they just put me over in the corner to collect cobwebs. So I said, 'I'm not satisfied with that, I'm worried and all upset.' So in 1933 I bought a guitar for two-and-a-half and I started to monkeyin' around with it. And I spent two or three years goin' roun' tryin' to get people to teach me to play it. And every time I went around they say, 'You cain't play no guitar 'cause you ain't no fingers to chord it right.' So I was just determined to play it so finally I met one blind feller who said, 'Well, maybe this idea will do.' So he tuned it up in Sevastapool, what he called 'cross-c' or something, I don't know anything about it. So then they say, 'Well you gonna have a problem because you don't know how to read or write, you cain't read braille and you cain't read music,' so I just started from ear like that. I just started to banging away. And I used to get more quarters for moving out the front of places than I did for stoppin' and playin' for them. They say, 'Here's a quarter, half-a-dollar, will you carry that noise on a little further.' I play with a bottleneck on my finger from a wine bottle. People years ago they used to have a system where they have a knife in their hand, held it some kind of way in their fingers and slide it up and down the strings. So I used to use a plain glass like you drink water out of. But then I had to lay my guitar down, so then I hit upon the bottleneck and I thought maybe this will do. Well, I come here to Chicago with one quarter in a tin cup and started to hustlin'. When the weather's good I play on the streets and in the winter I get on the street cars and make my money hustlin' on them.

A Quarter in a Tin Cup
Blind Arvella Gray begging
on the corner of Halsted and
Maxwell, Chicago

Cryin' strings
Daddy Stovepipe

You can figger it out; I'm ninety years old now, so I don't know exactly when I was born at but you can figger it. I been playin' on Maxwell for about ten years off an' on – I reckon. Playin' by myself. I'm a what they call a one-man band. Don't need no other fellers 'cause I play my own guitar and I got this harp on this rack round my neck so's I cin play it, and I stomp with my foot. So I jest set my box on the corner of Maxwell and Peoria and I'm a whole band. Some of us did have a band at one time, me and some of these other fellers. Tom Stewart, he's playin' trumpet on the street now and Eddie Hines who's playin' that ole rub-board. Eddie Hines's ole lady was burned to death in his house right here on Maxwell, he's had plenty trouble. Me and them had a li'l fallin' out but it don't make no difference 'cause I don't need no one playin' with me. I got lots of nice numbers like *The Tennessee Waltz* and *South of the Border*; play that one better than those Mexican fellers. Yeah, play the blues too – if you wanna. Hear them cryin' strings; that's when I slide 'em across, I make 'em cry the blues. And I got them Christian tunes too. Cause there's Christians you know, both white and black.

That Ole Rub-board Eddie Hines – Pork Chops – plays washboard and Tom Stewart, trumpet, in a Chicago street band while the guitar player rents current from the apartment above for his electric instrument

Best music ever was played

Blind James Brewer

When I was down in Mississippi there I didn't have one of these electric guitars, just one ole plain guitar. I heard them on the radio but I had never seen one to know what I was lookin' at. So when I came to Chicago some fellers was sittin' on the street there playin' as usually, down on Maxwell and Peoria and Sangaman and Newberry and all of them down on Maxwell Street – or some of them – was playin' these electric guitars and I thought that was the best music ever was played on a guitar. So by me never having seen them and by never having been round there I went up to the fellers – ask them to play a piece – they did. I got hold of the thing and it sound good but I didn't know what the name of this thing was from which the sound was comin' through, this amplifier. I wanted to ask but I didn't want to act like I didn't know anything – which I didn't know. So anyway, I bought a guitar and when I found out I put a pick-up on the outside of it and run it through one of those cheap amplifiers – don't cost over sixty-one dollars and twenty cents and that was the cheapest one that I could get and it taken me a couple of months to get that. But when I had got it I thought I had somethin' and I went around blowin' my top as usually. And I run up against a feller *did* have somethin', and I, blowin' my top says, 'Oh man, you ain't got nothin', let me show you what I got', and I had a guitar had one of those rubber pick-ups attached right back on the strings, quite naturally didn't have no sound to it. I went around from tavern to tavern, didn't go to church, and run on to this particular feller and he carried me home with him and he said, 'Well, you hook up yours and let me hear.' So I'm around beefin' with the women – quite a few women there at the time, waitin' to hear somethin' that I could play pretty good. So I commenced to playin' and they heard it and they all laughed at me because they knew electric guitars and I didn't. The man that had one, he made fun of me, which I didn't care for 'cause I thought I was gettin' some place. So he says, ' Now you played your guitar for me, now let me play my guitar for you.' And he goes back there in a room, his bedroom where he keeps it at and brings it out and hooks it up and he played. . . . Well, it did make me look quite cheap after all, I was gettin' nowhere. So I stood there and listened to him play and he asked me to play some more but I wouldn't because I hadn't anything to play *on*; just somethin' I botched up on my own. So I went and bought an amplifier right there on Jackson and Wabash and I owed a feller, blind feller I knew, some money, so I said, 'Would you take this ole amplifier for the money I owed you?' And he said, 'Yeah.' So after I got the amplifier I did the same thing, beefin' and goin' on, woofin'. Come to find I *still* ain't had nothin'. There's some guys here got better than I had.

Their only hope
Brother John Sellers

My aunt, Mrs Carrie Ferguson, carried me from Greenville, Mississippi, to Chicago in 1933. She'd been visiting my mother in New Orleans and she heard about me bein' in Greenville so she stopped off there, and didn't like the place I was livin' at and carried me to Chicago. Of course it was pretty hard in Chicago at that time and people were very poor on the South Side. Then jobs opened up, some sort of jobs anyway, and some were able to get work and the rest were on relief – assistance you know. Some of the churches had what they call 'thrift shops'; most of those churches were like Father Divine or Daddy Grace was but the Baptist churches didn't have that. But it was an idea for to help the poor because certain people like Ella Lucy Smith who was a big figure in Chicago and people who'd got rich homes would listen to broadcasts and they would give you – aw, sometimes they would give you shoes or clothes. And then you give them different things that you may give away to the poor or people who were less fortunate than you were and it would help them out. And sometimes you would sell it for a quarter or a dime – what have you, fifteen cents. If they didn't have the dollar or two dollars to pay for it, they'd pay the quarter or whatever they could afford. So it help them on. And policy – you know, it fed a lot of people during the Depression days in Chicago. Because that was their only hope. A lot of people wrote policy for their livin'. You know they had policy stations, they had different wheels like the 'Red Devil', the 'Wisconsin', the 'Green Gable' – they had all kinds of wheels. They had three drawin's – a.m. p.m. and midnight, and many people would win $2.50, three dollars, five . . . some didn't win at all but this helped many people even though many people got rich on this type of numbers because it wasn't legal. It made a lot of people believe in policy game, because I know my step-grandmother, we couldn't make her believe that policy wasn't true because she always had a nickel or a dime on it – she didn't care which way it came. It was illegal because it was forbidden to play it and it was run by syndicates as most rackets are run, but they played it anyhow – you know, slip around and play it. At one time it was kind of wide open because Ida Kelly had a place on Garfield Boulevard and it had all kinds of numbers to play, dice, crap shooting. But the Mayor cut that out because people began to kick.

Down so long
J. B. Lenoir

I been down so long, being down do not worry me no more,
I been down so long, being down do not worry me no more,
I'm goin' pack my suitcase, an' cross the way you know, I'll go.

Some people have their troubles, but I have been havin'
    mine all my life,
Some people have their troubles, I've had mine all my life,
Well one day I will be lucky, Oh Lord, before I die.

One day I was sittin' down here; I was broke and din't have no money and I said to myself, 'Oh, Lord, I haven't got no money, oh Lord what *is* I gonna do?' So my mother she 'ceased oh, about

My Luck Will Change
Numbers Books, Policy Dream Books, Jinx Removing Bath, Money Drawing Powder, Power Incense and John the Conqueror Root are among these items for sale in a *gris-gris* (charm) store, New Orleans

eighteen years ago and she came to me in my sleep about ten years ago when I was livin' on 1813 39th East and she give me a number to play on the 'Buffalo' – that's the time when the 'Buffalo' was goin' you know. And she told me, she said, 'You get up in the mornin' and put this number on the " Buffalo".' And so, in the mornin' I wakes up and I had done forgot that number, the last one: I could only think of two of them. So it rocks on about ten years until about four months ago I was sitting down here again, didn't have no money and I said to myself, 'Lord, I needs some money!' So I lays on down to sleep and whatever this thing was, this voice, I could see the numbers just as plain . . . and the number was on this 'Panama'. And this voice told me, 'J. B., you play this number 45–25–35,' so I turns round and I says to myself, 'You better get on up and write these numbers down so as you won't forget them like you did on 1813 East 39th Street.' And so then I raises up and writes the numbers down and goes back to bed – I guess it must have been about four o'clock in the mornin'. I didn't have no money so I had to call down here on Vermont and get some money from my cousin to play it, and the same way I put the numbers in that's the way I called it. You know, it's a funny thing how things will happen to human beings. That number sure came up.

A pretty rough boy

Shaky Jake

When I came here I was about seven years old, from Ellis, Arkansas, but I was raised in Chicago. When I was a kid I used to work in news stands, drug stores, wash dishes and did all of that. Then I used to polish cars, work at gas stations, fix flats and then I done a little chauffeurin' too. I liked to play poker, shoot the bones, pitty pat and I played all games – used to shoot pool lots; got so good I had to give some guys balls off. And I'd play poker anywhere, any place you know. Go to houses or different clubs and play poker; give parties myself at my home, play poker. Well I quit playin' poker 'cause it took a guy too long you know. To bet, you know, he had to have aces, kings or somethin' backed up, so I quit playin' it, start to shootin' dice. I never did use nothin' crooked, I was just good in the wrists. And so I know how to even-roll the dice, pad-roll, combination of the dice . . . and the boys used to holler, 'Shake 'em Jake, shake the dice!' and so I would give them a little click – click, click, click you know. Never did shake them, just hittin' them together and the boys used to argue, 'Shake 'em Jake,' and so they just started to callin' me Shaky Jake. I didn't play Georgia Skin, I was scared of the cup you know – all together, or three together and put one in the bottom, see – so I always borrowed the cup. And I wouldn't mind playin' anyway if I could play with a lot of guys who were slick because they would watch one another so that nobody would do nothin' you know. So I was a professional dice-shooter, poker-player for fifteen years. I used to get drunk, I used to drink a lot of whisky, brandy called Forbidden Fruit – I used to be a pretty rough boy. Well every time I'd win a lot of money I'd tip off from the boys to keep from splittin' with them and I'd get stuck up – and so finally I beat a guy for about, oh, – $800 and another guy tol' him, say, 'You know Shaky Jake he done somep'n to you. He put somep'n crooked on you.' And so the guy met me and said, 'Gimme the money,' and I said, 'I'm not goin' to give you none,' and he said 'Well, I'm gonna take it.' I said, 'No, you're not gonna take money away from me,' and so he pulled out a li'l ole pistol you know, a .32. I said, 'Well, you'd better put that water gun back in your pocket before you skeet water all over yourself,' – you know I thought he was kiddin'. And he was cryin' – I see a little water comin' from his eye so I got kinda scared then and I said a few wrong words to him and so I turned around and he shot me in the side. So I ran off – he still didn't get the money – so I goes to the hospital and they puts me in jail! They puts me in the Bridewell Hospital and then that cost me $10 to get out on bond. The guy – he's walkin' the streets, they didn't hit him. So after that, well, I picked some guys up and told one he could play guitar, and I got his brother – he was workin' at a steel mill – for my bass player. So we started playin' for $8 a night, we didn't have no drums at that time. They was gettin' $8 – I wasn't gettin' nothin'! Because I was shootin' dice in the back; I was takin' all the craps so I was makin' the money. So even the boss wasn't payin' us – I was payin' them out of my own pocket but was makin' good money in the game. So finally my harmonica-blower – I wasn't even blowin' a harp at that time, see – my harmonica-player, he was late, been to see a fight. And I had been stealin' his harps, tryin' you know, to learn how to play. And so when he come in I was wailin'. So I told him, 'Well, you're fired!' and I reached in my pocket and paid him off, and I been playin' ever since.

Very Poor on the South Side
Black housing behind South State Street, Chicago

They ganged him

Lonnie Johnson

First club I played in Chicago was the Three Deuces on North State with Baby Dodds on the drums and after that – lots of them. That's right I played a couple of places on East 51st Street. I played at the Boulevard Lounge there on East 51st Street and then at Square's at 931 West 51st Street – I was there about five years, something like that. Then I went into the Flame Club at 3020 South Indiana. I tell you who I was workin' with. Roosevelt Sykes. Workin' right on Indiana. And Sonny Boy Williamson was workin' just around the corner. So we would alternate on our intermission time and go round to the Plantation Club and keep him company and play with him, and on his intermission time he'd come round to the club where I was workin' at, place called the Flame. So he just come round, and then he went back, went round the corner. He said, 'Well, I'll see you after a while, when you get off. Come on round to the club.' I say, 'O.K.' And about five minutes later a feller come round and say he's dead. And we thought he was kiddin' you know? He had seventeen holes in his head with an ice-pick. They ganged him. He was 'bout one of the finest fellers I know. They never did find out who killed him. At least they knowed but nobody would tell anything. Sonny Boy – I'll tell you what he did. He worked to help the people with somethin' to eat and somethin' to drink. When pay-day come

he didn't have anything – he had no pay-day. He was just good – he bought everything they wanted to drink; everything they wanted to eat. He was good to the crowd around him. That's all he did, was work for them. And why they would kill a great guy like that I don't know but they did. Don't know today who killed him. Well . . . a little later on I went on work for Ruby Gatewood on West Lake and North Artesian Avenue. Ruby Gatewood's Tavern – only we called it the Gate. There was always a bunch of blues singers at Ruby's . . . well she had Kokomo Arnold after he finished at the Club Claremont on 39th and Indiana . . . and Big Bill was there, and Memphis Minnie. But they wouldn't stay too long you know . . . Ruby Gatewood was a hard person to work for. That's right. You work all right – but try and get your money! Memphis Slim was the only one could get it, he'd go behind the bar and get it. Go to the cash register and just take it. He was the only one would do that. The union got behind her – and still didn't make no difference. She still wouldn't pay, that's all. So I worked for Gaston on West Lake. I worked a year for him at $105 a week! And he paid every week, he was a great guy. He's still in business. He don't have music but he still has the same crowd he had on Lake – they follered him out there to 79th and Wentworth. Great crowd.

Raise a big mess
Brother John Sellers

Memphis Minnie – really those Blue Monday Parties in those days were too much! She was a very funny woman and she always wore those great big ear-rings . . . and she was a very fine guitarist. But she was so stern sometimes and Memphis Minnie would always say, 'I drink anywhere I please!' Cause Minnie was used to a rough life. She had a rough life and she lived rough. You know they don't talk about Memphis Minnie like they do Bessie Smith but she was a great artist and she knew the guitar and play it well and she used to be the tops. With all her greatness and her songs and her Blue Monday parties that she gave she was still a singer to be remembered. Big Bill would never do anything unless'n he called Minnie. 'Let me call Minnie on the 'phone and see what she say about it,' he'd say. And she'd say, 'Aw . . . well, all right Bill . . . I'll come over. . . I'll see . . .' in her gruff way. But she would come because she was big in her heart even though she could be rough. You know, blues singers on the South Side work in small spots and they can be very tough. And I can remember especially Lil Green, and she had brought out a song 'You had plenty money 1922, let other women make a fool of you . . .' and Big Bill did a lot of backing for her and wrote a lot of songs for her. But she was tough too, like Minnie. She wouldn't take nothin' because she had been shoved and pushed around so. And I'll never forget what Alberta Hunter said to me one time: you know she worked in a place called the Sunset on 35th and State years ago, and she said when she was workin' in this club she met so many rough people; pimps and the like would come up to her till she found to be a lone woman in the place you had to be rough and tough in a place and act as they did even if you weren't as tough as they were. That's what it was like with most of the singers here. Of course, Big Bill was different, he always did have a modest way about him – he never did raise his voice any. Tampa Red, Big Maceo – don't say nothin' to them! They would raise a big mess! They would want to square it up all over the place. Ready to fight – especially Tampa Red – he used to be a mess in *his* day!

If you want to do jazz
Sunnyland Slim

I had so much ups and downs at one time. Every time I set up a little bit somethin'd go wrong and every time I cultivate a little money and things go to happenin' and the women that I been dealin' with been eatin' black-eyed peas and neck-bones – they turn around and order steaks and want to go out for dinner and all things like that. I was workin' with Lonnie Johnson at the time, but nothin' would go right for me and it seemed to me that the Devil is a busy man . . . so I made a blues about it:

> You know the devil is a busy man, looks like he stays on
>   my trail,
> Yes the Devil is a busy man, boys he stays on my trail,
> And no matter what I try the Devil he gets right in my way.
>
> You know the Devil's got power and don't you think he ain't,
> Yes the devil's got power and boys, don't you think he ain't.
> Well if you ain't mighty careful he will lead you to your grave.
>
> I'm goin' over, I have decided to change my way,
> You know I'm goin' over, I have decided to change my ways,
> But no matter what I try the Devil gets right in my way.

That made me feel better about it. The blues make you think good; the blues is the way you feel and the blues make you feel good. Cause blues is a feelin' and you can't be jazzy with the blues. If you want to do jazz, do jazz, that's the way I feel about it. But you can't get jazzy with the blues. And at certain parts of the night the blues sound better, and there's a certain crowd, a certain class of people make the blues seem better. I don't know the hows about it but there's a certain spot there and the blues'll hit it and make you feel better. I don't care who he is, it'll move somethin' about you.

I met fellers
Muddy Waters

Come on up
Little Walter Jacobs

Big Bill had been around a long time in Chicago when I come up in '43 so he helped me to get my start. Of course I wasn't playin' music for a livin' then – I got a job at the Chicago Mill – paper mill, with those fork-lift trucks; and then I got a li'l job workin' for a firm that made parts for radios. That was wartime then and they needed a lot of those pieces I guess. So you know, I met fellers and played at house parties and things – everybody give house parties. I had a few of my folks here because Otis – he was goin' on about seventeen or eighteen then, but he was here with his folks and he's my half-brother. And then my uncle Joe was here, the one that gave me my first electric guitar. He's from Mississippi too and he was my nach'l uncle because his mother was my grandmother Della Jones: she was my grandmother on my mother's side and his name was Joe Brant. So he had been in Chicago a long time and everybody played those electric guitars and he told me I ought to play one and he bought me one. Then Big Bill introduced me to Sylvio and I played at Sylvio's along with Sonny Boy Williamson and old Tampa Red and Doctor Clayton and all those fellers. Doctor Clayton come up with Robert Junior you know, and Sunnyland used to play for him. All his folks got burned up in a fire in St Louis I heard and he was a funny kind of guy, always drunk and couldn't work dates. He come up from St Louis and he passed about '46 I think it was. A lot of those guys come up from St Louis – like Robert Nighthawk, I played a quite a bit with him; he's a good blues man. And of course there's old St Louis Jimmy – now Jimmy's *old*-time, and he writes great blues still, and he lives with me at my home. Well I met all these guys and I got me a rockin' band. Had Little Walter on the harp – I picked him up in Chicago 'cause he was playin' on the streets then. He's *real* tough, Little Walter, and he's had it hard. Got a slug in his leg right now! But he's the best damn harp player there is.

My home's in Alexandria, Louisiana, and I started in to playin' the harp when I was eight years old behind Sonny Boy Williams. No, I wasn't playin' *with* him but I heard his records. Then I went to New Orleans and I played in spots and I guess I was about twelve-thirteen years old; come up to Monroe, Louisiana, and played at the Liberty Inn for a spell. I was just on my own, playin' where I could get me some work. . . beat around Helena, Arkansas, for a few years and come on up to St Louis . . . Chicago. That was in 1947. Well I didn't find it too easy then; I played mostly in the streets for about three years . . . played on Maxwell Street and places. And Big Bill took me up and then Muddy Waters. I made a couple of tunes for a feller had a record company right on Maxwell there but they didn't do much; didn't even pay me for 'em. I got my real break with Muddy and then I had my own band at the Club Zanzibar and Ricky's Show Lounge. Yeah, Little Walter and His Night Cats and Little Walter and His Jukes I call 'em. And right now I'm doin' all right; played a one-nighter in New Orleans; flew up to Cincinnati, played a one-nighter there, come on up to Chicago.

He take me as his son

J. B. Lenoir

You take . . . I always said, when I growed up to be a man I was just goin' to leave and got to go to town. I have had a lot of relations here in Chicago and I just wanted to be around them. The way they do's you down there in Mississippi it ain't what a man should suffer, what a man should go through. And I said, after I seen the way they treat my daddy I never was goin' to stand that no kind of way. So I just worked as hard as I could for to get that money to get away, and be workin' and playin' music too. So I goes up North and when I gets to Chicago I started to work at Swift's, meat packin', and I still be workin' and playin' too. And the first person I ran into playin' here was Big Bill Broonzy. He was playin' here out on Lake Street, in fact the number was 2254 at Sylvio's. And Big Bill he had a guy on drums by the name of Arthur and *he* was the first one to introduce me to Big Bill and his guitar. So Big Bill he take me as his son and I played with him just as long as I wanted to play. And the next person I went around with was Memphis Minnie. She used to give cocktail parties you know – those Blue Monday parties at the Gate you know, and I actually found she would ask me to play a number for her. And the next person was Muddy Waters – he was playin' at a little place over there at 3609 Wentworth; he was playin' there and Little Walter was playin' with him. Walter, he wasn't doin' no recordin' at that time. And St Louis Jimmy, he was over with Muddy, and I used to go there and we'd have ourselves a wonderful time. So I had a style of my own and I used to go to movin' on the flo' there; rockin' and weavin' and Muddy, he latched on to that. He didn't play guitar no more so he could shout and move aroun'. But that's really my own partic'lar style and now this Chuck Berry and this white boy Elvis Presley and everybody got it. Well, then about ten year ago I formed my own band which I called J. B. and His Bayou Boys and I had Sunnyland Slim on piano and Alfred Wallace he played the drums. So later on Joe Montgomery become my regular pianist, he's Little Brother's *brother* and he's a very fine blues pianist only you don't hear too much about him. He's still my pianist – at least, I'm out of work right now, but I don't get worried too much because I reckon some of the place'll – you know, open up in the fall. So everytime I *do* get bluesy and worried I play this number of Maceo's and that make me feel better:

Oh Lordy, Lord, oh Lordy, Lord,
It hurt me so bad, for us to part,
But someday baby, I ain't gonna worry my life any more.

You on my min', every place I go,
How much I love you nobody knows,
But someday babe, I ain't gonna worry my life any more.

This is my story, this is all I got to say,
Bye-bye baby, and I don't care what you do,
But someday baby, I ain't gonna worry my life any more.

Places Will Open up
J. B. Lenoir and Eddie Boyd,
Mississippi blues singers living
in Chicago, waited for their
luck to change

Five long years
Eddie Boyd

I come up here and did all kinds of work and follered aroun' with differen' guys and after a while I met this feller Lester Melrose who was a talent scout for Victor. And I got a few sessions with Sonny Boy Williams' and recorded with him and with Big Maceo. I had a couple of sessions with Big Maceo after he had a stroke and couldn't play too well with his right hand – he was a real swell feller and a real good artist too. Then after I made a couple of sessions with him and I made some recordin's with Jazz Gillum. That was before I started out by myself, and then in the last of '52 I made this recordin' of *Five Long Years* and that's when I made my little name.

If you ever been mistreated, well you know jus' what I'm
talkin' about,
If you ever been mistreated, you know jus' what I'm talkin'
about,
I worked five long years for one woman, she had the nerve
to put me out.

I got a job in a steel mill, a-truckin' steel like a slave,
Five long years, every Friday I went straight home with all
of my pay,
Have you ever been mistreated? – You know what I'm
talkin' about,
I worked five long years for one woman and she had the
nerve to put me out.

I finally learn' a lesson I should've known a long while ago,
The next woman I marry must work and bring me some
dough,
I've been mistreated, you know jus' what I'm talkin' about,
I worked five long years for one woman and she'd the nerve
to put me out.

I made *Five Long Years* on J.O.B. label and then I went right on with Chess and from there to Bea & Baby and from there to Oriole. But I haven't had a big record out now for about a year and a half. See the field is so full of new artists and so many different types of records that you have to have a really hot record out that's really movin' to keep touring a lot now. Because a record don't last too long now – about six months is about the limit for a big record, so I'm gonna go and try to get a big one out. Because these days, if you ain't got a record that's movin' you ain't doin' nothin'.

I didn't write a blues
St Louis Jimmy

I was getting along pretty good; singing with Muddy Waters and Sunnyland and Eddie Boyd and all those fellers. Nothin' big but makin' my way, and I was writin' a lot of blues for Muddy. Then I had this accident see, in '57, 17 March. Me and Eddie Boyd – Boyd made *Five Long Years* – we were together and we were goin' to Kenosha, Wisconsin, and a truck was the cause of the whole accident. He lost control of the truck and we went over to the left of the road – it was a dual highway. Then we ran into a tree. And that feller left the scene of the accident. I had a broken foot, a broken leg, I had to have a plate put in my knee. I had to have two operations on my knee, so therefore I'm walkin' pretty good but still I have a stiff leg. And he had three broken ribs, Eddie Boyd did, and eye – he was cut over the eye. And a broken foot. Well, I didn't write a blues about it . . . Eddie Boyd did, he made a blues on it, but I didn't. Since then I haven't got around so much but I'm still workin' and I still sing with Muddy. But there's lots of young fellers comin' up so we older blues singers sort of move back.

I put on a show

Shaky Jake

I was playin' at Sol's place; he had a little place called The Congo Village. It was on 55th and Ingleside. So I was waitin' for him on a weekend and he came in on Monday and he said, 'Shaky, I want you at The Beehive.' I said, 'Oh man . . . the balls . . .' – you know. He said, 'Yeah, I want you at The Beehive Wednesday night.' I said, 'Oh.' I thought he was tryin' to make a fool out of me or somep'n, 'cause you know I don't suppose no one plays The Beehive with the blues. A big-shot joint you know; well there was Bud Powells and Thenolius Monks and all them was there. And so this guy called up – I think it was Monks – and say he couldn't make it so I had to take his gig. And that's the most money I made in my life in one night – playing *music*, you know. But I thought Sol was just jivin' me so I went on home, sat aroun' the house and I tol' my mother, I say, 'You know what, Sol tol' me he want me to work at The Beehive.' Mama say, 'Oh, is you crazy? You know you ain't goin' in no Beehive and playin' no harp and singin' the blues! You just forget it, the man's tryin to make a fool out of you.' So I went on the beer and went to sleep and so about 8.30 Sol called up and asked me what time I'd be down. He said he wanted me there at ten o'clock; he said he wasn't kiddin'. So that tol' me to get the boys together but when I got there it was twelve o'clock – 'cause I could've called the boys in time but I thought he was kiddin' me. I knowed I ain't got no business in The Beehive. So anyway, I was playin' there – ladies come in there with them little poodle dogs you know, and I had an extra harp . . . I let the dog blow the harp! I mean I put on a show; it was pretty good I mean. The first night and pretty good. I was kinda scared 'cause I ain't never played for that kinda people in my life before, see, and so after that I went back to the Congo Village. So Sol, he put me in business and I worked for him for a year and a half and so finally I run out of jobs, so I called up the Union Hall. Well I asked them, 'What about a job – I ain't got no job.' They say, 'We'll get you a job.' So they got me a job – out at Leo's place out at Lime and Lake. That's a white folks place, but this guy he tol' me I'm supposed to play it. So I said, 'Now *they're* tryin' to make a fool out of me too.' I ain't never played for all-white before in my life, see. So I thought they wanted that merry-go-round stuff, you know, hillbilly. Course, I couldn't play that – I don't know none of 'em; all I knowed was *Sixteen Tons* by

this guy called Tennessee Ernie. And so that's all I know how to sing. So I went out there and give an audition and he liked it. And so I was out there for about four months until the people started runnin' me away you know. Guys call me different names and every time I get ready to go, a guy would throw bricks at the boys in the band and get at them and all that kind of stuff. So I quit.

Blowin' a Harp Shaky Jake played both 'crossed' and chromatic harmonica

They don't mean nothin'
James Cotton

You know I've been pretty lucky, because I come up to Chicago in 1954 and went right in to play with Muddy Waters. I was only nineteen then and I've been playin' with him ever since. Muddy is a wonderful guy to work with and the way he sings he really brings them down. He hasn't played much guitar for the past few years – doesn't need to, because Pat Hare is a terrific guitar player and Jimmy Rogers and other guys have played in the band. And when Muddy starts to hollerin' he doesn't need a guitar ! Well I joined the band right after Little Junior Wells – he come in when Little Walter lit out on his own. But I'd been playin' harmonica a long while before then – about nine years because I started when I was ten years old or so, playin' on the streets. Then when I was just about twelve years old I was playin' regularly – you might say professionally – at least I was makin' my way. I'd been raised on a farm – my folks had a farm in Tunica, Mississippi, which is about forty miles out from Memphis on Highway 61. Well I cut out from home when I was ten, when I started playin' harmonica. Went up to Memphis and across the River to West Memphis, Arkansas. That's where I met up with this boy Rice Miller – well

Muddy Waters Sings over WOPA
Pat Hare plays second guitar, James Cotton plays harmonica, broadcasting from the Club Tay May

he wasn't no boy 'cause he was well over forty then. You know he's from Mississippi too – Glendora. Well he just knocked me out the way he played and he looked after me and I played second harp with him, and we had Willie Love on piano. Fact I played drums for Willie Love on *Nelson Street*. Then I had my own band and I'd been playin' with Howlin' Wolf too out in West Memphis and that's when I met Pat Hare and he joined me in my little group. I made that *Cotton Crop Blues* for Sun then

> Ain't gonna raise no mo' cotton, I'll tell you the reason
> why I says so,
> Ain't gonna raise no mo' cotton, tell you the reason why I
> says so,
> Well you don't get nothin' for your cotton and your seed's
> so dog-gone low.

> Well raisin' good cotton crop's just like a lucky man
> shootin' dice,
> Raisin' good cotton crops is just like a lucky man shootin' dice,
> Work all the summer to make your cotton, fall comes and
> still ain't no price.

> I've ploughed so hard baby, till corns have got all over my
> hands,
> I ploughed so hard baby till I got corns all over my hands,
> I wanna tell you people it ain't nothin' for a poor farmin' man.

I was just about sixteen then but like I say, I'd been raised on a farm and I knew about these things. And that record did pretty good. I made some sides with Memphis Willie Nix too about that time. Later on he come up to Chicago too. Of course blues like that don't go in Chicago; they don't mean nothin' to the people who comes to Smitty's. It's not their kind of blues you see. But whatever it is, it's all blues to me. I never did want to do anything else or play anything else and Muddy's is a blues band, period. They don't come better than that, so I'm happy doin' what I'm doin' here.

Hey! Hey! Hey! He's Back Magic Sam returns to the Club Tay May on West Roosevelt. Muddy Waters and Buddy Guy play regularly until 4 a.m.

I had my break

Willie Nix

One time I had it real good – you know, I had my own band in Memphis and we played some rockin' numbers. Had a ball in those days. That was oh, about ten years ago I guess. So I made it for Chicago, tried my luck there. It was a bit hard goin' at first but I started playin' one night a week at Smitty's Corner, you know, where Muddy Waters had his band? Well he used to go over and play a one-nighter at Gary, Indiana, so that gave me a chance and I held that one-night spot down. Then I had my break; my real break come when Muddy Waters went to England, went on that trip. The band broke up for a while or somethin' – maybe went on tour; anyway I had Smitty's to myself then, and I really packed 'em in! Oh man . . . . But it's been a bit tough of late. You know, I lost that job, played a few clubs on Wentworth and Rush and Lake – did the rounds. So then I guess my dice didn't play so I decided I'd cut out. I'm on my way out to the West Coast now. Monroe ain't my home.

The Dice Didn't Play
In Monroe, Louisiana, Willie Nix
wearing second-hand pants, breaks
his hoboing trip, from Chicago to
California

We'll make it

Ernest Roy

I don't belong in Louisiana – it's just that the rattler I was on brought me here! So I had to stop off and scrape up a little loot you know; I mean you gotta eat and I cain't give many pounds away! But man, ain't this a hell of a hole? Monroe! They ain't even heard of radio here, I'm tellin' you. So I'm gonna catch me a fast rattler and try and make Bakersfield, California. Get there in time for the pea crops if I work it right.

I used to play one of those twelve-stringers – git-tar. I just about busted it up though. I give it to a feller who wanted to try and play it. Don't know right now where it went. Anyway I've got an electric guitar now and I'm workin' hard on that. Me and a bunch of fellers in Clarksdale have got this little band; we've got bass guitar, and drums and one guy's got a tenor sax, one's got an alto. And I play lead. So we're rehearsin' – fact we got a rehearsal tonight and we'd really like for you to hear it. You know there's lots of fellers have gone up North from here and they're big shots now, playin' blues. Most of the good ones have gone. So I reckon if we keep up with our rehearsals we'll make it. I don't want to be raisin' cotton all my life. And I've got a woman and four kids to look after, now.

Working Hard on It
Ernest Roy in Clarksdale hoped to follow other Mississippi blues guitarists who had gone north

On our kick

Sil Johnson

My real name's Sylvester Thompson but I taken Sil Johnson for what you call my professional name. I've been a professional for two years now but I've been playing guitar for quite a few years. I wasn't born in Chicago; I came with my folks about fourteen years ago from Centerville, Tennessee, which is my home state. I was just about nine years old then and I'm twenty-three now. When I started I played with Junior Wells and I played with Shaky Jake too in bands they had – I played guitar behind Shaky. Then I worked with Tiny Topsy and Elmore James; played with them on station WGES. Now I've got my own groups and I have Rufus Forman on tenor; he's a good sax man and he was workin' with Buddy Guy before he joined my group. You know, Buddy Guy's a good blues singer – he plays guitar and he's about a year older than me. Buddy comes from Louisiana and he plays quite a few of the spots that I play. Right now I'm playin' instead of Magic Sam; this was his spot but he had the appendicitis and they operated on him and then when he came out a guy threw a bottle at him and he couldn't move. So that put him back in hospital again. But I hear he's playin' again up at the Tay May on West Roosevelt. Now my lead guitar is Fat Man Morrison – his name's Leonard Morrison only they call him Fat Man 'cause he's so thin. And Fat Man comes from Corinth, Mississippi, and he played a year with B. B. King in St Louis. So we have a rockin' group. We play more of a blues with a beat you know, what they call this rock 'n roll or somethin'. It's just blues but it's got a beat to it 'cause that's what the kids want today – they don't want that old-style blues like Muddy Waters and Chuck Berry and Howlin' Wolf and those old-timers play. They're great of course and Muddy Waters has been real good to me and I play over in Gary with him at the F & J Lounge and places. And my folks go for their kind of blues you know, but the kids like it on our kick.

F & J Lounge Steel mill workers and their women with a sprinkling of
army personnel form the audience at the principal blues centre in Gary, Indiana

A Rocking Group Sil Johnson, a young blues singer and guitarist, leads
his group at a Rush Street club. Leonard Morrison plays bass guitar, James
West, drums, and Rufus Forman, saxophone, in the accompanying band

I never did latch on

Lee Collins

Yeah, Lee Collins was the name of my father. He was the great trumpet player. We did all we could for him but he just kep' on slippin' and slippin' back, and so finally he passed. He taught me to play trumpet – at least he tried but I couldn't do the fingerin' right and I never did latch on to his kind of playin'. You know he tol' me he used to back up blues singers years ago but I don't know too much about it. ' I can't remember any of the singers,' he said. But that give me an interest in the blues I guess, though I'm a professional basketball player – was, I should say. I played with the Harlem Globetrotters and I went over to England a few years ago and played there. But I didn't like that travelin' too much so I come back to Chicago and started to play the drums. I gigged around and right now I'm playin' here at the Green Door with Little Otis, sockin' the skins for him. We call this The House Rockers and we've got James Green on bass guitar and James Wheeler playin' lead guitar and Blues Blowin' Mickey on sax. Mickey Bolls I think his name is – he was with Willie Dixon's combo you know, and he played with Shaky Jake on *Roll Your Money Maker*. Little Otis don't play anythin' – he couldn't do all that and play an instrument too! I guess I'm not much of a drummer but I can beat the skins hard and that's what they want. Yeah, it's a loud, shoutin' band all right . . . maybe I'll go back to playin' basketball.

They should get together

Shaky Jake

Here's the idea of musicians today: someone come up for a request and tell the band to play that request, but the first thing they do – they play another song that they want to hear. I think they're no good now, I mean musicians now, because they want to do what *they* want to do, not what the audience want them to do. And it's the audience that makes 'em, you know what I mean? So I guess it's easier for a singer these days if he's goin' to do what he's supposed to do – not be too big, but try to do what the audience want. And the same with the lead guitar-player – he don't have to play so loud. Instead he wants to play so loud he don't want to have nobody hear anyone but *him*. The drummer want you to hear *him* – so the lowest player is as good as the highest player and the highest player's as good as the lowest player. So they should come together and come down, not go up – it's too loud. You can't even hear yourself talk you know, and how can you enjoy yourself? You can't enjoy yourself with your girl friend or nothin'. And the musician, he just gets too big – and he ain't got a quarter! I mean he can't pay his rent, but he's still big because he's up on the bandstand before the public. Now me, I could live off gamblin' far as that's concerned, if I wanted, but I just play music 'cause I like it. I'm gonna be a preacher in the next couple of years anyway. I'm gonna retire, be a minister. Minister – because I want to preach the truth you know. I'm gonna go from house to house and preach. Not the church, just from house to house and read to people, be a reader. No, I'm not doin' it now; I got somebody readin' to *me* now, some nights. What I would like – I just likes the Bible – I want to find out who is who . . . like today, I don't think anybody exactly know who is who, you know.

Store-front Church
The Greater Bethlehem
Gospel Singers. Tickets
25¢ at the door

I seen a very rough time

John Lee Hooker

Why that I have such a big soul when I start singin' the blues,
spirituals, anythin', is because I was normally a spiritual singer.
I reversed from spirituals to the blues and when I get that big
feelin' look like it's somethin' like a bombshell hit me. You
know, you can turn it right aroun'. The spirituals and the blues
is based on just about the same pattern. So I used to sing with
the Fairfield Four and some of the Quartets – spirituals you
know. And I come from Memphis to Cincinnati and I worked
in some factories there and then I come on to Detroit. That's
where I really made my first big hit, that was *Boogie Chillen*.
That was my tremendous hit. I was workin' at that factory at
Fords for that five or six years. So that was a little hard goin'.
Some I seen was real rough. I was goin' from place to place
tryin' to get a start. After I was through workin' at that Ford
factory for the day I be right on at the Club Basin and the Forest
Inn, places like that. See I was playin' little gigs for parties and
I messed around. Then I played for these clubs here in Detroit
and go right back to workin' at Fords the next day. So I was
goin' here and there all tryin' to get a break with this record
company and that record company and so finally a little
company out on the Coast they discovered me – Modern
Records – they got a big population now. So I got that hit
Boogie Chillen and right behind that I got *I'm in the Mood for
Love* – that was a big one. And I was certainly on my way. And
I seen a very rough time gettin' a start. And I can tell any blues
singer or any spiritual singer that at the time that I got my start
it was very, very rough, but nowadays, it's not as bad as it was,
because things have changed more modern now. There's more
people takin' on more artists and everything; breaks is much
easier now but when I got my break I really
got it the hard way and that's for sure.

You develop your own

Boogie Woogie Red

My family's artistic – I mean they do paintin' and letterin'.
My brother's a sign painter and he wrote my name – Boogie
Woogie Red – on my car there. But you ought to see his car –
he's got letterin' and pictures all over it. But my leanin's was
to playin' music so I was playin' boogies and blues in bars and
joints when I was too young to be really allowed in them you
know. Of course for who influenced me the most it's hard to
say because Detroit has always been a jumpin' town. But I guess
it was Big Maceo. My style is somethin' after Macey's style.
He was playin' at Brown's Club on Hastings for six years
straight and I learn a lot from him. And of course you develop
your own. Well then I got with John Lee and I played with
him for about ten years as his regular pianist.

Boogie and Blues
At the back of Joe Von Battle's
music store in Detroit, Boogie Woogie
Red played piano while Little Eddie
Kirkland sang a blues

So people can understand
Little Eddie Kirkland

When I come to Detroit I guess I was about fifteen years old. I was born in New Orleans and I used to sing in the Sanctified Church there, you know, gospel groups. Well I started out to be a professional boxer and I was fightin' for about a year, eighteen months. I didn't like that so much and I'd played a little harp and a little guitar since I was about eight years old, so when I got to Detroit I got me some job playing in clubs. Then later on I got with John Lee Hooker and went on tours with him all over. I had to manage the band in a manner of speaking, and I'd go on ahead, make arrangements and see they got the places right for us to play in. So we went down to Atlanta, Georgia – that's where I really started to play the harp, picked it up one day and started in to playin'. We played in Houston, Dallas, Texas; Tulsa, Oklahoma – came back up North to Chicago and Detroit; stay a bit, go on the road again. Well finally I quit that tourin' because I've got a wife and twelve children and I didn't like leavin' my family all the time. Every man needs a good woman just to be by his side. When he's worried and tired she can make him satisfied. When he comes home from a hard day's work come and pat him on the back and say, 'Don't worry darlin', everything's gonna be all right.' I'm a lonely man so I like to have someone by my side. About love in a man's life, you know the way I think about it, a man's nowhere unless he has it. It takes love to keep the world goin'. That's why I say, I'm expressing my feelings so people can understand the amount of feeling of the blues. I sing the blues to otherwise get all my heart's feeling off my chest. So that's why I stay in Detroit and why I sing the blues, and right now I have a nice little band at the Apex Club, which is a spot for all those men that's workin' at Fords can go to, and I got a group at Swann's Paradise Bar on Grand Rapids.

Swing brother
Eddie Burns

I got my start playin' with Sonny Boy Williamson. We had a little band and I was playin' the washboard then. So Sonny Boy give me the idea to play the harp and I followed him on. Then when I came up to Detroit about twelve years ago I used to sing spirituals and I had a group of my own I called The Friendly Brothers. But when I started in Detroit I worked with Washboard Willie for a while and then – I was playin' harp then – so I started in to playin' guitar, and that was about ten years ago. I've been playin' guitar mostly since and for the past couple of years I've been backin' up Little Sonny Willis at the Club Carribe. He blows the harp and we have a swingin' group. Little Junior Thomas sits in on second guitar sometimes – he's from Memphis, Tennessee. My home's in Belzoni, Mississippi – I guess most of the boys come from the South. Little Son comes from Greensbro', Alabama – that's about fifty miles from Mississippi. Washboard Willie's from the South too and he still sings those old blues – you know, *C. C. Rider*, *Every Day I Have the Blues* and those old numbers? He's old-time. He plays the boards but he's got those cow bells and snares and skillet pan and all kinds of stuff on them – they call him The Fantabulous Washboard Willie and he's got his Super Suds of Rhythm I think it is, up at the Calumet Show Club on 12th Street right now. Little Son played with Willie too – I guess just about everybody played with Willie and right now he's got Evans McClennan with him on guitar. He don't go in for recordin' though. I made some myself for Sensation, they put them out under the name of Swing Brother; and I made some for Joe Von Battle and I was on a couple of sides with John Lee.

Every day I have the Blues The Fantabulous Washboard Willie was a popular blues singer in Detroit, who was not interested in recording

Record star

Sam Price

You know, let me tell you. Today a guy can go into a studio and make a record, just any guy. Today you're judged by your records. You make a record overnight. A guy makes a record and overnight he's a big recording star and you can't say anything to him. And most of the time he can't even carry his instrument.

The inside story

Lil Son Jackson

You take playin' for a recordin' company. You try recordin' you more or less tryin' to do the best you can and your nerves would be a little tight and you couldn't produce like you could if you really was blue – like you had the blues, because if you had the blues I mean you wouldn't care – you wouldn't know where or what have you. You would be more or less playin' what you feelin', but then in recordin' I believe it's often a little different. Because whole lots of those songs is actually made up because lots of people that's makin' those blues don't even feel them. But a lot of people that do make 'em, do feel 'em. Because they have actually lived the life. And I mean, I think one of those records that is made from a guy who's in the mood who's really got the blues then I think he's makin' a good record. I think that's the onliest way you can make a good record. I think the people that buys the records I think they're bound to have some kind of a feelin' – think that the person that's makin' the record is tryin' to get over a story to him which they would like to get on the inside of, in other words, to know. And I think they understand just about as good as the feller that made the record, blues or whatever you may call it. Because, if I buy a record I buy it for somethin' specially; I buy it because there's somethin' I want to hear. I think that peoples who buys records that is the blues, they think they want to get the inside story of the guy that's makin' the record.

Some Kind of a Feelin'
Lil Son Jackson spoke and
sang with earnest conviction

This is very touchable

John Lee Hooker

You can hear a certain type of record be playin'. You can be feelin' very normal, nothin' on your mind, period. But it's somethin' on that record hits you. It hits somethin' that have happened in your life, and sometime if you can't stand to listen to the record you take a walk or take a ride or get in your car because you don't want to be hurt so deep that it cause heartaches and things. Because you'd rather *not* to hear it than to hear it. Because there's some places in them records, there's somethin' sad in there that give you the blues; somethin' that reach back in your life or in some friend's life of yours, or that make you think of what have happened today and it is so true, that if it didn't happen to you, you still got a strong idea – you know those things is goin' on. So this is very touchable, and that develops into the blues.

I would sing about them

Henry Townsend

There's several types of blues – there's blues that connects you with personal life – I mean you can tell it to the public as a song, *in* a song. But I mean, they don't take it seriously which you are tellin' the truth about. They don't always think seriously that it's exactly you that *you* talkin' about. At the same time it could be you, more or less it *would* be you for you to have the feelin'. You express yourself in a song like that. Now this particular thing reach others because they have experienced the same condition in life so naturally they feel what you are sayin' because it happened to them. It's a sort of thing that you kinda like to hold to yourself, yet you want somebody to know it. I don't know how you say that two ways: you like somebody to know it, yet you hold it to yourself. Now I've had the feelin' which I have disposed it in a song, but there's some things that have happened to me that I wouldn't dare tell, not to tell – but I would *sing* about them. Because people in general they takes the song as an explanation for *themselves* – they believe this song is expressing *their* feelin's instead of the one that singin' it. They feel that maybe I have just hit upon somethin' that's in their lives, and yet at the same time it was some of the things that went wrong with me too.

That's what makes it sin

Lil Son Jackson

Whether a man sing the blues or ballads or what have you, there's no way in the world that he can get round and not make a sin out of it in some way. In other words, there's so many ways he can make it a sin, and there's too many different ways the average entertainer *will*. He cain't go wrong and keep himself clean with singin' ballads or blues or boogie woogie, because it's on the wrong side. It's a two-sided road and you on the wrong side all the time. A man who's singin' the blues – I think it's sin because it cause other people to sin. But church music is from the Lord and I never knowed anybody to sin over that. I don't think it's sinful to sing of a wrong done to you, but it's the *way* you do it. I mean you *could* sing it in a spiritually form. You see it's two different things – the blues and church songs is two different things. If a man feel hurt within side and he sing a church song then he's askin' God for help. It's a horse of a different colour, but I think if a man sing the blues it's more or less out of himself, if you know what I mean, see. He's not askin' no one for help. And he's not really clingin' to no-one. But he's expressin' how he feel. He's expressin' it to someone and that fact makes it a sin you know, because it make another man sin. Make another woman sin. Say for example, I get worried; somethin' come up wrong. If I was praisin' the Lord on a spiritually kick instead of me takin' a drink or somethin', well I'd go and say my prayers, I mean I'd go on my knees and pray. See, that's the two different things about it; in singin' the blues you take a drink, then you sing the blues. And then I mean, you're tryin' to get your feelin's over to the *next* person through the blues, and that's what makes it sin. But on a spiritually kick – you never take a drink to say your prayers!

Pavin' her way

Emma Williams

I wasn't interested in blues and such and I didn't like that country music and dancin' so well. I wanted to be with God. She got religion, my daughter, when she was twelve years old but after she got up to be a pretty goodsize girl, well she went enjoyin' like the rest of the young people. Well I worked and got along very well to be a widder-woman, and after she got up into middle age she started to make records and made a little money like that and you know, we got along pretty fair. But I wanted her to come on back to the Church and serve God like she had been. So finally, she decided she would do that. But when she was singin' them blues I told her – she was pavin' her way to Hell.

Scripture from the Bible

Mary Johnson

I had always gone to church with my mother and she said, 'I know you tryin' to get money and help mother but I'd rather see you in church.' So I went to church with her one Sunday and the preacher he preached very good scriptures from the Bible and I liked it very much and I decided right there, I would go back to the church; quit singin' the blues. Then I tried to make a couple of numbers but I didn't do so good on spiritually recordin's – I didn't make good on them. Made a couple of recordin's but didn't do no good on them. Well the Devil always give you a good send-off. Looks like the Lord is stronger than him but I never did no good with those spiritually records. Well I was a singer just around here in the city – just for groups in church like that. Don't bring you very much. You make good on Sundays. Well, I go to Chicago, Kansas City and places and sing there, and I worked meantime for the Bell Telephone Company out on Linden for a while. But I had to stay out there and I didn't like that so I left. So I just goes to work doin' day work to help my mother and then last year I take a little stroke. And I haven't tried to sing any more, but I'm goin' to, I'm gettin' stronger now. It affected my vocal chords, and my teeth is out and they don't fit.

It stayed on my mind

Walter Davis

It was a nice trip I had with R.C.A. Victor, nice contracts and everything, but finally we ended up in a lawsuit and I guess I came out on top – anyway I don't fret no more about it. So then I got with another little company they got down in Nashville, Tennessee, they call Bullet, but after that contract run out on me and their manager Mr Lester Melrose had a little misunderstandin'. I pulled Bullet out of a hole so to speak – well that's what *he* said – but he didn't want to pay me too much. So I finally dumped him and I quit. Well in '54 I did make one more recordin' and that was *Vacation Time, Everybody's Gone*. That sold all right so R.C.A. wrote me another letter but I never would go back no more, because preachin' had taken a great effect on me then. So I just went on, started preachin'. See I had come out of the recordin' studios that day; wasn't thinkin' about preachin'. I just came out of the studio in Chicago, the Mart building, and there's a bookstall downstairs. And there was a Bible there and the Bible was open at the twentythird psalm and I went in there and bought the Bible and an encyclopaedia. And from then along – why, it was just about the end of my career in recordin'. And finally I started to thinkin' about it, and I had took a stroke which affected my hand and I couldn't play the piano no more. So it stayed on my mind all the time, about preachin'. And finally I started preachin' and from that time on I've been a preacher. I preaches here in the city of St Louis in different places and at different other cities. And I have a church in Hannibal, Missouri.

Jack-leg Preacher
Blind James Brewer, straw-hatted, playing for a preacher and his congregation on Sangamon Street, Chicago

Store-front churches

Blind James Brewer

Now I don't only play the blues; I play for different churches and things, and the churches I play for are very small churches. The large churches got their own musicianers – such as Reverend Cobbs and Reverend Body and Reverend Clay Evans and Reverend Paxton – they've got their own musicianers, but these little small churches what they call store-front churches, they like my playin' and they hear me and they say, 'Well, we'd like you to play for us.' Well, I went to playin' and they give me a dollar-and-a-half, two dollars. Well I didn't know how expensive these git-tars are, but I'm catchin' on more and more. Well lots of people say, 'What profit you in the world if you gain the world and lose your soul?' – Well I realize that's true too. But you got to live down here just like you got to make preparations to go up there. You cain't go there until you do get there; that is you cain't cross the bridge until you get to it. So they say – well, they try to get out a little propaganda stuff. I know it's right to serve God; I know it's right to go to church. But goin' to church ain't gonna save no one – I realize that. You got to live this life, and you got to obey God. And God give me this talent and he knew before I came into this world what I was goin' to make out of this talent.

He ain't aginst God

Willie Thomas

Some people say blues is nothin' but a feller with a sad feelin'.
All right. Another feller, he may not have a sad feelin' at all,
but he say he sing the blues, he sing the blues because he love
the *sound* of it. He love the sound of it, and the rhythm of it
and everything – how it goes. He ain't aginst God at all, he just
want to hear somethin' with a sound to it. It ain't nothin' to
do with bein' aginst God. That's the thing that church people
have aginst it. 'Oh look! What he do! Oh, he's singin' the blues!'
But what's that? It don't mean nothin'. He sings a church song
– if it comes nach'al, *church* people sing the blues! See, this is
what some people do in our churches – if not so in the white.
They sing:

> Lord – have mercy . . . .
> Lord – have mercy . . . ooooh,
> Lord – have mercy . . . save poor me.

He's in the church singin' that! He got the blues in church!
He's feelin' so bad and everybody's down on him and he ain't
gettin' his right wages and his neighbour gonna mess him up
and everything. He feels so broke down that he got the blues
himself. Why should he be angry with a feller out somewhere
because he may go out somewhere with a social bunch, takin' a
social drink and sing the blues? Those things ain't aginst God.

Just as deep a feelin'

John Lee Hooker

Way back before you and everybody else and all the peoples
was born, spirituals was the thing. Nobody can reach way back
and find out just when it was born. But when spirituals was
born it was born on the blues side. You can compare spirituals
and blues almost along together because both of them got a
very, very sad touch. Because that's why you could take some
spirituals and some blues and compare them together and you
get a sad feelin' out of each one. So that's why I sing the blues.
I used to be a spiritual singer. But I get just as deep a feelin'
from the blues as I would from the spirituals, because I do it
sad and I do it so satisfaction until the whole thing reaches me
what happened to other people and I get that real deep down
sad feelin'.

Move back for what?
Brother John Sellers

What have I committed?
Henry Townsend

The Holy Roller Church – you know they call them Sanctified Holy Rollers – well this is the church that I belong to where we play the tambourines and the guitars and the horns. And the reason we play these instruments is because we get it from the 150th psalm of David, you know: ' Praise the Lord with the handclapping, with the shakin' of cymbals, with the tambourines and the guitars,' and one particular gospel song we sing is that 'everybody ought to pray sometime':

Everybody, everybody, everybody ought to pray some time,
You ought to fall down on your knees,
Cry, Lord have mercy on me.

Every gambler, every gambler, every gambler ought to pray
some time,
He ought to fall down on his knees,
Cryin', Lord, have mercy on me.

And every liar, every liar, every liar ought to pray some time,
Ought to fall down on his knees,
And cry, Lord, have mercy on me.

And we believe that's true, because the Church should take in everyone. Now take most blues singers – they have lived rough lives, or they have been rough in their lives before they changed, because hard struggles and hard times – it makes people hard and mean towards each other regardless of who they are. If you have poverty you must have hard times and roughness – because if you come up a rough way it makes you tough and ready to battle at anything. Maybe people been talking about you and you get an achin'. Maybe you with a gang of people and some person, especially some white person say, 'Move back!' Well you automatically think they're talkin' to you. Move back? Move back for what? What have I got to move back for? Poverty makes you rough; it makes you like that – and that's part of the blues.

Some people think that the blues is something that is evil – I don't. Some people feel that a religious song is great – I do too. But now, here's the thing about it. Even if the blues is of evil and a man surmise to go ahead and sing a religious song, which is good – now how could you fault him? So tomorrow, if he want to sing the blues, he go back. If it's a good mood or a bad mood it's still a mood, and I think that the truth itself will touch anything. I mean, whether – if it's anything that has the knowledge of the truth. I think the truth will have some kind of bearin's on it. If the blues is delivered in the truth, which most of them are, they are told exactly as the story go and as the feelin' that they have – so I think it'll touch. And as I was sayin', if I sing the blues and tell the truth, what have I done? What have I committed? I haven't lied. So it's just a tone – it's just a frame of mind that people are in. But you can't just build it out of thoughts, that's for sure. You have to have some kind of experience for this. And if you don't have a feelin', you can't do much with it.

They Can Be Tough Places
Outside the Stumble Inn on West Lake
Street a light-skinned woman solicits

To have the blues within
Edwin Buster Pickens

The only way anyone can ever play blues – he's got to have them. You got to have experienced somethin' in life. You been troubled, you been broke, hungry, no job, no money, the one you love is deserted you – that makes you blue. Blues don't derive from a person's makin' up his mind: 'I'm gonna sing the blues.' He's got to have a feelin', he's got to have somethin' within, so he can bring it *out*. Just how he feels about it. Blues ain't nothin' but a good man feelin' bad – that's all they say it is. But he's feelin' bad over *somethin'*. No man in good spirit, no man in good heart can sing the blues, neither play them. There never has been, never will be. But nach'al blues come directly from a person's heart: what's he's experienced in life, what he's been through. Whether he's been troubled, whether he's ridden freight trains, where he's been put in jail; been beaten up by railroad dicks and everythin' else you understand – pushed around in life. That makes you blue. You have a tough way in life – that makes you blue. That's when you start to sing the blues – when you've got the blues.

Conversation with the Blues
Three generations of blues singers talk in front of Lightnin Hopkins's home: L. C. Williams (front right), Luke Long Gone Miles (left) and Spider Kilpatrick (back right)

Ayo, Sam

Ralph Peer, Eli Oberstein, Lester Melrose, J. Mayo Williams
– these are well-known names among the men who have made
the recording of blues and folk singers the basis of their careers.
Dan Hornsby, Lester Hearne, Sam Ayo are less familiar though
they were responsible for the recording of many of the outstanding blues singers of the 'thirties. Sam Ayo organized the sessions,
managed the musicians, sought the talent in East Texas and
even operated his own label. A representative of Wurlitzer
Music – 'Musical Fun for Everyone' he was a well-built,
typical Texan businessman. We met him at a roadhouse
near Galveston. (Page 123.)

Barrett, Sweet Emma

Lean to the point of emaciation, Emma Barrett had limbs
like sticks but she played powerfully swinging ragtime piano,
and the bells that she wore on her shoes and gartered knees
jingled as she stomped her feet. The Bell Gal was pianist
with the Original Tuxedo Jazz Orchestra in the 'twenties and
played with Louis Armstrong on the S.S. Sidney riverboat.
In the summer of 1960 she was playing with Willie and Percy
Humphrey at Brennon's Absinthe House on Bourbon Street,
New Orleans. With a similar band she recorded on Riverside
RLP 364 but though she made *The Bell Gal's Careless Blues*
she had a certain contempt for the blues that is shared by many
New Orleans musicians. Sweet Emma recorded for Southland
in 1967, but she suffered a stroke three years later, though she
continued to play with one hand. She died aged 86 in 1983.
(Page 87.)

Black ace

Pseudonym for B. K. Turner, q.v.

Blunt, Hillary

Small shacks line the unmade roads of the folk community
of Scotlandville, Louisiana, where Hillary Blunt lived. An
amiable, casual, stockily-built truck-driver he played at Saturday night dances with Smoky Babe (Robert Brown) and other
blues singers from the area. He was recorded by Dr Harry Oster
and played guitar on Sally Dotson's *Your Dice Won't Pass* on
Arhoolie CD 372. (Page 10.)

Boogie Woogie Red

Pseudonym for Vernon Harrison, q.v.

Boyd, Eddie

An elevated railroad of the Chicago Transit Authority ran
beside the wall of Eddie Boyd's tenement apartment on East
53rd Street and in the peak hours the expresses that passed
every few seconds shook the building to the foundations.
He played at many clubs in Chicago and out of town gigs,
sometimes with Lonnie Graham or Robert Lockwood on
guitar. Well esteemed as a blues pianist he played for Big Maceo,
Jazz Gillum, Sonny Boy Williamson and L. C. McKinley in
the 'forties. *Five Long Years* was issued on JOB 1007 and another
version appeared on Oriole 1316. On several of his recordings
poor balance did not do justice to his fine rolling blues piano.
Eddie Boyd was born in Clarksdale, Mississippi, on the 25
November 1914, and moved to Memphis when he was
twenty-two. Eddie toured in Europe in the 1960s and later
moved to Switzerland, Finland and Sweden, where he died.
(Pages 100, 160.)

Brewer, Blind James

We first heard Blind James Brewer playing with a Gospel
group which was holding a service under the guidance of a
fiercely exhorting 'jack-leg' preacher on the broken sidewalk
of South Sangamon Street, Chicago, a short step from Brewer's
home. He was playing electric guitar, for the owners of the
buildings fronting the streets near Maxwell rented out the use
of an electric cable to street musicians for a dollar a day. On
another day we heard him with Blind Gray and recorded him
playing *I'm So Glad Good Whisky's Back* (Heritage HLP 1004).
Born in Brookhaven, Mississippi, on 3 October 1921, he had
been almost totally blind from childhood, but his slight vision
enabled him to travel and beg in many states. An excellent
Mississippi guitarist, he was fascinated by instruments and
was content with the life of a street singer. (Pages 44, 104,
149, 179.)

Brown, Henry

Tall and gangling, Henry Brown in his white jockey's cap stood out in the milling throng on Easton Avenue in St Louis. With Charlie O'Brien of the Police Department we found Henry in a pool-room and he willingly led us to Pinkey Boxx's Beauty Parlour, where, on a tiny piano he rolled off his *Henry Brown Blues*. We recorded it on the BBC machine and it is included in the enclosed CD. Later we arranged a session which produced his first solo recordings in over thirty years. He had a curiously strangled voice, talked in short sentences and reminisced in this vein on *Blues for Charlie O'Brien*. Henry Brown's 1929 recordings with his trombone-playing partner Ike Rodgers and accompanying Alice Moore and others were reissued on Document DOCD-5103. A simple, introspective blues pianist, he played with undiminished feeling and ability. Henry Brown was born in 1906. (Pages 104, 110.)

Burns, Eddie

A Mississippi blues singer from Belzona, where he was born on 8 February 1928, Eddie Burns played washboard for Sonny Boy Williamson and Pinetop Willie Perkins, later taking up the harmonica. He moved to Detroit in 1948 and played harmonica on John Lee Hooker's *Miss Eloise* (Sensation 34). Joe Von Battle, for whom he also recorded, took us to hear him playing with Little Sonny Willis. A stocky, serious man, Eddie Burns was an excellent blues artist. (Page 172.)

Cage, James Butch

Missing a few front teeth, Butch Cage talked with a blurred, hollow enunciation but for a man who was born in 1894 – 16 March – he sang adequately and played wild exciting fiddle music in a raw country tradition, holding the instrument against his chest. He also played good blues guitar in the Mississippi 'jukin' style, reflecting his origins in Franklin County, Mississippi. He lived on the Old Slaughter Road in Zachary, Louisiana, when we called on him at the suggestion of Dr Harry Oster who had recorded him (Folk-Lyric FL III). An all-day session of country music, at which half the children and a fair proportion of Zachary's population were present at one time or another, produced some rough, thrilling music, including *44 Blues* on Arhoolie CD 372 'Country Negro Jam

Session'. and a solo *'Tween Midnight and Day*, self accompanied with guitar, on the enclosed CD. (Pages 22, 36, 57.)

Cannon, Gus

Veteran medicine show entertainer, Gus Cannon was happy to recall the routines that he would use on the improvised show pitches. He was a spirited old man with bird-like features and movements and fingers still fairly nimble as he picked his banjo. Born in Red Banks, Mississippi, on 12 September 1883, he did most menial jobs and was digging a sewer in Memphis a few days before we met him. As Banjo Joe he made some fine folk recordings for Paramount including *Can You Blame the Colored Man?* (Paramount 12571) a narrative on Booker T. Washington. *Charmin' Betsy* was apparently never released but the recordings of the Cannon's Jug Stompers are outstanding examples of the jug band idiom. They are available on Compact Disc, Document DO CD 5032/33.

Gus Cannon was 96 when he died in 1979. The Rooftop Singers' recording of *Walk Right In*, an old Cannon composition, brought him unexpected royalties and recognition and in 1963 he made a number of concert appearances. (Pages 50, 92.)

Carter, Bo

Sharing a corner in the bare, shot-gun building on South 4th Street where Will Shade lived, was an ailing, blind, light-skinned man whom the occupants knew only as Old Man. By a lucky hunch I guessed he might be Bo Carter and the sick man brightened to hear his name. At first he could hardly hold down the strings of his heavy steel guitar with its worn fingerboard. But he slowly mastered it and in a broken voice, that mocked the clear and lively singing on his scores of recordings under his own name and with the Mississippi Sheiks, he recalled incidents from his varied life and some of the songs that had made him one of the most famous of blues singers. *Baby When You Marry* he had recorded nearly thirty years before (OK 8888) in 1931 and in the years since he had worked on medicine shows, farmed and begged. He was born in Bolton, Mississippi, in 1898 and christened Armenter Chatman. 'Bo' died in September 1964, but his beautifully played blues have been reissued on Document DOCD 5078-5082. (Pages 47, 56, 90, 127.)

Chatman, Sam

Not as well-known as his brother Bo Carter, Sam Chatman was one of the large and talented family who called themselves the Mississippi Sheiks, with whom he played and recorded, 'bassin' on guitar. The seventh son of a slavery-time fiddler he was born in Bolton, Mississippi, in 1899. From his long experience and longer heritage he has an inexhaustible supply of blues and pre-blues songs, of which *I Have to Paint My Face* is one which had not been recorded before – understandably perhaps (Arhoolie CD 432). It is made the more startlingly effective coming as it does from a light-skinned African American. Living in a small frame house in Hollandale, Mississippi, Sam Chatman supported a paralysed wife by doing labouring jobs and working as a carpenter. He enjoyed a wider fame in the 1970s and died in Hollandale in February 1983. (Pages 35, 46, 47.)

Collins, Lee

Two men with open razors in their hands were circling in the road outside the Green Door, a hole-in-the-wall club in the tough neighbourhood of West 63rd Street, as John Steiner and I called in on my first night in Chicago. It was a salutary introduction and the music of Little Otis and his band was fierce and deafening. The six-foot-four drummer turned out to be the son of the New Orleans trumpeter, Lee Collins, once a basketball player and now providing the socking rhythms that were liked by the Chicago blues singers of the younger school. Shirt-sleeved Black police looked in but the band members gave us a friendly welcome in the intermission before leaping on the splitting bar to belt out another blues. (Page 168.)

Cotton, James

A tall, heavily-built young man, James Cotton was quiet in speech and manners, wild in his harmonica playing. He was a strong member of Muddy Waters's band and with guitarist Pat Hare established a fine rapport at Smitty's Corner and the F & J Lounge in Gary, Indiana. Born in Tunica, Mississippi on 1 July, 1935, he played in the streets from the age of ten, moving to West Memphis, Arkansas, and becoming a well-appreciated musician at an early age. *Cotton Crop Blues* was originally issued on Sun 206 and made when James Cotton was about

eighteen years old. In 1961 he made a brief visit to England and appeared at the Beaulieu Festival. He continued to work with Muddy Waters and later as a featured artist on college and concert dates. (Page 162).

Crump, Jesse

Ida Cox's celebrated accompanist, Jesse Crump, was working at the Kewpie Doll with the late Marty Marsala's band in San Francisco when I interviewed him in the dismal kitchens in the rear of the building. He was justifiably proud of his association with the singer, with his thirteen years on the road touring the TOBA theatres, and of his compositions. 'I have not only blues tunes but I have pretty ballads and jump tunes too, but I don't get anywhere with them,' he said. 'I had one tune that was published in England that Ida sang. It's called the *Last Mile Blues*. It didn't do so good but I got a cheque from England – I think it was for six cents! These things kinda hurt you know.' He re-joined Ernie Figaro and the band to roll out a couple of fine choruses of *Chicago*. A saddened man, Jesse Crump was reported to be seriously ill in 1964. He was born in Paris, Texas in 1906 and died in April 1974. Many of his accompaniments to Ida Cox (1927) can be heard on 'Ida Cox' Volume 4, Document DOCD 5325. (Pages 133, 136.)

Daddy Stovepipe

Pseudonym for Johnny Watson, q.v.

Davis, Walter

Still the broadly-smiling man who beamed contentedly from the Bluebird catalogues, Walter Davis had put on weight in recent years. When the Calumet Hotel, where he had been working as a night clerk, was destroyed, he moved to the Albany Hotel, St Louis, where he operated the switchboard and the reception desk. A slight stroke caused him to lose complete control of his left hand and ended his career as a blues pianist. When he spoke he had a warmer and more expressive voice than many of his recordings would suggest, a quality that must have aided him in his preaching. Walter Davis was born in Grenada, Mississippi, on 1 March 1912, and made his first record, *M and O Blues* (Victor 38618) when he was eighteen. He died early in 1964. A very popular blues artist in the 1930s his recordings have been reissued on seven CDs: Document DOCD 5281-5287. (Pages 76, 113, 127, 178.)

Gray, Blind Arvella

We got off the street-car at Halsted and Maxwell within ear-shot of Blind Gray's stentorian voice and thundering steel guitar. With his white stick tapping a sewer-vent for orientation and a tin cup pinned to his suit he was singing and playing a fierce blues. For thirty years a street singer, Blind Gray was a tough and powerful man who had come to terms with the sudden tragedy of his blindness. He was born in Texas in 1906 and lived under conditions of almost unbelievable hardship and violence. With John Steiner we recorded him at the old building at 4403 South State Street, now destroyed, where he was living on the top floor. The work songs (page 59) and blues (pages 32, 138) together with an outstanding version of *John Henry* are issued on the accompanying CD. Blind Gray was a proud man who refused a helping arm to guide him to the bus termini or street corners where he played. As we left his home he felt the light bulbs to see if the lights were on and strode unhesitatingly into the street. (Pages 23, 30, 62, 80, 132, 142, 146.)

Harris, James D.

' I was in a big crap game last Saturday morning; I win a hatful, about $150 – the tavern owners wanted to play me – thought I had a lotta money you know, so I beat 'em,' Shaky Jake remarked. A professional gambler for fifteen years before he became a musician, he has kept his hand in and if he was wavering at the time did not follow his declared intention to become a minister. Born in Arkansas in 1924, he came to Chicago at the age of seven and only in recent years had he played music professionally. Nevertheless he was respected by the younger musicians, whom he actively encouraged. An LP for Prestige (Bluesville BVLP 1027) did him credit but he is more at home on *Call Me If You Need Me* (Artistic 1506), or *Love My Baby* which he recorded whilst in Europe on tour with the American Folk Blues Festival in 1962. (Pages 152, 161, 168.)

Harrison, Vernon

Though born in Louisiana in 1926, Boogie Woogie Red was brought by his father to Detroit before he was two. He lived with his father and brothers and sisters but his house on Leland in Detroit was due for demolition in 1960. Boogie Woogie Red played piano on many records made by John Lee Hooker and he also recorded himself for Jack Brown's Fortune label. He had a strong style as his nickname implied and showed the influence of his chief mentor, Big Maceo Merriweather, though *So Much Good Feeling* finds him in more reflective mood. His pinkish, mottled complexion accounted for the name of Red. (Pages 20, 22, 171.)

Henry, Robert

A native of Memphis, Robert Henry had lived on Beale Street since 1913. Robert Henry's Place – a semi-flophouse - was across the street from his pool-room at 335 Beale, where we interviewed him above the clamour of the players. Close friend of W. C. Handy and an agent who booked the jug bands for Boss Crump, Robert Henry sponsored many of the bands, blues singers and entertainers who played at the Palace. He was a champion for Beale Street but sadly admitted, ' Like Jerusalem in the Bible you could put a wall round it these days and call it "Holy Memphis". But we're hopin' that times'll get better and life'll come back to Beale.' The ageing, brown-skinned Robert Henry was unable to help it to regain its former vitality. (Pages 96, 98.)

Hooker, John Lee

John Lee Hooker's stepfather William Moore was a guitarist and John's initial inspiration. Hooker was born in Clarksdale, Mississippi, on 22 August 1917, and at the age of eleven sang in the Big Six gospel group, later joining the Delta Big Four. He ran away to Memphis – eventually successfully – and worked in factories there and in Cincinnati, going to Detroit to work at Ford's in 1948. He had been working in clubs and in 1949 commenced a long, successful recording career with some of his best material appearing on Modern and Sensation. We met him at Martha Ledbetter's Brooklyn home and later in Detroit, where he sang and played powerfully and passionately. He talked with intensity and conviction but because of a slight impediment, sometimes with difficulty. Recently John Lee

Hooker has been lionized by enthusiasts who have discovered the blues. He still remains one of the most important of blues singers of modern times, even if some of his later recordings were disappointing. Hooker came to Europe with the 1962 American Folk Blues Festival and toured the English rhythm and blues clubs in July 1964; thirty years later he represented one of the last links with the early phases of blues. (Pages 21, 94, 171, 176, 180.)

Hopkins, Sam Lightnin

Worthy successor of Texas Alexander and Blind Lemon Jefferson from whom he learned much, Lightnin Hopkins was one of the most poetic and inventive of blues singers, commenting on his immediate world and experiences in his blues. He played clear arpeggio guitar – sometimes fiercely extrovert as we heard him at Irene's on Houston's Buffalo Bayou; sometimes introspectively as he was at the Sputnik Bar when the ill-fated L. C. Williams, who died of T.B. a year later, was playing drums. King of the Third Ward he held court on the porch of his home near West Dallas Street, surrounded by friends and other bluesmen. With Mack McCormick we joined Lightnin, Luke Long Gone Miles, Williams and Spider Kilpatrick there in many hours of conversation. Lightnin bore the scars of past scrapes, of the chain gang shackles and of the stabbing that put him in hospital on the eve of being drafted. Born in Centerville, Texas, on 15 March 1912, he only became widely known outside Texas in the 1960s, meeting his fans on a European tour in 1964. He died in 1982. Lightnin's historic Gold Star sessions are reissued on Arhoolie CD8s 330 and 337. (Pages 44, 57, 89.)

Jackson, Melvin Lil Son

Taut, tense, sincere, Lil Son Jackson was greatly concerned with the morality of the blues, the more so since he was involved in the car wreck that decided him to discontinue playing blues for a living. He worked in a car-wrecking yard which proclaimed its nature by the decoration of hub-caps that almost constituted a folk art of motorized America. He made an attractive home for his young wife and family and it was there that we talked at length and there that Chris Strachwitz persuaded him to record a final set of blues, *Gambler Blues*

(Arhoolie CD 409) amongst them. His father was a sharecropper and it was on his share that Lil Son was born near Tyler, Texas, on 17 August 1916. He spent some time in Wales, France and Germany during the war and on his return made a couple of recordings in a booth which eventually led him to a career in blues singing. He fell ill in the 70s of cancer, from which he died in May 1976. (Pages 20, 31, 174, 177.)

Jacobs, Little Walter

The toughness of the diminutive Little Walter became something of a legend in Chicago, and his features had deep scars that gave it support. When we met him at Muddy Waters's home and at Smitty's Corner he was recovering from a bullet wound in the ankle. Little Walter was born in Alexandria, Louisiana, on 1 May 1930, in conditions of extreme poverty which forced him to fend for himself at an early age. He moved to Chicago at the age of seventeen. There he begged on Maxwell Street, came under the protection of Big Bill Broonzy and joined Muddy Waters in 1940. In his condensed career he became widely admired and copied; generally acknowledged by blues singers to be in the forefront of harmonicists, his Chess recordings demonstrated his later, rocking style, much as he played on his tour in England in 1964. Beligerent as ever, Little Walter was involved in a street brawl early in 1968 and died from thrombosis as a result in February that year. (Page 155.)

John, Henry

The pseudonym conceals the identity of a prisoner on Parchman Farm, sentenced to twenty years for murder following a fracas at a juke in Drew, Mississippi. He had fifteen years to go and was hoping for some remission of his sentence. Since the Lomaxes made their remarkable recordings in the midthirties on Parchman Farm, conditions at the notorious, featureless, penal farm had improved. 'A Great Institution in a Great State, 20, 000 acres, 17 Units', read the bland notice at the gates. We were admitted and allowed to drive across its vast acreage of cotton fields and crops; the special detention compound and the watch-towers of the guards were firm reminders of its purpose and the station presented a bleak image to the arriving, manacled prisoners. (Page 60.)

Johnson, Edith

In her mid-fifties when I met her, Edith Johnson was the widow of the promoter Jesse Johnson whose activities as talent scout and organizer she assisted in the 'twenties and 'thirties. Later she devoted much of her time to social work in St Louis but in the late 'twenties she made a small number of important blues records when her *Honey Dripper Blues* (Paramount 12823) made her famous at the time. The original backing *Nickel's Worth of Liver* may be heard on the reissues Agram CD 2016. Edith North Johnson shared the management of her husband's De Luxe music shop and after his death, operated for some time her De Luxe Restaurant. She was an animated person with a very expressive and musical voice, and it is unfortunate that she was not recorded more extensively when she was at the height of her abilities. She died in February 1988. (Pages 117, 139.)

Johnson, James Stump

Short and stocky, James Johnson was inevitably called Stump and retained the name on many of his recordings. His *The Duck Yas Yas Yas* (QRS 7049, Paramount 12842) was an instant success and under various pseudonyms he recorded for many labels. Many of his blues, especially with Dorothea Trowbridge, were mildly pornographic but others were more serious in intent, all of them distinguished by his simple but effective piano-playing. After the death of his brother Jesse Johnson, he opened a shoe-shine stand. 'Now,' he said, 'I'm at the city of St Louis hall in the tax collection department and I'm also a policeman in the Wellston area, a little town right out of St Louis, Missouri. I thought I was cute when I was young and wasn't working then; I had a lot of girl friends and I knowed nothin' about work, and I didn't ever thought I would ever have to work. And when I was recordin' I was getting hold of so much money, gamblin' and playin' the races and what-not – but it's altogether different now!' An army veteran, Stump Johnson died in 1969 at the age of 67. His early recordings have been reissued on Document DOCD 5250. (Pages 101, 115.)

Johnson, Lonnie

A native of New Orleans where he was born on Rampart and Franklin on 8 February 1894, Alonzo 'Lonnie' Johnson has been one of the most celebrated, most widely admired and extensively recorded of blues singers. As a child he worked in a lumber yard but after learning to play the violin, joined his father's band in 1914. He came to England with a small stock company in 1917 – and returned again to England thirty-five years later. His family of twelve was decimated by an epidemic in 1922 and after that he said, 'I got to ramblin' – usually people get that way. I couldn't keep my feet still so I just started travelling.' He worked in Texas, made his way to St Louis and spent several years with Charlie Creath's band, later working both as a solo blues singer and as a member of small band groups. At intervals throughout his career Lonnie Johnson did heavy manual work, and when we met him in Chicago he was enjoying a brief break from working as a janitor at the Benjamin Franklin Hotel in Philadelphia. He was the oldest member of the 1963 American Folk Blues Festival but was still able to demonstrate his remarkable command of the guitar. Fifteen CDs DOCD 5063-69 and DOCD 6024-26 sum up his early achievements. After an automobile accident Lonnie Johnson died in June 1970. (Pages 84, 107, 122, 140, 145, 153.)

Johnson, Mary

Living with her mother Emma Williams in an apartment on Biddle Street, St Louis, above the premises of a wholesale dealer in live fish, Mary Johnson had known considerable poverty for many years. She was born near Yazoo City, Mississippi, in 1905 and was brought by her mother to St Louis where she eventually commenced a career as a blues singer. Though not possessing a strong voice she had a low moaning quality in her singing which made her popular with her audiences and on record. *Barrel House Flat Blues* (Paramount 12996) and its original backing, *Key to the Mountain Blues*, are among the items reissued on Document DOCD 5305 which includes accompaniments by Henry Brown and Roosevelt Sykes. A stroke affected her speech and her singing but she still sang for the church. Mary Johnson was the wife of Lonnie Johnson with whom she worked in the 'twenties (Pages 103, 121, 178.)

Johnson, Sil

Pseudonym for Sylvester Thompson, q.v.

Kelly, Oscar

Enjoying a fair local reputation as a guitarist, even as a one-man band, in East Baton Rouge County, Louisiana, Oscar Kelly proved hard to find. We finally located him in a tiny cabin, buried in undergrowth, near Baker a few miles from Highway 61. With the contents of a bottle of wine inside him Oscar Kelly was hospitable but disinterested in recording or very much else but another bottle of locally brewed wine. About thirty years of age he worked sporadically and played guitar and sang when the spirit in one form or another, moved him. (Page 125.)

Kirkland, Eddie

As he removed his tight, white cap Eddie Kirkland presented a somewhat wild appearance when we met him at Boogie Woogie Red's home, his hair standing out in an aura of long, tight ringlets. Eddie Kirkland was in fact a professional boxer for a short while. A family man with twelve children he had a gentle voice and pleasant disposition. An excellent harmonica player and guitarist, and occasional organist – he played the instrument on John Lee Hooker's *It Hurts Me So* (Modern 867) – he has not been well represented on record though he made sides for King and Fortune. Though born in New Orleans (Jamaica has also been given), 16 August 1928, he settled in Detroit, where we recorded him in the back of Joe Von Battle's record shop on 12th Street. (Pages 20, 172.)

Lenoir, J. B.

Christened simply J. B. with no forenames, J. B. Lenoir was the son of a Mississippi farmer, born at Monticello on 5 March 1929. His father was a blues guitarist and J. B. could recall the old-style blues that he had heard and learned at an early age. He worked in many jobs on the farm, on the railroad and later, meat-packing in Chicago where he settled in his teens. J. B. recorded fairly extensively for Chess, JOB, Parrot and other labels. *I Been Down So Long* on the enclosed CD is more contemplative than many of his recordings. Other records, with Sunnyland Slim, Joe Montgomery and other Chicago

musicians are excellent, including *Deep In Debt Blues* and *Korea Blues* (Chess 1463 and Chess 1449). J. B. got his inspiration 'like through a dream, as I be sittin' down, or while I be sleepin'. He talked with warm Mississippi accents and sang in a surprisingly high voice, accompanying himself with rapid arpeggios or boogie guitar. He had a fondness for zebra-striped, yellow velvet or similarly bright jackets and wore a small ear-ring. J. B. took much time and trouble to introduce us to a number of blues singers in Chicago. Sadly, he died at the age of 38 after an automobile accident. (Pages 26, 150, 159.)

Lipscomb, Mance

Texas sharecropper and songster with a reputation that extended widely in Grimes, Washington and Brazos counties, Mance Lipscomb was discovered by Mack McCormick and Chris Strachwitz in July 1960. A few weeks later we joined them in recording him for the first time (Arhoolie CD 306) in his two-roomed cabin. A man of great dignity and natural culture, Mance Lipscomb was a veritable storehouse of blues, ballads and songs of more than half a century, who had remained unembittered by a hard and unrewarding life as a sharecropper. He had many grandchildren whom he raised with his patient, maternal wife and the proceeds of a belated fame he put to building them a better home. *Evil Heart Blues* and *Blues in the Bottle* were made at his first session. Later he appeared in Houston and on the West Coast, remaining unaffected by the wide acclaim accorded to one of the most important discoveries in the field. He was born on 9 April 1895 and was 81 when he died in Navasota. (Pages 24, 37.)

Lockwood, Robert Junior

Born in Marvell, Arkansas, in 1914, Robert Junior, as his associates frequently called him, was the stepson of the famous blues singer Robert Johnson. A quiet round-faced man, he was very much absorbed in his playing and widely respected by blues singers in Chicago where he lived. Though he accompanied such blues singers as Eddie Boyd, Sunnyland Slim, Otis Spann and others on record, it was only later that Robert Lockwood earned the general recognition he deserved. He was a strong, taut singer and was accompanied by Sunnyland Slim on *Take a Little Walk With Me*. His comments and those of other singers here on Robert Johnson were recorded more than a year before the appearance of Johnson's blues on l.p. and the immensely popular CDs, and differ in many particulars from the picture drawn of the singer by Don Law, recording executive in Texas in the 'thirties. Instead of the shy, teenage singer who remained solely on the plantation of Robinsonville, Mississippi, they speak of a restless, widely influential, youthful artist who precipitated modern trends in blues rather than the culmination of the old styles. Robert Johnson remained something of a mystery; his stepson did not deserve to remain in similar obscurity. (Page 73.)

Long, Jewell

In the inhospitable township of Sealy, Texas, we spoke to the blind and semi-paralysed manager of a liquor store whose infirmity made him indifferent to the colour consciousness that was generally evident amongst the inhabitants. He told us of Jewell Long, an illiterate, tough Negro worker, who played both guitar and piano, and in spite of threats of calling the police, which we received from an irate white owner when we joined the singer at table in a local joint, we encouraged him to play. *Muddy Shoes Blues* (VJM VEP 4) is one of the small number of items Jewell Long recorded for us before the difficulties wore him down. All his life he lived in Sealy, where he was born on 30 June 1908. (Page 39.)

Love, Charles

Across the Mississippi River from New Orleans lived Charles Love in a small, neat frame house on Thayer Avenue, Algiers. A board sometimes stood on the plank bridge that spanned the weed-grown ditch separating his yard from the rough road and the bumping freight wagons on the railroad sidetrack beyond. It bore the sign: 'At Lib. Dixxie Land Band'. But Charles Love was a ragtime-jazz player best at home with the contents of the *Red Book of Rags*; He was born in 1885 in Placquemine, Louisiana, played in Placquemine and later in New Orleans from childhood; took a band when he was thirty to Vera Cruz and two years later was playing in Shreveport at the Star Theatre. A long career led to recording in 1949 with Big Eye Louis De Lisle including *Black Cat on the Fence* (AM 537) and later, after recovering from a stroke, with Albert Jiles

in the Love-Jiles Ragtime Orchestra in June 1960. We visited him with Herb Friedwald a couple of months later when he reminisced at length on working in tent shows and minstrel troupes and expressed the ragtime player's distrust of the blues. (Pages 83, 88, 89, 131, 133, 137.)

Love, Jasper

'Right now, I'm a pay-hand on a farm. Other words kinda like I drives a tractor; and I chops cotton – 'most anything you know. Well the cause of me bein' on a farm now was: it was a bad winter and I were here in Clarksdale and couldn't get no job no kind of way, so I stomped through the country and then this feller hired me as a tractor driver. I mean until the jobs properly open up and then maybe I can be back in town. Later on go back to the seed-mills, soya beans . . . grind 'em up, make this oil and this lard . . . I do's all type of work like that.' In such terms, Jasper Love, barrelhouse pianist in Clarksdale, described his occupation. Born in Lambert, Mississippi, in 1915 he was partly raised in Wabash, south of West Helena, Arkansas, later returning to Mississippi. For a while he had a band in West Memphis but did not achieve the fame of his cousin Willie Love. Jasper Love is included solo and with Columbus Jones on Arhoolie CD 432. His *Santa Fe Blues* is characteristic. (Pages 58, 69, 75.)

Luandrew, Albert

A tall and powerful man, Sunnyland Slim had a voice of great volume and a boogie-blues piano style that was in keeping. He was born in Vance, Mississippi, on 5 September 1907, and obtained his first job in Lambert, a few miles north, when he was seventeen. Later he moved to Memphis, Tennessee, where he remained for fifteen years until 1942. During this time he played with Sonny Boy Williamson, Doctor Clayton and innumerable blues singers and short spells with Ma Rainey and other celebrated singers. It was as Doctor Clayton's Buddy that he first recorded in 1947 after he had been living in Chicago for some five years. We met him at Muddy Waters's home, at Jump Jackson's and at the Buckingham Club at 3030 West Madison where he was playing with a group that included Robert Lockwood and Eugene Pierson on guitars. The *Devil Is a Busy Man* and *Prisoner Bound* were amongst the items that we recorded of his playing and singing (77 Records LA 12–21 . Sunnyland Slim visited Europe in 1964, and continued playing for nearly thirty years. He died in 1995. (Pages 41, 73, 97, 154.)

Mason, Norman

Though little recorded, Norman Mason was a veteran of the riverboats and the tent shows, having played with Fate Marable on the Streckfus Steamer *St Paul* in Marable's first riverboat band. With him were Louis Armstrong, Davey Jones on mellophone, Sam Dutrey on clarinet and Johnny St Cyr amongst others. Later, Morris White, Sidney Desvignes and Zutty Singleton joined the band. Early in his career, Norman Mason played saxophone but in later years after doubling clarinet, switched for a while to trumpet. He played with the Rabbit Foot Minstrels for a number of seasons and accompanied Ma Rainey, Ida Cox and other blues singers who played with the Minstrels. When we talked with him at his pleasant St Louis home he was working in the evenings at The Gaslight with Singleton Palmer's Band with which he subsequently recorded. Playing clarinet in the current Dixie idiom rather than in any extension of the native St Louis style was a source of some regret to Norman Mason. He was present on the extremely rare recording by Fate Marable's Society Syncopators made in New Orleans in 1925. Born in Florida in 1895 he was 72 when he died of a stroke. (Pages 129, 132, 136.)

Miller, J. D.

'Around here in this part of Louisiana, I'd say within a hundred miles radius of Crowley, we've got more blues singers than any other spot in the United States,' declared J. D. Miller, whose office and home were in Crowley. Responsible for the recording of Lightnin Slim, Lonesome Sundown, Lazy Lester and other Louisiana blues singers, as well as the first records of Clifton Chenier and the ill-fated Harry Choates, he had a respect for the talents of the singers and musicians he managed. He died in 1991. (Page 125.)

Montgomery, Eurreal

'I was born in the state of Louisiana, in 1906, Kentwood, on 18 April', stated Little Brother correcting the usual date given. Learning to play piano at the age of four or five he stayed in Kentwood until he was eleven when he ran away to play piano at barrelhouses in various parts of Louisiana, staying a while at 419 Saratoga in New Orleans and subsequently moving to a number of river towns. In Jackson, Mississippi, he joined Clarence Desdune's band and toured with this group as far as Omaha, where he left to come to Chicago and record in 1929 his original *Vicksburg Blues* and *No Special Rider* (Paramount 13006). He returned to Mississippi in the early 'thirties and led a band in Jackson until 1939 when he moved to Hattiesburg. The outbreak of war brought him back to Chicago where he played intermittently at the Hollywood Lounge at Randolph, between Clark and Dearborn. At his home on South Wabash, in a blues milieu, his immense reputation as a blues pianist amongst other blues singers was self-evident and it was unfortunate that his visit to England later did not show him at his best. We were happy that his *44's, Vicksburg Blues* and *Dud Low Joe* did him justice. (Pages 66, 67, 74, 144.)

Moore, Alexander Herman

Whistling Alex Moore was curled up in the dark corner of a screened porch when I finally traced him to a dusty, deserted street in North Dallas. When he had mastered his bewilderment at being asked about his blues recordings of thirty years before, he became animated and enthusiastic to play again. We tried out pianos, beat down instruments in saloon, dive and brothel labelled 'Strictly for Colored' and after many vicissitudes secured the use of a piano at Madamme Pratt's private music school. One of the most poetic blues singers on record, Alex Moore had developed as a remarkable pianist in the boogie and blues tradition with an eccentric inventive flair both in his vocals and his playing. Between blues he reminisced about the wild days of Dallas's lurid past, days for which he longed. His voice was husky, his playing vigorous on *Come and Get Me* on this CD, on *Pretty Woman with a Sack Dress On* and his moving *West Texas Woman* (Arhoolie CD 408). Born on 22 November 1899, Alex Moore lived all his life in Dallas and rarely ventured far away. For many years he drove a hack through the streets of the city and when I found him he worked as a hotel porter. He died at the age of 90. His early recordings are collected on Document DOCD 5178. (Pages 55, 60.)

Morganfield, McKinley
Muddy Waters was first recorded by Alan Lomax and John C. Work in Stovall, Mississippi, where he was working in the cotton fields. His personal holler *I Be's Troubled* (Library of Congress 18) he recalled from those days. After a brief spell with the Silas Green Minstrel Show – playing harmonica – he moved to Chicago in 1943 where he worked in various jobs until he commenced to record for Aristocrat and Chess. Though born on 4 April 1915, he was regarded as a veteran blues singer by the younger men, having held down Smitty's Corner for several years. We stayed with him at his home, had day-and-night sessions with many blues singers in the basement and travelled with him to Gary, Indiana, and to other dates. Still a simple man, Muddy Waters lived in a pleasant, modest home on South Lake Park and was restrained when not performing; frighteningly powerful when working. When he visited England in 1958 he gave only a hint of the impact of his shattering blues band or of his electric guitar which he still played on occasion. Muddy took his band to Pepper's Lounge on 43rd Street, but later he made frequent college tours and concert appearances coming to England in both 1963 and 1964. Muddy Waters' first recordings are on Document DOCD 5146, while his classic Chicago blues are on several albums. He died in 1983. (Pages 26, 50, 70, 155.)

Muddy Waters
Pseudonym for McKinley Morganfield (see above).

Nix, Willie
Monroe, Louisiana, was a dismal town and the effects of a cloudburst on unmade roads and leaking terrace shacks made it more so. A hint that a blues singer could be found at the home of a trombonist on one such street led us unexpectedly to Willie Nix. Native of Memphis, Tennessee, where he was known as the Memphis Blues Boy he was born in 1923. He led a band which once included James Cotton and Elmore James

and had worked with Willie Love and Pinetop Perkins. Cotton and Love were probably with him on *Seems Like a Million Years* (Sun 179), made in 1951. A few years later he left for Chicago, played at various clubs and replaced Muddy Waters at Smitty's Corner when Muddy came to England. Now, times were bad. He was making for Bakersfield, California, to catch the crop-picking. Monroe wasn't exactly on the way – but it was the way the train on which he had hoboed his way was going. (Page 164.)

Oden, James
'You know it's hard to come up by yourself when you only eight year old but I had to because my daddy died when I was just a kid see, and I don't hardly remember my mother,' explained St Louis Jimmy in the yellow-walled cellar beneath Muddy Waters's house, where he was living. He came to St Louis at the age of fourteen, having been born in Nashville, Tennessee, on 2 June 1905, the son of a dancer. Jimmy Oden worked in a barber shop and came in contact with the many blues singers in St Louis. He learned to play the piano but was discouraged by the large number of excellent blues pianists and devoted himself to singing and composing blues. He toured extensively with Roosevelt Sykes and later with Eddie Boyd who was with him when he had the automobile crash which caused him to cease travelling. St Louis Jimmy was one of the most original composers of blues, his *Going Down Slow* (Bluebird 8889) being a classic example of the idiom. It is on a 2 CD collection of his work, Document DOCD 5234/5. He died in December 1977 in Chicago. (Pages 107, 160.)

Oldham, Marion
An active member of the St Louis Branch of the National Association for the Advancement of Colored People at 3529 Franklin, Marion Oldham had also spent twelve years with the Congress for Racial Equality and when interviewed in the street was picketing a large store in downtown St Louis. (Page 1.)

Perryman, Rufus

I was in Memphis, playin' at a joint on Pauline and a feller by the name of Jim Jackson heard me playin' and got his boss to come out and hear me and they asked could I make it pretty decent? I said 'I guess so'. And did I want to make any money to make a record. I said, 'Sure, I want to make money any kind of way!' So Speckled Red made his record of *The Dirty Dozen* (Brunswick 7116) in 1929 – he was then thirty-eight. Though he had given Hampton, Georgia, as his birthplace, he was brought there as a small child, being born in Monroe, Louisiana, on 23 October 1891, an albino. His father was earning 40¢ a day as a field-hand and he was soon fending for himself. He went to Detroit, learned to play the piano, hoboed South to Memphis and spent an adventurous life as an itinerant near-blind barrelhouse pianist for more than thirty years. He came to Europe in 1960 and returned to settle quietly at his home on Newberry Terrace, St Louis, where we visited him. Speckled Red's uproarious piano playing is to be heard on Document DOCD 5205. He died in St Louis in January 1973. (Pages 65, 81, 90, 100.)

Pickens, Edwin

Buster Pickens was virtually the last of the barrelhouse and saw-mill pianists, for his contemporaries were nearly all dead. He owed his survival to the advice of 'a notable pianist named Foster,' who 'used to lecture me all the time. He'd say, "Look son, whatever you do, when you play in them places, I don't care whether it's the middle of July or August, you get you a coat and put it on before you go out in the air".' The heat of the barrelhouses, the chill rides on 'the blinds' and 'the rods' of the 'rattlers' took a heavy toll amongst the juke players of the Texas Piney Woods. Pickens, born in 1915, was younger than many of them though he shared the work, and small, compact and tough, he was playing still. His world had been one of railroad routes and this is reflected in many of his blues. His description of hoboing a ride, told to a slow train blues appears on the accompanying CD (*Santa Fe Train*). *Colorado Springs Blues* and others we recorded with the help of Mack McCormick and Chris Strachwitz, were issued on Heritage 1008. Buster Pickens later recorded with Lightnin Hopkins for Prestige. Tragically, he was shot and killed in a bar-room argument in November 1964. (Pages 56, 63, 67, 77, 123, 183.)

Pierce, Billie

Née Billie Gootson, the wife of Dédé Pierce was born on 8 June 1907, in Marianna, Florida, but came to Pensacola with her parents as a baby. All her family played piano and Billie joined Joe Jesse's orchestra, following this with spells with travelling groups. In 1929 she replaced her sister Sadie Gootson briefly playing with Buddy Petit on the S. S. Madison and a year later came to New Orleans to stay, joining Alphonse Picou. In the ensuing years she played at a bewildering variety of places in New Orleans, even working with a Filippino band. In 1935 she married Dédé Pierce and toured with him in Ida Cox's company. From then on her career closely paralleled that of her husband. Billie Pierce had a tough, honkytonk piano style and a blues voice in the classic tradition. She sang and played 'Primitive Piano' on Tone 1, *Gulf Coast Blues* on Folk-Lyric EL 110 and with Lawrence Tocca on *Shake It and Break It* on Folkways FA 2463. Devoted to her husband she was one of the last of the blues singers of the classic style. She died in New Orleans in September 1974. (Pages 84, 86, 88, 137.)

Pierce, Joseph la Croix Dédé

'They call me Dédé for what you call a nickname but as far as I can remember my father and mother spoke French but the Creole come in by me not talkin' French so good; broke it up in a kinda dialeck,' explained Dédé Pierce when we visited him and his wife in their tiny brise-block home in a back yard. New Orleans born on 18 February 1904, he learned to play the trumpet when 'a cousin who was a player, Baby Rand he followed different shows and he give me one. That's been forty years. I picked up music by ear'. He idolized the blues-playing trumpeters Chris Kelly and Kid Rena and absorbed much of their quality. After his marriage to Billie Pierce they worked together. During the war they worked at a club in Bunkie, Louisiana, and it was there that Dédé's sight failed. They returned to New Orleans to play at the small Luthjen's dance hall until forced by ill-health to retire for a while. Playing frequently in the 1960s they are to be heard to advantage in their blues-based jazz on Arhoolie. Dédé died in November 1973 in his home city. (Pages 83, 86, 89.)

Price, Sam

A local politician in Harlem where he lived on 138th Street, Sam Price had a long career as a blues and jazz pianist. He was born in Honey Grove, Texas, on 6 October 1908, moved to Waco and thence to Dallas where he commenced his career as a dancer, later becoming a pianist on the TOBA. He played in Kansas City with Lips Page, moved to Chicago in 1933 and five years later, after a spell in Detroit, settled in New York. He was house pianist on scores of Decca blues records in the 'thirties which were enriched by his slow blues, and boogie piano. He visited France many times since 1948, touring with Milton Mezzrow, Jimmy Archey and with his own group. He was playing with Henry Red Allen at the Metropole in 1960 when he proved an excellent host to us at his home and offices and an informative guide in Harlem. We met again in 1988 shortly before he died. (Pages 33, 134, 174.)

Roy, Ernest

Ernest Rogers – or Ernest Roy – played at first a twelve string guitar which he had made himself, but his ambition was to be a blues singer in the current idiom and to this end he bought an electric guitar which he plugged into the only light socket of his tiny Clarksdale cabin, when we visited him. Later we joined him with several of his friends who were battling manfully with their instruments in crude, out-of-tune rhythm and blues. As yet they were inept but they had the determination to master their instruments as generations of blues musicians had done before them. Married and with a family, Ernest Rogers was then about twenty-five years old and hoping to make his way North. (Page 165.)

St Louis Jimmy

Pseudonym for James Oden, q.v.

Sellers, Brother John

The circumstances of an unusually broad range of associations made Brother John Sellers almost unique in the ease with which he moved freely to and from the blues, gospel music, jazz and the stage – a modern counterpart of the role of the classic singers of the 'twenties. He was born in Clarksdale, Mississippi, on 27 May 1924, and raised in the Mississippi townships of Burdett, Leland and Greenville. He had contact with travelling shows and later, in Chicago where he moved in 1933, he sang in the Sanctified Church with Mahalia Jackson and Rosetta Tharpe. As a youth he was encouraged by Big Bill Broonzy, Sonny Boy Williamson and Memphis Minnie and sang with Sam Price in New York in 1945. Two years later he toured with Don Archer's band, recorded with Memphis Jimmy Clark and in subsequent years with accompanists as varied as Sir Charles Thompson, Schoolboy Porter and Sonny Terry. He came to England with Big Bill Broonzy in 1957 and was singing at churches in Chicago when he acted as a generous host to us in 1960. His associations with the Chicago blues singers remained close though a world tour with the Alvin Ailey Dance Company in 1962 enforced a separation and a wider public, the company playing in London in 1964. Vanguard PTT 12017 and Decca LK 4197 illustrated aspects of his work. (Pages 128, 150, 154, 161, 181.)

Shade, Will

Known as Son Brimmer, having been raised by Annie Brimmer, his grandmother, Will Shade was born in Memphis, Tennessee, on 5 February 1898 and continued to live there in conditions of acute poverty. Will Shade was a medium-height, tough man with a gritty voice and he recalled in detail the lawless days of Beale Street with not a little regret at their passing. Once the leader of the Memphis Jug Band, one of the best groups to have recorded in this idiom, he sang with a rugged, strong delivery and played guitar. He first recorded *Newport News Blues* in 1927 (originally Victor 20576) and he was happy to record it again, for me. In 1956, Will Shade was working in a tyre re-treading plant but when we talked with him four years later he was living on relief. He died in September 1966. (Pages 51, 93, 96, 98.)

Shaky Jake

Pseudonym for James D. Harris, q.v.

Smith, Robert Curtis

'Maybe there'll be some little job but mostly there ain't nothin' to do but hunt,' said Robert Smith explaining how he tried to support his wife and family of nine children during the winter. He lived in a one-room shack with his family in brutal conditions. A sharecropper, tractor-driver, farm-hand, he was burdened by the blues in its stark, unromantic realism. He played guitar in a natural, easy Mississippi style and sang movingly in a warm, soft voice *I Hope One Day My Luck Will Change*. Born in 1930 he was resigned to a life of penury, of gruelling toil interspersed with periods of wasteful inactivity and as in the past, probably jail without trial. (Pages 19, 40, 76.)

Spann, Otis

The pianist in Muddy Waters's band, Otis Spann was his half brother. He talked with a slight lisp, sat three-quarters-on to the piano and rolled out boogie and blues with a strength that recalled Big Maceo. He was born in Belzoni, Mississippi, on 21 March 1930, and started to play the piano at the age of eight under the tutelage of Friday Ford, whose *Poor Country Boy* he recorded for me. Working in Mississippi until the age of fifteen he moved to Chicago after the death of his mother. In Chicago Otis worked as a plasterer and his contact with many blues pianist there rapidly matured his playing. He accompanied Bo Diddely on a few recordings and when Muddy Waters established his band became a mainstay of the group, winning many admirers on European tours. Otis was only 40 when he died in Chicago. (Pages 42, 54.)

Speckled Red

Pseudonym for Rufus Perryman, q.v.

Spivey, Victoria

Black Snake Blues (OK 8338) was a remarkable success when Victoria Spivey at the age of sixteen recorded it in May 1926. It was followed by band and vocal versions by innumerable artists and established the basis of her long career. Victoria moved from Houston to New York where she played at the Lincoln Theater. *T.B. Blues* was made that year, 1927, and two years later she was given a part in *Hallelujah*, the all-colored King Vidor film. She joined Hunter's Serenaders from Omaha in 1931 and in the ensuing years toured widely. In 1940 she was in a Dallas club and in 1948 at Smalls' Paradise New York, joining Olsen and Johnson in *Hellzapoppin'* two years later. She retired and in 1959 made a few church appearances. We met her at the home of her manager Harrison Smith, accompanied by Len Kunstadt who was currently working on her biography. Animated and expressive, Victoria Spivey was every inch the blues singer and in the 1960s made appearances with her old partner, Lonnie Johnson. Reissues of her earlier work are on Document, and she made some notable recordings for her own label Queen Bee. Victoria came to England on a package tour in 1963. She died thirteen years later in New York. (Page 118.)

Sunnyland Slim

Pseudonym for Albert Luandrew, q.v.

Sykes, Roosevelt

We first met Roosevelt Sykes at the Tay May Club, appropriately on West Roosevelt (12th Street) Chicago, and many times thereafter. Generously built he had a light, freckled complexion and talked with a rich Southern voice that his early records scarcely suggested. Born in Helena, Arkansas, in 1906 he moved with his parents to St Louis at the age of three, but spent all the time he could with relatives in Helena where he learned to play the blues and came in contact with many of the fine bluesmen from that area. He recorded *44 Blues* (OKeh 8702) in June 1929 thus commencing a long recording career with Okeh, Decca, Victor and other companies. The 'Honeydripper' as he was frequently called, was one of the most famed and admired of blues singers, whilst as a talent scout he was himself responsible for the recording of many blues artists. We recorded him at John Steiner's Chicago home and at Muddy Waters's, playing for me the *44 Blues* and Jesse Bell's *West Helena Blues*. Later he visited England. Roosevelt Sykes was a singer who performed and played with immense gusto and his continued popularity lay largely in his ability to mould himself to changing trends in blues. In 1963 he decided to return South and died in New Orleans twenty years later. (Pages 72, 75, 109, 113, 122.)

Taylor, Floyd

One of the many excellent blues pianists who remained little known outside their own environment in Detroit, Michigan – Floyd Taylor recorded little. Born in Tennessee in 1909 he was brought by his parents to Detroit in 1918 when the Northern industrial expansion attracted Southern Blacks. He was the confrere of Will Ezell, Charlie Spand and Pinetop Smith and could recreate the individual and local styles of boogie piano of the 'twenties with skill. He worked with Sippie Wallace and during the 'thirties at various clubs, strip joints and drag shows featuring female impersonators who fortunately required blues for a musical setting. He later accompanied Dinah Washington, wrote *The Hucklebuck* and was still actively playing in Detroit in the 1960s. (Page 143.)

Thomas, Percy

A plow-hand all his life, Percy Thomas was born in the country near Clarksdale, Mississippi, in 1896. Lean and muscular he gestured as he talked with large, calloused hands which had not fingered a guitar to any extent for some years. With his fiddle-playing friend Will Johnson he attempted to re-create the sound of the Mississippi Corn-Shuckers, the country band which they had led in the 'twenties and 'thirties. Lack of practice prevented them from evoking more than a ghost of the sound that once rocked the jukes of Louisa, Rome, Bobo and Hushpukena and sent feet shuffling at fish-fries on the banks of the Sunflower River. With Son Simms, Percy Thomas accompanied Muddy Waters when he recorded for the Library of Congress in 1942. (Page 48.)

Thomas, Willie B.

When his parents were taking their belongings to their new home in Zachary, Louisiana, Willie Thomas was crushed by slipping furniture. He was badly injured and his growth was stunted as a result. That was in 1925 when Willie was thirteen years old. He was born on 25 May 1912, at Lobdell, Louisiana, just across the river from Scotlandville, and started life as a gleaner of cane on the Bellemont Plantation where his family were sharecroppers. Later he became a water- boy for a construction gang and when we met him at Butch Cage's house in Zachary he was a factory janitor. Willie played kazoo with

Butch Cage for ten years before commencing to play guitar in 1939. A few years later he started to preach after seeing a vision. Though a limited guitarist he was an impassioned and eloquent speaker, pouring forth a stream of ideas as he warmed to his subject. He joined Butch Cage on a unique recording of an early African American protest song, *Kill That Nigger Dead*. It is included on the accompanying CD. (Pages 22, 46, 53, 180.)

Thompson, Charles

Almost the last of the ragtime pianists from St Louis, Charley Thompson, who died in 1964, aged seventy-three, had played the piano since the age of twelve, learning by ear. He worked as a chef cook on the Illinois Central railroad and in later years was a cook for country clubs in the St Louis area. With Robert Hampton, Charley Thompson used to play at the notorious Aunt Kate Gryder's in Lovejoy, Illinois, a short distance from East St Louis, before the First World War. In 1916 he won the State Ragtime Championships with *Lily Rag,* which he later recorded (American Music 527) and a couple of years after met James P. Johnson in Toledo, Ohio, who greatly influenced him. They wrote a tune – *Asia* – which they performed often in Toledo. In the 'fifties Charles Thompson had his own bar at 3005 Lawton Boulevard and in 1960 was still playing at Gaslight Square, St Louis, at an espresso bar. He recorded *Hop Alley Dream* (Circle 1071) and *Buffet Flat Rag* (Circle 1069) and both his memories and some of his compositions are instructive of the links and disparities between blues and ragtime. (Pages 101, 103.)

Thompson, Sylvester

Though a young blues singer Sil Johnson had already made a name for himself in Chicago. He had a good rocking band with him when Bob Koester and I heard him playing at a small club at 1804 South Rush Street, a group that included Rufus Forman, Joe Hill and Leonard Morrison. Sil Johnson, as he is now known, was born in 1937 in Centerville, Tennessee, and came to Chicago in 1946. He learned to play guitar and though he had only become a professional in 1958, he had recorded with Shaky Jake on Cobra, under his own name for King and had worked with Little Junior Wells, Elmore James and many other younger generation Chicago bluesmen. Later, when we heard him as a solo singer at Gary, Indiana, he showed himself to be a strong and personable blues singer. His star continued to rise and in the 1990s Sil Johnson was regarded as one of the most creative of the 'soul-blues' genre. (Page 166.)

Townsend, Henry

A debt-collector by way of regular employment, Henry Townsend still played at week-ends in clubs in St Louis and East St Louis. 'I don't go in for it exclusive but I can never let the guitar go, it's just a part of me and if I have to play for myself then I go to it. But I manage to play some place every week-ends, and still have a pretty good demand, but the job I have kinda holds me down,' he explained. Coming from Shelby, Mississippi, to Cairo, Illinois, when he was a child he moved later with his parents to St Louis where he has remained, apart from tours, ever since. We visited him in his sparsely furnished, rather dark apartment and he talked seriously about aspects of the blues with which he was greatly concerned. He was eighteen when he recorded *Poor Man Blues* (Columbia 14491) in 1929 and his deep voice later contrasted with the high vocal on his earliest records or even those with Sonny Boy Williamson made in 1937. Henry Townsend accompanied Walter Davis for several years and in the mid-fifties was playing with Roosevelt Sykes and later, Sonny Boy Williamson No. 2. (Pages 20, 105, 112, 176, 181.)

Turner, B. K.

'I am the Black Ace, I'm the boss card in your hand,' Babe Kyro Turner used to sing on Station KFJZ out of Fort Worth, and it was as the Black Ace that he became known. His birthplace was Hughes Springs, Texas, and he stayed on his father's farm until he was thirty, in 1935. He had made a guitar for himself as a child, later picking up an old one and playing and singing at country suppers. In the worst of the Depression years he moved to Shreveport, Louisiana, where he was influenced by Oscar Buddy Woods whose steel guitar style he adopted. When we met at his neat home in Fort Worth he had not played for some years but rapidly responded to reminders of the early Decca recordings. He was probably the last surviving player of the flat guitar and bottle bar which his *Bad Times*

Stomp instrumental shows at its best. *New Triflin' Woman*, *I Am the Black Ace* and *Golden Slipper* are amongst the items we recorded (Arhoolie CD374.) Black Ace worked with a photographic firm in Fort Worth, Texas. He chose not to pursue music and died in Fort Worth in November 1972. (Pages 36, 53.)

Walton Wade

The proprietor of the Big Six barber shop on 4th Street, Clarksdale, Wade Walton had the traditional centre for blues singers in a Southern community. His wife was a prominent church member and above the peanut stand hung a sign 'Mississippi QUARTETT UNION Head Quarter & Booking Office' and the posters advertising visiting groups were displayed inside. An intelligent, witty man he was born in the little township of Lombardy in a sharecropping family in 1925. From childhood he was determined to be a barber and after qualifying he moved to Clarksdale. Wade's energies were seemingly inexhaustible and he worked often from 8 a.m. to midnight, his actions as rhythmic as his *Barber Shop Rhythm* played with a razor and strop (Arhoolie CD432). Wade Walton played guitar and harmonica, sang, danced, told tall tales and enjoyed a well-earned local reputation. (Pages 19, 28, 51.)

Watson, Johnny

Resplendent in a royal blue jacket with gold epaulettes and shiny-peaked cap Daddy Stovepipe sat on a wooden crate on Maxwell Street playing guitar and harmonica, the latter held by a frame around his neck. He was a wizened, diminutive but spirited old man who looked as if he could have been born in 1870 as he claimed. Hailing from Mobile, Alabama he had been a street singer and occasional field-hand most of his life. During the 'thirties he lived in Greenville, Mississippi, with his wife Mississippi Sarah and they both recorded for Vocalion and Bluebird. With the death of Sarah in 1937 he went south to Mexico and played with Zydeco bands in Galveston and Houston, Texas later returning to Mississippi and moving on to Chicago. After some prompting he recalled *Sundown Blues* (originally Gennett 5459) but was more anxious to play *The Tennessee Waltz* (Heritage HLP 1004). Daddy Stovepipe died in 1963. (Pages 68, 148.)

Williams, Emma

Firm of lip and of voice, Emma Williams was the mother of the blues singer Mary Johnson. She was born and raised in Eden Station eleven miles north of Yazoo City on Highway 49 East under old plantation conditions. As she was 'house-workin'' she fared somewhat better than some of her neighbours but the minimal wages and conditions of living after her young husband died made her decide to move to St Louis with her daughter. There she did factory work and the earnings of Mary Johnson as a blues singer, though she deplored the occupation, helped them along. A devout church member Emma Williams lived with her daughter on Biddle Street. (Pages 23, 177.)

Wynn, Albert

New Orleans born, on the 29 July 1907, Al Wynn came to Chicago as a boy, learning to play the trombone at the age of eleven and joining Gertrude Ma Rainey on tour when he was seventeen. Returning to Chicago he soon formed his own band which he was leading at the Dreamland in 1926. He played with Charlie Creath and Louis Armstrong and had Punch Miller in his recording band of 1928 which made *Parkway Stomp* and *She's Crying for Me*. In 1928 he came to Europe, toured with Sam Wooding and returned in 1932 to Chicago. He played with Carroll Dickerson and later in the bands of Jimmy Noone and Fletcher Henderson. Soft of speech 'broad and smooth in his playing, Al Wynn looked back nostalgically on his years spent with Ma Rainey. We talked with him at his home and at the Catfish Row club where he was leading his own group. (Pages 138, 140.)

Contents of the CD

The CD included at the end of this book contains a selection of extracts from the songs, blues and narratives of the blues singers recorded by Paul Oliver in the field in 1960. Certain of the extracts have been edited in the interests of brevity. The full texts will be found in the book, if quoted there, on the pages indicated.

Included in the anthology are:

Boogie Woogie Red (spoken, with own piano)
Detroit, 7 July
So Much Good Feeling (Harrison) Copyright Control (pages 20, 22)

Willie Thomas (spoken)
Zachary, Louisiana, 7 August
A Little Different (page 22)

James Butch Cage (vocal and fiddle) accompanied by
Willie Thomas (vocal and guitar)
Zachary, Louisiana, 7 August
Kill That Nigger Dead (Cage; Thomas) Copyright Control (page 22)

Lil Son Jackson (Melvin Jackson) (spoken)
Dallas, Texas, 29 July
The Onliest Way (page 31)

J. B. Lenoir (vocal and guitar)
Chicago, Illinois, 17 July
My Father's Style (Lenoir) Copyright Control (guitar solo)
So It Rocked On (spoken)
Move to Kansas City (Jim Jackson) Peer Music (UK) Limited (vocal and guitar) (page 26)

Otis Spann (vocal and piano)
Chicago, Illinois, 14 July
When She come Back (spoken)
Poor Country Boy (vocal and piano) Copyright Control (pages 42, 43)

Lightnin Hopkins (Sam Hopkins) (spoken)
Houston, Texas, 12 August
Ain't No Easy Thing (page 57)

Mance Lipscomb (vocal and guitar)
Navasota, Texas, 13 August
Evil Heart Blues (Lipscomb) Copyright Control

Blind Arvella Grey (spoken)
Chicago, Illinois, 9 July
A Roughneck (page 62)

Roosevelt Sykes (vocal and piano)
Chicago, Illinois, 16 July
West Helena Blues (Bell: Sykes) Bug Music Ltd (page 72)

Will Shade
Memphis. Tennessee, 20 July
Days of 1900 (spoken)
Newport News Blues (Shade Williamson) Peer Music (UK) Ltd (vocal and guitar) (pages 93, 99)

Whistling Alex Moore
Dallas. Texas, 30 July
Chock House Days (spoken)
Come and Get Me (Moore) Copyright Control (vocal and piano) (page 55)

Brother John Sellers (spoken)
Chicago, Illinois, 17 July
Move Back! For What? (page 181)

J. B. Lenoir (vocal and guitar)
Chicago, Illinois, 17 July
I Been Down So Long (Lenoir) Jewel Music Pub. Co. Ltd (page 150)

James Stump Johnson (spoken)
St. Louis, Missouri, 29 August
A Place They Call Boots' (page 96)

Henry Brown (piano and speech with Pinky Boxx, comments)
St. Louis, Missouri, 28 August
Henry Brown Blues (Brown) Copyright Control

Blind Arvella Gray (vocal and guitar) with
Blind James Brewer (guitar)
Chicago, Illinois, 9 July
They Called Us Gandy-Dancers (spoken)
Work Songs and *John Henry* (Traditional) Copyright Control (vocal and guitar) (page 62)

Edwin Buster Pickens (piano and speech)
Houston, Texas, 9 August
Santa Fe Train (Pickens) Flyright Music (page 77)

Robert Curtis Smith (spoken with guitar)
Clarksdale Mississippi, 24 July
Most Reason I Sing (page 19)

Jasper Love (vocal, piano and speech)
Clarksdale, Mississippi, 23 July
Santa Fe Blues (Love) Copyright Control (page 75)

John Lee Hooker (spoken)

New York, N.Y., 26 June

Somewhere Down The Line (page 21)

Robert Curtis Smith (vocal and guitar)

Clarksdale, Mississippi, 24 July

I Hope One Day My Luck Will Change (Smith) Copyright Control

Otis Spann

Chicago, Illinois, 14 July

Only Places They Can Go (spoken)

People Calls Me Lucky (Spann) Copyright Control (vocal and piano)

(page 54)

Henry Townsend (spoken)

St Louis, Missouri, 28 August

What Have I Committed? (page 181)

James Butch Cage (vocal and guitar)

Zachary, Louisiana, 7 August

'Tween Midnight and Day (Cage) Copyright Control

Little Brother Montgomery

Chicago, Illinois, 15 July

Walking Basses and *Dud Low Joe* (Montgomery) Copyright

Control (spoken, and piano solo)

The First Vicksburg Blues (Montgomery) Prestige Music Ltd (vocal

and piano) (page 74)

Roosevelt Sykes

Chicago, Illinois, 16 July

They Call Him 'Pork Chops' (spoken)

Forty-Four Blues (Green; Sykes) Bug Music Ltd (vocal and piano)

(page 75)

Mance Lipscomb (vocal and guitar)

Navasota, Texas, 13 August

Blues In The Bottle (Trad./arr Lipscomb) Bug Music Ltd (page vi)

Edwin Buster Pickens (spoken)

Houston, Texas, 9 August

To Have The Blues Within

Colorado Springs Blues (Pickens) Flyright Music (vocal and piano)

(page 183)

Recorded and produced by Paul Oliver

Album compilation with Michael Vernon and technical supervision
by Bill Price and Derek Varnals, 1965. Originally released under the title
of *Conversation with the Blues* on Decca LK 4644

Additional material compiled with John Cowley and technical
supervision by Richard Ashcroft, 1997

The following is a list of recordings made by the author which have been released to date, together with recordings made in association with Chris Strachwitz and recordings made by him during the joint field trip in 1960.

Black Ace (vocal, steel guitar)

Fort Worth, Texas, 14 August

Hitchhiking Woman (Arhoolie FS 101, Arhoolie CD 374)

I am the Black Ace, Bad Times Stomp (guitar solo), *Drink on Little Girl, Santa Fe Blues, New Triflin' Woman, Farther Along, Evil Woman, 'Fore Day Creep, Little Augie, Your Leg's Too Little, No Good Woman, Santa Claus Blues, Golden Slipper* (Heritage HLP 1006. Arhoolie F 1003)

Blind James Brewer (vocal, electric guitar)

Chicago, Illinois, 11 July

I'm So Glad Good Whisky's Back (Heritage HLP 1004, Collectors Issue C 5527)

Henry Brown (piano)

St Louis, Missouri, 28 August

Henry Brown Blues (25 August), *Got It and Cain't Quit It, Bottled in Bond, Blues for Charlie O'Brien, Deep Morgan Is Delmar Now, Henry Brown Boogie, O'Fallon Blues, My Blues Is in the Bottle, Papa Slick Head, Handyman Blues, Scufflin' Boogie* (77 Records LA 12–5)

James Butch Cage and Willie Thomas (vocals, fiddle and guitar)

Zachary, Louisiana, 7 August

One Thin Dime (Arhoolie FS 101)

44 Blues, Butch's Blues (Arhoolie F 1005, Arhoolie CD 432)

Sam Chatman (vocal, guitar)

Hollandale, Mississippi, 25 July

God Don't Like Ugly (Arhoolie FS 101)

I Have to Paint My Face, You Shall Be Free, I Stand and Wonder, Lay My Burden Down (Arhoolie F 1005, Arhoolie CD 432)

Blind Arvella Gray (vocal, steel guitar)

Chicago, Illinois, 11 July

Corinne Corinna, Have Mercy Mr Percy, Railroad Songs and John Henry, Have Mercy Mr Percy No. 2 (Heritage HLP 1004, Collector's Issue C 5527)

Lil Son Jackson (vocal, guitar)

Fort Worth, Texas, 29 July

Johnny Mae (Arhoolie FS 101)

Blues Comes to Texas, Cairo Blues, Ticket Agent, Louise Blues, Sugar Mama, The Girl I Love, Santa Fe Blues, Turn Your Lamp Down Low,

Groundhog Blues, Gambler Blues, Charley Cherry, West Dallas Blues,
Rollin' Mill Went Down, Red River Blues, Roberta Blues
(Arhoolie F 1004, Arhoolie CD 409)

Mance Lipscomb (vocal, guitar)
Navasota, Texas, 11 August
Back Water Blues Arhoolie FS 101 *Freddie, Sugar Babe It's All Over Now,*
Going Down Slow, Baby Please Don't Go, Rock Me All Night Long,
Ain't Gonna Rain No Mo', Jack O' Diamonds Is a Hard Card to Play,
Shake Shake Mama, Ella Speed, One Thin Dime, Going to Louisiana,
Mama Don't Allow, Aint' It Hard, 'Bout a Spoonful (Arhoolie F 1001,
Arhoolie CD 306)

Jewell Long (vocal, piano, or vocal, guitar – 1)
Sealy, Texas, 11 August
Frankie and Albert, My Pony Run Blues – 1, Sealy Rag – 1,
Muddy Shoes Blues (VJM/VEP4)

Jasper Love (vocal, piano)
Clarksdale, Mississippi, 23 July
Love's Honeydripper (Arhoolie FS 101)
Desert Blues, The Slop (with Columbus Jones) (Arhoolie F 1005)

Little Brother Montgomery (vocal, piano)
Chicago, Illinois, 14 July
Trembling Blues, My Electronical Invention, That's Why I Keep
Drinkin', Bob Martin Blues, No Special Rider (77 Records LA 12/21)

Whistling Alex Moore (vocal, piano)
Dallas, Texas, 30 July
Wake Up Old Lady (Arhoolie FS 101)
Whistling Alex Moore's Blues, Pretty Woman with a Sack Dress on,
Rubber Tired Hack, You Say I'm a Bad Feller, From North Dallas to the
East Side, Miss No-Good Weed, Black-Eyed Peas and Hog Jowls, Boogie
in the Barrel, Goin' Back to Froggy Bottom, July Boogie, West Texas Woman,
Frisky Gal (77 Records LA 12–7 Arhoolie F 1008, Arhoolie CD 408)

Edwin Buster Pickens (vocal, piano)
Houston, Texas, 9 August
Santa Fe Train, Rock Island Blues, Ain't Nobody's Bizness If I Do,
Colorado Springs, She Caught the L. & N., Remember Me, Women in
Chicago (17 August), The Ma Grinder, You Better Stop Your Women, Jim
Nappy (17 August), Mountain Jack, D.B.A. Blues, Hattie Green, Backdoor
Blues, Santa Fe Blues (Heritage HLP 1008, Flyright FLY LP 536)

Robert Curtis Smith (vocal, guitar)
Clarksdale, Mississippi, 24 July
Stella Ruth (Arhoolie FS 101)
Going Back to Texas, Lost Love Blues, Lonely Widow (Arhoolie F 1005,
Arhoolie CD 432)

Sunnyland Slim (vocal, piano)
Chicago, Illinois, 14 July
One Room County Shack, Prison Bound, Brownskin Woman, La Salle St
Boogie, I Got the Blues about My Baby, Devil Is a Busy Man, Every Time
I Get to Drinkin' (77 Records LA 12/21)

Wade Walton (vocal, guitar)
Clarksdale, Mississippi, 24 July
Rooster Blues, Barber Shop Rhythm (with Robert Curtis Smith)
(Arhoolie F 1005, Arhoolie CD 432)

Brief details are also given in the Notes on the Speakers of
recordings made by them which are quoted in the text. As
all the transcriptions are of performances played, sung and
occasionally recited to the author, the quoted words and
verses differ in a number of instances from commercially
issued versions.

Index